Church Catholic

The lesser hours of the Sarum breviary

Church Catholic

The lesser hours of the Sarum breviary

ISBN/EAN: 9783744741484

Printed in Europe, USA, Canada, Australia, Japan

Cover: Foto ©Lupo / pixelio.de

More available books at **www.hansebooks.com**

THE LESSER HOUR

OF THE

SARUM BREVIARY

Translated and arranged according to the Kalendar of the Church of England

LONDON:
SWAN SONNENSCHEIN & CO.
PATERNOSTER SQUARE
1889

PREFACE.

The present volume is an attempt to present a faithful rendering in English of the Hours of Prime, Terce, Sext, None, and Compline, according to the Use of the English Church of Sarum, together with such of "the Rules called the Pie" as apply to our present Kalendar. The work has been undertaken, not merely in the spirit of the antiquary, but mainly with a practical view. In our present Prayer-Book the old Sarum services of Mattins, Lauds, and Evensong are retained in a modified form: the present English Liturgy is the crippled child of the venerable Liturgy of Sarum, in its own day "famosissimæ ac inter occiduas nominatissimæ ecclesiæ"; the Kalendar is a somewhat expurgated version of that of Sarum; while the preface in well-known words claims for the whole book continuity with the past, and showers not unpointed anathemas on those who at any time have made their "vain attempts and impetuous assaults" upon the little which the book yet retains of the worshipful past, whether in ceremonial or in substance; seeing that they have "always discovered a greater regard to their own private fancies and interests, than to that duty they owe to the publick."

Those who retain any reverence for the utterances of that Church to which they owe a filial obedience, or have any the least appreciation of what is fit according to the ancient order of the Church Catholick, cannot but feel that in completing their daily round of worship with the five Services of the Breviary which are scarcely or not at all represented in the Book of Common Prayer, those Services should be drawn from the source to which the Prayer-Book throughout directs attention, and from which the public services of the present day take their origin.

One or two more or less mutilated translations of the English Breviary have already appeared: the present work aims at a faithful and fearless rendering of the whole Service, as our forefathers in the Faith of Christ and of His holy Church used the same, without any recognition of "private fancies." Where however authority has altered the order of Service, such alteration is recognised in this translation. Thus the Kalendar of the Prayer-Book has been followed throughout, and the Prayer-Book Collects have been added where they differ from the old ones, besides other minor alterations. The Appendix contains some services, unrecognised in the Prayer-Book, for Feasts which are still locally observed; and it must be allowed that Dedications such as those of Corpus Christi and All Souls' Colleges at Oxford University, or of the Churches of St. Thomas of Canterbury and others, are sufficient authority for the restoration, at least locally, of the Feasts connected with their names, if it be lawful to keep the Feast of the Dedication of a church, or the Patronal Feast, at all. Where Relics of the Saints have been allowed to remain undisturbed in shrine or tomb, there seems to be double reason for honouring their memory; for they must have been saints indeed who were able to weather the fury of the fanatical sixteenth and seventeenth centuries. Hence the Hour Services for the Feast of Relics also find their place in the Appendix.

The editor's chief aim has been to avoid that modern Anglican Charybdis of *private judgment*, to which the Hagiology[1] of the old Service books is often made to play Scylla: the only case in which he has consciously varied from the Breviary is that of the Feast of St Britius, the Antiphons for which hardly accord with modern notions of propriety.

The rubrics, which are often verbose, and sometimes refer to parts of the Service which the Prayer-Book has superseded, have been shortened and paraphrased.

---

[1] It may not be widely known that for the principle at any rate of Invocation of Saints we are able to quote, among higher authorities, the Thirty-nine Articles themselves. Article XXXVI., "Of Consecration of Bishops and Ministers," says that the Ordinal of Edward VI. contains nothing "that of itself is superstitious or ungodly." And yet the "Oath of the King's Supremacy," therein directed to be administered to Bishops, Priests, and Deacons alike, ends with the words, "So help me God, all Saints, and the holy Evangelist"; *i.e.* the particular Evangelist of that Gospel upon which the oath was sworn. It is witness to the legitimacy of calling upon the Saints for aid in any particular crisis, and to the power of a particular Saint, by his intercession with God, to render the same. The Articles therefore deny such a practice to be either superstitious or ungodly.

In bringing to a close this part of a difficult work, it would be too much to hope that the aim with which it was taken in hand has been wholly achieved; and there is probably much still to be desired in point of translation, for which the editor can only ask the indulgence of those who may use the book.

H. G. W.

Brixton.

OF QUIRE SERVICE.

OF STANDING AND KNEELING IN QUIRE.—All shall stand throughout the Service, except during the singing of a Responsory or Alleluia, when they may sit. Also it is permitted to sit during the Lections; and when the Psalmody is very long it is permitted to every alternate Clerk to sit.

All shall kneel whenever the Petitions are said at the Hours; but at Prime and Compline the Petitions are said standing on all days when they are omitted at the other Hours, save when it is otherwise directed in the Rubrics.

In Lent the Choir shall kneel at the beginning of every Hour while saying privately the Lord's Prayer, the Angelic Salutation, and the Creed, whenever the service is of the Feria; at all other times of the year let them stand. [The "Myrroure of Oure Ladye" shows that by the beginning of the sixteenth century *Our Father*, etc., was always said kneeling; this was perhaps the monastic rule.] The Penitential Psalms and Litany are said kneeling in Lent, unless said in Procession.

During Eastertide, and from Christmas Eve to the Octave of Epiphany, let everything be done standing; also on all Sundays and Festivals, and within Octaves.

OF TURNING AND BOWING TOWARD THE ALTAR.—
The Choir shall stand turned towards the Altar at all
services until the first Antiphon is begun. Whenever
Glory be to the Father is said, they shall stand turned
toward the Altar, and bow towards the same. So also
at the commencement of all Responsories, Chapters,
and Collects, and at the end of the last Psalm until the
Responsory or Lection is begun.

At Mattins the Choir shall face the Altar until the
Invitatory and Canticle is finished, at the beginning of
Te Deum and *Benedicite*, and during the singing of
the last verse of each. Let all bow at " Holy, holy,
holy," etc. : " Since angels praise God with great
reverence, ye bow down yourselves when ye sing their
song " (" Myrroure" lxxiii.). Also at the words, "When
Thou tookest upon Thee," etc., in veneration of our
Lord's incarnation; and at " We therefore pray Thee,"
etc., in veneration of " that most rich liquor, the
reverend and holy Blood of our Lord Jesus Christ."

" When a bow is ordered, it should be made not side-
ways, obliquely, but straightforward, towards the Altar;
and the person bowing should bow the whole body."

OF THE SIGN OF THE CROSS.—" Ye bless ye with
the sign of the holy Cross, to chase away the fiend
with all his deceits; for, as St. Chrysostom saith,
'Whenever the fiends see this sign of the Cross, they
flee away, dreading it as a staff wherewith they are
beaten withal.' And at this blessing ye begin with
your hand at the head downward, and then to the left
side, and after to the right side, in token and belief our
Lord Jesus Christ came down from the Head—that is,
from the Father unto earth, by His holy Incarnation;

OF QUIRE SERVICE.

and from the earth unto the left side—that is, hell, by His bitter Passion; and from thence unto His Father's right side, by His glorious Ascension. And after this ye bring your hand to your breast, in token that ye are come to thank Him and praise Him in the inmost of your heart for His benefits."

OF RULERS OF THE CHOIR.—On all double Feasts there shall be four Rulers of the Choir; on Sundays and Feasts not doubles, two. The Octaves of certain Feasts also have Rulers, as hereafter noted. Let the Rulers be habited in silk copes, with caps on their heads, and in their left hands batons with which to rule the Choir.

ORGANS shall not sound in Lent except on Sundays (including the First Evensong on Saturday), Double Feasts, Evensong on Wednesday in Holy Week, and at Mass on Maundy Thursday.

OF LIGHTS.—On all Principal and Greater Doubles eight candles are lighted round about the Altar at all sung services; *i.e.* six on the Altar and two in standards. On Lesser and Inferior Doubles, on Simples of the first class, on Advent Sunday and Palm Sunday at both Evensongs and Mattins, at Evensong on Wednesday in Holy Week, on Maundy Thursday, and during Easter and Whitsun weeks, four candles are lighted at sung services. On all other occasions two candles are lighted. Candles should be lighted at Compline, but not at Prime, Terce, Sext, and None.

OF THE PREPARATORY PRAYERS.—Before each service let there be said secretly, "In the Name," etc., the Lord's Prayer, the Angelic Salutation, and the Creeds. At the *V.* "O God, make speed" all sign themselves with the Cross. This $V., R.$ are in the singular number, " because we begin our prayers and praises in the person of holy Church, which is one, and not many."

OF ANTIPHONS.—The Antiphon should indicate the tone in which the Psalm or Psalms following are to be sung; thus the first few words are sung before the Psalm by the Cantor alone, the whole is repeated by the Choir at the end. When the words of an Antiphon are taken from the beginning of the following Psalm they are not repeated, but the Psalm is begun from the point where the Antiphon ended.

An Antiphon is said to be "*doubled*" when the whole is sung before as well as after the Psalm. According to the ancient use of the Church, it appears that no antiphon except that over Magnificat was ever doubled, and that only at first Evensong of the greater Feasts, when all the side altars were censed. And this is the Sarum rule.

The doubling of antiphons has properly nothing to do with double Feasts, which seem to have been so called because on certain very great Feasts, when no Memorial was allowed, the Offices had to be doubled —*i.e.* the Festival and Ferial services said separately in their entirety;—whereas on smaller days it was permitted to make a memorial of the Feria or Sunday in the Festival Service. In later times this prolongation of the service was avoided (*a*) by dropping the ferial service altogether, (*b*) by a memorial, or (*c*) by transferring the Festival.

OF THE PSALMS.—According to ancient use (represented in the Sarum Breviary), all the Passion Psalms —*viz.* Pss. xxii.-xxvi., together with Pss. liv., cxviii., cxix. 1-16, 17-32—are sung under one Antiphon on Sundays at Prime, except between Christmas and the Octave of Epiphany, between Easter and Trinity, when any Festival is observed with full service on a Sunday, or when the Service of Octaves is performed on Sunday: for at such times Pss. liv. and cxix. are alone sung. On Sundays between Septuagesima and Easter Ps. xciii. takes the place of Ps. cxviii. On weekdays Pss. liv. and cxix. are said.

At Terce, Sext, and None the Psalms are invariable throughout the year. At Compline Pss. iv., xxxi., xci., cxxxiv. are sung under one Antiphon, and *Nunc Dimittis* under its own Antiphon; except from Maundy Thursday to the first Compline of Low Sunday, when Ps. xci. is omitted, and Pss. iv., xxxi., cxxxiv., and *Nunc Dimittis* are all sung under one Antiphon.

N.B.—If for convenience the Psalms at Prime are said according to the modern Roman use, one each day of the week, it would seem better to say Ps. xxiii. in the place of Ps. liv. on Sundays when the ANT. *The Lord is my Shepherd* is said. But neither method has any authority in the English Church.

TE DEUM according to ancient custom was said at Mattins on Sundays and Festivals only: except that it was not said on Sundays or Festivals during Advent; nor from Septuagesima to Easter; nor on Feasts of three Lessons falling on the Eves of Feasts or in Ember seasons, saving only the Eve of Epiphany falling on a Sunday, and the Whitsun Embertide.

The Altar and Choir should be incensed at *Magnificat* and *Benedictus*.

OF QUIRE SERVICE.

The Creed of Athanasius is said daily at Prime, except from Maundy Thursday to Low Sunday.

The Chapter ended, let the Choir always respond *Thanks be to God;* and the Clerk then begins the Responsory, as is more largely expressed at Terce on Advent Sunday. On Septuagesima, Sexagesima, and Quinquagesima Sundays, also during Lent, the mode of saying the Responsory differed, for which we see directions at Terce on Septuagesima.

Of the Kyrie.—Thus Cardinal Bona: "Dicunt Latini in missa *Kyrie, eleison* Græce; dicunt etiam Hebraice *Amen, Allelujah, Sabaoth,* et *Osanna:* quia fortassis sic ab initio ecclesiasticarum precum institutores voces istas usurparunt, ut ostenderent unam esse ecclesiam, qua ex Hebrais et Græcis primum, deinde ex Latinis coadunxta est," etc. (Tom. iii., p. 73).

The Lord's Prayer is always said silently throughout, which finished, the Priest repeats again aloud, *V. Lead us not,* etc., and Choir respond, *But deliver us,* etc. The Apostles' Creed is recited in a similar manner.

Of the Penitential Psalms.—The fifty-first Psalm is recited without note at every Service on Ferias throughout the year, except in Christmas and Eastertide, when the Petitions are not said. On Ferias in Lent it is followed by one of the Penitential Psalms at each service in order, except that at Sext it is followed by Psalm lxvii.

The custom of saying Psalm li. seven times daily arose towards the end of the tenth century, when it was a common belief that the world would come to an end in the year 1000 A.D.

Of Collects.—The Collect of the day is always preceded by *V. The Lord is with you*, *R. And with thy spirit*, *Let us pray*, except on Good Friday and Easter Eve. All Collects addressed to the Father conclude, *Through Jesus Christ our Lord, Who liveth and reigneth with Thee in the unity of the Holy Spirit, one God world without end.* Collects addressed to the Son conclude, *Who livest and reignest with the Father in the unity*, etc. If in the Collect the Son has been named, *through the same*, etc. If the mention of the Son occurs at the end, *Who liveth and reigneth with Thee*, etc. If the Holy Ghost has been named, *In the unity of the same Holy Ghost*, etc.

When a number of Collects are said in the Litany, the first and last shall have their full ending, and the intermediate ones have no set ending. *Let us pray* is said before the first two only. However, when Collects are said as Memorials, the intermediate ones end *Through Jesus Christ our Lord*.

OF MEMORIALS.—No Memorials should be made at any service except Mattins and Evensong. When several Memorials are said, the following is the order of precedence: (1) Memorial of any Feast day; (2) of a Sunday; (3) of a day within Octaves; (4) of the Feria, in Advent or Lent; (5) season Memorials, as of the Resurrection in Eastertide.

Collects and Memorials together at any one service must not exceed seven in number, and at Mass the number should always be uneven, except within the Octaves of Christmas.

OF COMMEMORATIONS.—In every church in England it has been usual in times past to celebrate on Saturdays the Commemoration of the Blessed Virgin; or if

Saturday be not vacant, on any other vacant Feria of the same week. Also where the church was not dedicated to our Lady, the Commemoration of the Feast of the place was made once every week on some vacant Feria, if practicable, and except as after mentioned. The commemorative service at the Lesser Hours was the same as on the Feast itself. There was never second Evensong of the Commemoration.

Such Commemorations were omitted during the third week in Advent, from Christmas Eve to the Octave of the Epiphany, from Ash Wednesday to Low Sunday, from the fifth Sunday after Easter to the Octave of the Ascension, during Whitsuntide, on Feasts and Octaves with Rulers, on Eves and Ember Days.

OF OCTAVES.—It was usual in times past to speak of a Feast having " Octaves," not " an Octave." " An Octave " denotes merely one of the seven days next succeeding particular Feasts of importance, whose celebration was prolonged during eight days.

According to the Sarum Use the following Feasts were kept with Octaves and Rulers of the Choir throughout:

All Principal Doubles; also the Feasts of Corpus Christi, Visitation, Holy Name, St. Stephen, St. John the Evangelist, Holy Innocents, St. Thomas of Canterbury, and the Nativity of B.V.M. The Dedication of a church ranks as a Principal Double; but if it fall between Septuagesima and Easter, it should have Rulers on the Octave day only.

Sarum Feasts with Octaves, but without Rulers through the Octaves, are as follows:

Nativity of St. John Baptist, St. Peter and St. Paul,

St. Laurence, St. Andrew, St. Martin. The Feasts of St. Peter and St. Andrew had Rulers on the Octave day.

On the Sunday within Octaves with Rulers the whole service is of the Octaves, *i.e.* the same as on the Festival, except certain modifications at Lauds and Evensong; Memorial of the Sunday is made.

On the Sunday within Octaves without Rulers the Service is all of the Sunday, or of any Feast falling on that day and taking precedence of the Sunday, together with a Memorial of the Octaves. If the Sunday be superseded by a Feast, then a Memorial of the Sunday shall be made before that of the Octaves.

On weekdays within Octaves all is said as on the Feast, except that at Prime the Antiphon over the Athanasian Creed and the Chapter change as is noted in the Psalter; and at Lauds and Evensong there are certain modifications.

On the Octave day all is done as on the Feast at the little Hours.

N.B.—Mattins and Evensong, according to the modern Anglican use, should be said throughout Octaves as on the Feast, with a Memorial of the Sunday on the Sunday within the Octaves. If the Octaves have no Rulers, then the Sunday service should be said throughout with Memorial of the Octaves. More detailed directions will be found in the Rubrics.

N.B.—"Procession before the Cross" was the ordinary Procession at Evensong on all Saturdays from Easter to Advent. It went down the Quire into the Nave, singing the Antiphon of the day; made a station before the Rood, where the *V. R.* and Collect were said;

and then immediately returned into the Quire, singing the Antiphon of St. Mary.

"Solemn" Memorials are those which are said aloud.

The Capitular Office after Prime was said in all Cathedral and Collegiate bodies.

The prayer, "May the souls of his faithful," etc., with which the offices of the Roman Breviary conclude, is not found anywhere in the Sarum.

When a Feast or Sunday has a first Evensong, then Compline on the Eve or Saturday is always of the following day, unless there be a special Compline appointed.

DIGNITY OF FEASTS.

Principal Doubles.—Christmas Day, Epiphany, Easter Day, Ascension Day, Whitsun Day, the Assumption of B.V.M., Feast of the place, Dedication of the church.

Greater Doubles.—Purification, Trinity Sunday, Corpus Christi, Visitation, Holy Name, Nativity of B.V.M., All Saints.

Lesser Doubles.—St. Stephen, St. John Evangelist, Holy Innocents, Circumcision, Annunciation, Easter Monday, Tuesday, and Wednesday, Whitsun Monday, Tuesday, and Wednesday, Low Sunday, Invention of the Cross, Nativity of St. John Baptist, St. Peter and St. Paul, Transfiguration, Exaltation of the Cross, Conception of B.V.M.

Inferior Doubles.—St. Andrew, St. Thomas Apostle, St. Thomas of Canterbury, St. Matthias, St. Gregory, St. Ambrose, St. George, St. Mark, St. Philip and St. James, St. Augustine of Canterbury, St. James, St. Bartholomew, St. Augustine of Hippo, St. Matthew, St. Michael and All Angels, St. Jerome, Translation of St. Edward, St. Luke, St. Simon and St. Jude, All Souls.

Simples of First Class. (Nine Lessons.)—Octave day of Epiphany, Conversion of St. Paul, St. John before the Latin Gate, St. Barnabas, Commemoration of St. Paul, Octave day of St. Peter and St. Paul, Octave day of the Visitation, St. Mary Magdalen, St. Anne, Lammas, St. Laurence, Octave day of the Holy Name, Beheading of St. John Baptist, St. Martin, St. Nicholas.

Simples of Second Class. (Nine Lessons.)—St. Lucy, St. Silvester, St. Agatha, St. David, St. Chad, St Benedict, St. Richard, St. Dunstan, St. Alban, Translation of St. Martin, St. Swithun, St. Margaret, St. Remigius, St. Denys, Translation of St. Etheldreda, St. Crispin, St. Leonard, St. Hugh, St. Edmund, St. Cecilia, St. Clement, St. Katherine.

Simples of Third Class. (Three Lessons.)—Octave days of St. Stephen, St. John Evangelist, and Holy Innocents.

Simples of Fourth Class. (Three Lessons.)—St. Blasius, St. Valentine, St. Perpetua and St. Felicitas, St. Alphege, Ven. Bede, St. Nicomede, St. Boniface, Translation of King Edward, Octave day of St. John Baptist, St. Enurchus, St. Lambert, St. Cyprian, St. Faith, St. Britius, St. Machutus.

Principal privileged Sundays.—First Sunday in Advent, Passion Sunday, Palm Sunday.

Greater privileged Sundays.—Second, third, and fourth Sundays in Advent, Septuagesima, and all from that day until Passion Sunday.

Lesser privileged Sundays.—First Sunday after the Octave of Epiphany, Rogation Sunday, first Sunday after Trinity.

Inferior privileged Sundays.—All others throughout the year.

Principal Ferias.—Ash Wednesday, Maundy Thursday, Good Friday, Holy Saturday, Whitsun Eve.

Greater Ferias.—All week-days between Passion Sunday and Maundy Thursday.

Lesser Ferias.—All week-days between Ash Wednesday and Passion Sunday, the first and third Rogation Days, and the last nine days of Advent.

Inferior Ferias.—Week-days in Advent before *O Sapientia*.

N.B.—When two Antiphons are printed or referred to at Prime, the second is always the Antiphon over the Athanasian Creed.

I. TABLE OF OCCURRENCE OF FEASTS.

(*i.e.* when one Feast occurs on the same day as another.)

	Day within Octaves without Rulers	Octave-day without Rulers	Day within Octaves and Octave-day with Rulers	Simple of the Fourth Class	Simple of the First Three Classes	Lesser and Inferior Double	Principal and Greater Double
Principal Sunday	B	B	B	B	A	A	A
Greater Sunday	B	B	B	B	A	A	C
Lesser Sunday		D	D	D	A	C	C
Inferior Sunday	D	D	C	D	C	E*	E*
Principal & Greater Double	B	B	D	B	A	A	F
Lesser and Inferior Double	B	D	D	D	A	F	G
Simple of the First Three Classes	D	D	D†	D	F	G	G
Simple of the Fourth Class	D	C	C		C	C	E
Day within Octaves and Octave-day with Rulers . .	D	D	H	D	C†	C	C
Day within Octaves without Rulers		C	C	C	C	E	E
Octave-day without Rulers .	D		C	D	C	C	E
Principal Feria	B	B	B	B	A	A	A
Greater Feria	B	B	B	B	A	C	C
Lesser and Inferior Feria .	D	D	C	B	C	C	C

A. All of I., Translation of II.
B. All of I., nothing of II.
C. Service of II., memorial of I.
D. Service of I., memorial of II.
E. All of II., nothing of I.
F. All of the higher, Translation of the other.
G. All of II., translation of I.
H. Service of the Octave-day, memorial of the other.

* When a Double Feast falls on a Sunday in Eastertide, a memorial is made of the Sunday.
† A simple Feast above the lowest class falling on the Octave-day of Ascension or Corpus Christi is translated.

II.

I. TABLE OF CONCURRENCE OF FEASTS.

(*i.e.* when second Evensong of one Feast falls on the same day as first Evensong of a Feast following.)

	Octave-day without Rulers	Octave-day with Rulers	Simple of the Fourth Class	Simple of the First Three Classes	Lesser and Inferior Double	Greater Double	Principal Double	Lesser and Inferior Sunday	Greater Sunday	Principal Sunday
PRINCIPAL SUNDAY		C	D	C	A	A	A			
GREATER SUNDAY		A	C	A	A	A	B			
LESSER & INFERIOR SUNDAY	C	A	C	A	B	B	B			
PRINCIPAL DOUBLE	D	D	D	D	C	A		D	C	A
GREATER DOUBLE	D	C	D	C	C		A	D	C	A
LESSER DOUBLE	D	C	D	C	A	A	A	D	C	A
INFERIOR DOUBLE	C	C	C	C	A	A	A	D	C	A
SIMPLE OF THE FIRST THREE CLASSES	C	A	C	A	A	A	B	A	A	B
SIMPLE OF THE FOURTH CLASS	B	B	B	B	B	B	B	B	B	B
OCTAVE-DAY WITH RULERS	C	A*	C	A*	A*	B*	B*	A*	A*	A
OCTAVE-DAY WITHOUT RULERS	A	C	A	B	B	B	A	A	B	
PRINCIPAL FERIA	D	D	D	D	D	D	D			

A. Service of II., memorial of I.
B. All of II., nothing of I.
C. Service of I., memorial of II.
D. All of I., nothing of II.

* The Octave-days which rank as Simples of the first class have their second Evensong with a memorial of the Feast following, unless such a Feast is unable to have its own second Evensong; viz. Octave-days of St. Andrew, Epiphany, Ascension, Corpus Christi, St. Peter, Visitation, Holy Name, Assumption and Nativity of B.V.M.; also the Octave-day of the Dedication of the church, if not kept in Advent, or between Septuagesima and Easter.

OCT 1 0 1995

ERRATA.

PAGE

12. The Collect at the Hours on the fifth and sixth days after Christmas (*i.e.* when the Feast of St. Thomas the Martyr is not kept), should be the same as on Christmas Day.

13. The Antiphon at Sext on the Feast of the Circumcision should end:
    O mother of God, pray for us.

20. On Monday before Ash-Wednesday let Evensong be of St. Mary, with full service on the morrow, if vacant; if not, let the service be performed on the Monday.

41. On Tuesday before Ascension Day let full service of St. Mary be performed in like manner.

50–53. All the Collects should end as is directed on p. xv.

99. *Glory be to the Father* is not said after Ps. xci. at Compline.

IN THE NAME OF THE HOLY AND UNDIVIDED TRINITY. AMEN.

Here beginneth the Order of Service according to the Manner and Use of the English Church of Sarum.

FIRST SUNDAY IN ADVENT.

No memorials are made on this day, except of holy Mary; and if the Feast of St. Andrew have been celebrated on this Saturday, a memorial is then made of it before that of holy Mary.

At Compline.

All as in Compl. i.

This Compline is said throughout Advent; on Double Feasts the Hymn only is changed, and Saviour who didst is said.

At Mattins. Te Deum is not said during Advent, whatever be the service. Neither is it said on Eves throughout the year, except on the Eve of Epiphany when it falls on a Sunday; nor is it said in Embertides, except the Whitsun Embertide.

And here it is to be noted that never in the Church of Sarum does the priest who executes the office begin the Lord's Prayer or the Creed aloud at any service, save only at Mass, when they are said or sung aloud throughout.

In Advent, when a Feast of nine Lessons falls upon a Saturday, it is celebrated on that day, and Second Evensong is of the Sunday with a solemn memorial of the Feast, unless it be a Double Feast; for then Evensong is of the Feast with a solemn Memorial of the Sunday following; yet on the Saturday before Advent Evensong is always of the Sunday, whatever be the Feast.

If a Feast of nine Lessons fall on a Sunday in Advent, it is always transferred to the morrow, even though it be a Double Feast. And when a Feast is so transferred, or if it fall naturally on the Monday, then on the Sunday Evensong shall be of the Feast, with a solemn memorial of the Sunday preceding that of blessed Mary.

And it must be noted that on all Feasts in Advent, always is made a solemn memorial of Advent and of holy Mary. Feasts of three Lessons in Advent are not observed even with a memorial, according to the Use of Sarum, except the Octave of St. Andrew.

And here it should be noted, that if the Feast of St. Andrew fall on Advent Sunday, it is always transferred to the morrow, even though the Church be dedicated in honour of St. Andrew.

At Prime.

Antiphon.—In that day the mountains shall drop down new wine, and the hills shall flow with milk and honey. Alleluia.

Psalm xxii. — My God, my God.

Psalm xxiii. — The Lord is my Shepherd. Glory be.

Psalm xxiv.—The earth is the Lord's.

Psalm xxv.—Unto Thee, O Lord. Glory be.

Psalm xxvi. — Be Thou my Judge.

Psalm liv.—Save me, O God. Glory be.

FIRST SUNDAY IN ADVENT.

Psalm cxviii.—O give thanks.
Psalm cxix.—Blessed are those. Glory be.
Psalm cxix.—O do well. Glory be.

The aforesaid Psalms are said at Prime in the above manner on all Sundays throughout Advent, and from the first Sunday after Epiphany to Easter, and from the first Sunday after Trinity to Advent, whenever the service is of the Sunday: except that from Septuagesima to Easter is said Psalm xciii., The Lord is King, instead of Psalm cxviii., O give thanks.

Whenever these Psalms are said at Prime, then over the Athanasian Creed is said the Antiphon, Thee, God the Father.

Chapter.—Now unto the King eternal.

For the rules for saying antiphons over the Athanasian Creed and Chapters, see the Rubrics in the Psalter.

At Terce.

Antiphon.—Rejoice greatly, O daughter of Sion; shout, O daughter of Jerusalem. Alleluia.

Chapter. Romans xiii. 11.
Now it is high time to awake out of sleep: for now is our salvation nearer than when we believed.

A clerk shall say the R.—Come and save us, O Lord God of hosts.
The choir repeat the same.
The clerk says the V.—Show the light of Thy countenance, and we shall be whole.
Choir.— *R.* O Lord God of hosts.
Clerk.—Glory be to the Father, and to the Son, and to the Holy Ghost.

Choir.—Come and save us, O Lord God of hosts.
The clerk says the verse.—The heathen shall fear Thy Name, O Lord.
The choir respond.— And all the kings of the earth Thy majesty.

Let this order be observed in all Responsories with their Verses in saying the Hours throughout the year, except in Lent and on Septuagesima, Sexagesima, and Quinquagesima Sundays.

Then let the priest say the Collect with—

V. The Lord be with you.
R. And with thy spirit.

Let us pray.

ALMIGHTY GOD, give us grace that we may cast away the works of darkness, and put upon us the armour of light, now in the time of this mortal life, in which Thy Son Jesus Christ came to visit us in great humility; that in the last day, when He shall come again in His glorious Majesty to judge both the quick and dead, we may rise to the life immortal, through Him who liveth and reigneth with Thee and the Holy Ghost, now and ever. Amen. [1549.]

Or this.

RAISE up, we beseech Thee, O Lord, Thy power, and come among us: that we, who, by reason of our sins, are set in the midst of so many and great dangers, by Thy merciful protection may be delivered. Who livest and reignest with the Father in the unity of the Holy Ghost, one God world without end.

SECOND SUNDAY IN ADVENT.

The above Collect is said at all the Hours of this day, and throughout the week when the service is of the season. And this rule shall be generally observed throughout the year, whether the service be of the season or of any Saint, that always the Collect which is said at Mattins is said at Terce, Sext, and None.

At Sext.

Antiphon.—Behold, the Lord shall come, and all His saints with Him; and in that day shall be great light. Alleluia.

Chapter. Romans xiii. 12.

The night is far spent, the day is at hand: let us therefore cast off the works of darkness, and let us put on the armour of light.

R. O Lord, show Thy mercy upon us. *V.* And grant us Thy salvation. *R.* Thy mercy upon us. *V.* Glory be to the Father, and to the Son, and to the Holy Ghost. *R.* O Lord, show Thy mercy upon us.

V. Remember us, O Lord, according to the favour that Thou bearest unto Thy people. *R.* O visit us with Thy salvation.

Collect as above.

At None.

Antiphon. — Behold, a great Prophet shall come: and it is He that shall renew Jerusalem. Alleluia.

Chapter. Romans xiii. 13.

Let us walk honestly, as in the day; not in rioting and drunkenness, not in chambering and wantonness, not in strife and envying. But put ye on the Lord Jesus Christ.

R. The Lord shall arise: upon thee, O Jerusalem. *V.* And His glory shall be seen upon thee. *R.* Upon thee, O Jerusalem. *V.* Glory be to the Father, and to the Son, and to the Holy Ghost. *R.* The Lord shall arise upon thee, O Jerusalem.

V. Turn us again, O Lord God of hosts. *R.* Show the light of Thy countenance, and we shall be whole.

Collect as above.

MONDAY.

At Prime.

Antiphon.—Come and deliver us: O our God.

Psalm liv.—Save me, O God.
Psalm cxix.—Blessed are those.
Psalm cxix.— O do well.

Antiphon. — Glory to Thee, Co-equal Trinity.

At Terce, Sext, and None all is said as is noted in the Psalter for Ferias in Advent. And so the Hours are said on Ferias until Christmas Eve, whenever the service is of the Feria, with the Sunday Collect.

At Evensong and Mattins on Ferias throughout Advent is made memorial (1) *of holy Mary;* (2) *of All Saints, whenever the service is of the Feria; and also on the Octaves of St. Andrew: except that no memorial of All Saints is made on December 16th, O Sapientia.*

SECOND SUNDAY IN ADVENT.

At Prime.

Antiphon.—Behold, the Lord shall come in the clouds of heaven: with great power. Alleluia.

At Terce.

Antiphon.—We have a strong city, even Sion: salvation will

God appoint for walls and bulwarks. Open ye the gates; for God is with us. Alleluia.

Chapter. Romans xv. 4.

Whatsoever things were written aforetime were written for our learning, that we through patience and comfort of the Scriptures might have hope.

RR., VV. as on the First Sunday in Advent; and so at all the Hours on Sundays in Advent.

Collect.

BLESSED LORD, Who hast caused all holy Scriptures to be written for our learning; Grant that we may in such wise hear them, read, mark, learn, and inwardly digest them, that by patience, and comfort of Thy holy Word, we may embrace, and ever hold fast the blessed hope of everlasting life, which Thou hast given us in our Saviour Jesus Christ. Amen. [1549.]

Or this.

STIR up, we beseech Thee, O Lord, the hearts of Thy faithful people to prepare the way of Thy only begotten Son: that so we may be found worthy to serve Thee with minds purified through His Advent. Through the same.

At Sext.

Antiphon. — The Lord shall appear and shall not lie: though He tarry, wait for Him; because He will surely come, He will not tarry. Alleluia.

Chapter. Romans xv. 5.

Now the God of patience and consolation grant you to be likeminded one toward another according to Christ Jesus: that ye may with one mind and one mouth glorify God, even the Father of our Lord Jesus Christ.

At None.

Antiphon.—Behold, our Lord shall come with power to enlighten the eyes of His servants. Alleluia.

Chapter. Romans xv. 13.

Now the God of hope fill you with all joy and peace in believing; that ye may abound in hope, through the power of the Holy Ghost.

THIRD SUNDAY IN ADVENT.

At Prime.

Antiphon. — The Lord will surely come, He will not tarry, and will bring to light the hidden things of darkness: and reveal Himself to all people. Alleluia.

At Terce.

Antiphon.—O Jerusalem, rejoice with great joy: for Thy Saviour shall come to thee. Alleluia.

Chapter. 1 *Cor.* iv. 1.

Let a man so account of us, as of the ministers of Christ, and stewards of the mysteries of God. Moreover it is required in stewards, that a man be found faithful.

Collect.

O LORD JESU CHRIST, Who at Thy first coming didst send Thy messenger to prepare Thy

FOURTH SUNDAY IN ADVENT.

way before Thee; Grant that the ministers and stewards of Thy mysteries may likewise so prepare and make ready Thy way, by turning the hearts of the disobedient to the wisdom of the just, that at Thy second coming to judge the world we may be found an acceptable people in Thy sight, Who livest and reignest with the Father and the Holy Spirit, ever one God, world without end. Amen. [1661.]

Or this.

INCLINE Thy gracious ears, O Lord, to our prayers: and lighten the darkness of our hearts by the glory of Thy visitation. Through.

At Sext.

Antiphon.—I will place salvation in Syon: and in Jerusalem My glory. Alleluia.

Chapter. 1 Cor. iv. 3.

But with me it is a very small thing that I should be judged of you, or of man's judgment: yea, I judge not mine own self.

At None.

Antiphon. — Live we righteously and godly: looking for that blessed hope, and the appearing of the Lord.

Chapter. 1 Cor. iv. 5.

Judge nothing before the time, until the Lord come, Who both will bring to light the hidden things of darkness, and will make manifest the counsels of the hearts: and then shall every man have praise of God.

FOURTH SUNDAY IN ADVENT.

At Prime.

Antiphon.—Blow ye the trumpet in Sion: for the day of the Lord is nigh at hand: behold, He shall come to save us. Alleluia, Alleluia.

At Terce.

Antiphon.—Behold, the Desire of all nations shall come: and the house of the Lord shall be filled with glory. Alleluia.

Chapter. Philippians iv. 4.

Rejoice in the Lord alway: and again I say, Rejoice. Let your moderation be known unto all men. The Lord is at hand.

Collect.

O LORD, raise up (we pray Thee) Thy power, and come among us, and with great might succour us; that whereas, through our sins and wickedness, we are sore let and hindered in running the race that is set before us, Thy bountiful grace and mercy may speedily help and deliver us; through the satisfaction of Thy Son our Lord, to Whom with Thee and the Holy Ghost be honour and glory, world without end. Amen.

At Sext.

Antiphon.—The crooked shall be made straight, and the rough places plain: come, O Lord, and tarry not. Alleluia.

Chapter. Philippians iv. 6.

Be careful for nothing; but in everything by prayer and supplication with thanksgiving let your requests be made known unto God.

At None.

Antiphon. — Thine almighty word, O Lord: shall leap down from heaven out of Thy royal throne. Alleluia.

Chapter. Philippians iv. 7.

The peace of God, which passeth all understanding, shall keep your hearts and minds through Christ Jesus.

CHRISTMAS EVE.

At Mattins Te Deum *is not said; and if it be Sunday, no memorial is made, save only of All Saints.*

At Prime.

Antiphon.—O Judah and Jerusalem, fear not, nor be dismayed: to-morrow go ye forth, for the Lord will go with you.

Psalm liv.—Save me, O God.
Psalm cxix.—Blessed are those.
Psalm cxix.—O do well.

Antiphon. — Glory to Thee, Coequal Trinity.

Chapter.—Lord, be gracious to us.

R. Jesus Christ, Son of the living God: have mercy upon us. Alleluia, Alleluia. *V.* Thou that sittest at the right hand of the Father. *R.* Have mercy upon us. Alleluia, Alleluia. *V.* Glory be. *R.* Jesus Christ.

The Petitions are said standing.

If Christmas Eve fall on Sunday, then the Antiphon to the Creed of St. Athanasius, Thee all Thy creatures, *and the Chapter,* Now unto the King eternal, *are said.*

At Terce.

Antiphon.—Ye shall know this day that the Lord will come: and in the morning shall ye see His glory.

Chapter. Isaiah lxii. 1.

For Zion's sake will I not hold my peace, and for Jerusalem's sake I will not rest, until the righteousness thereof go forth as brightness, and the salvation thereof as a lamp that burneth.

R. Stand ye still. Alleluia, Alleluia. *V.* And see the salvation of the Lord with you. *R.* Alleluia, Alleluia. *V.* Glory be. *R.* Stand.

V. To-morrow ye shall have help. *R.* Saith the Lord God of hosts.

The Petitions are not said at the Hours, and all is done standing.

Collect.

O GOD, Who makest us glad with the yearly expectation of our redemption; Grant that as we joyfully receive Thine only begotten Son as our Redeemer, so we may behold Him without fear when He shall come to be our Judge; through the same Jesus Christ, Thy Son our Lord, Who liveth and reigneth.

At Sext.

Antiphon. — To-morrow shall the wickedness of the earth be done away; and the Saviour of the world shall be King over us.

Chapter. Isaiah lxii. 2.

The Gentiles shall see thy righteousness, and all kings thy glory: and thou shalt be called

CHRISTMAS DAY.

by a new name, which the mouth of the Lord shall name.

R. To-morrow ye shall have help. Alleluia, Alleluia. V. Saith the Lord God of hosts. R. Alleluia, Alleluia. V. Glory be. R. To-morrow.

V. Ye shall know this day that the Lord will come. R. And in the morning ye shall see His glory.

At None.

Antiphon. — To-morrow ye shall have help: saith the Lord God of hosts.

Chapter. *Isaiah* lxii. 4.

Thou shalt no more be termed Forsaken; neither shall thy land any more be termed Desolate: but thou shalt be called My delight is in her, and thy land shall be inhabited.

R. Ye shall know this day that the Lord will come. Alleluia, Alleluia. V. And in the morning ye shall see His glory. R. Alleluia, Alleluia. V. Glory be. R. Ye shall know.

V. Stand ye still. R. And see the salvation of the Lord with you.

If Christmas Eve fall on Sunday, then the Sunday Mass is said in Chapter after Prime, before Terce, and before the Procession. And the Mass of the Eve is said after Sext in choir.

At Compline.

All as in Compline ii.

CHRISTMAS DAY.

At Mattins. Memorial of St. Mary is made: at the consummation of the whole mystery of the Incarnation.

At Prime.

The Hymns at all the Hours are said with this Doxology:

All glory, Virgin-born, to Thee,
Jesu, Incarnate Deity,
Whom with the Father we adore,
And Holy Spirit evermore.

And so until the morrow of the Purification, except during the Octave of the Epiphany.

Antiphon.—Whom saw ye, O shepherds? declare to us: say ye Who hath appeared upon earth. We have seen the Child amid choirs of angels, the Saviour, the Lord. Alleluia, Alleluia.

Psalms.—Save me, O God. Blessed are those. O do well.

Antiphon. — Thanks be to Thee.

Chapter.—Now unto the King eternal.

R. Jesus Christ, Son of the living God, have mercy upon us: Alleluia, Alleluia. V. Thou that didst not abhor the Virgin's womb. R. Have mercy upon us. Alleluia, Alleluia. V. Glory be. R. Jesus Christ.

V. O Lord, arise, help us. R. And deliver us for Thy Name's sake.

This Responsory is said daily till the morrow of the Purification, except during the Octaves of Epiphany, but without Alleluia after the Epiphany.

Petitions as usual, standing.

At Terce.

Antiphon.—A maiden hath borne the King, whose Name is everlasting: she hath the joy of a mother with the honour of virginity; none hath been seen like unto her, nor shall there be any such. Alleluia.

Chapter. Titus ii. 11.

The grace of God that bringeth salvation hath appeared to all men, teaching us that, denying ungodliness and worldly lusts, we should live soberly, righteously, and godly in this present world.

R. The Word was made flesh. Alleluia, Alleluia. V. And dwelt among us. R. Alleluia, Alleluia. V. Glory be. R. The word.

V. He shall call Me. R. Thou art my Father.

Collect.

ALMIGHTY GOD, Who hast given us Thy only begotten Son to take our nature upon Him, and as at this time to be born of a pure Virgin; Grant that we being regenerate, and made Thy children by adoption and grace, may daily be renewed by Thy Holy Spirit; through the same our Lord Jesus Christ, Who liveth and reigneth with Thee and the same Spirit, ever one God, world without end. Amen. [1549.]

Or this.

GRANT, we beseech Thee, Almighty God, that as we believe our Lord Jesus Christ at this time to have been born of a pure Virgin and made man; so, by this new birth of Thine only begotten Son, we who are tied and bound with the old bondage and yoke of sin, may be mercifully delivered; through the same.

At Sext.

Antiphon.—The angel said unto the shepherds, Behold, I bring you good tidings of great joy: for unto you is born this day the Saviour of the world. Alleluia.

Chapter. Titus iii. 4.

The kindness and love of God our Saviour toward man appeared, not by works of righteousness which we have done, but according to His mercy He saved us.

R. He shall call me. Alleluia, Alleluia. V. Thou art my Father. R. Alleluia, Alleluia. V. Glory be. R. He shall.

V. The Lord declared. R. His salvation.

At None.

Antiphon.—Unto us a Child is born this day: and His Name shall be called the Mighty God. Alleluia, Alleluia.

Chapter. Hebrews i. 1.

God, Who at sundry times and in divers manners spake in time past unto the fathers by the prophets, hath in these last days spoken unto us by His Son.

R. The Lord declared: Alleluia, Alleluia. V. His salvation. R. Alleluia, Alleluia. V. Glory be. R. The Lord.

V. Blessed is He that cometh in the name of the Lord. R. God is the Lord Who hath showed us light.

At Second Evensong memorial of St. Stephen is made, unless there be a Procession of St. Stephen. And no memorial of St. Mary is made at Mattins until the morrow of the Circumcision; nor yet at Evensong, unless there be a Procession.

At Compline.
All as in Compline iii.

ST. STEPHEN'S DAY.
At Mattins memorial of the Nativity is made.

At Prime.
Antiphon.—And they stoned Stephen, calling upon God, saying: Lord, lay not this sin to their charge.

At Terce.
Antiphon.—The stones of death were sweet unto Stephen: him do all righteous souls follow.

Chapter. Acts vi. 8.
Stephen, full of grace and power, did great wonders and miracles among the people.
R. Thou hast crowned him with glory and worship: Alleluia, Alleluia. V. Thou makest him to have dominion of the works of Thy hands. R. Alleluia, Alleluia. V. Glory be. R. Thou hast crowned.
V. Thou hast set upon his head, O Lord. R. A crown of pure gold.

Collect.

GRANT, O Lord, that, in all our sufferings here upon earth for the testimony of Thy truth, we may stedfastly look up to heaven, and by faith behold the glory that shall be revealed; and, being filled with the Holy Ghost, may learn to love and bless our persecutors by the example of Thy first Martyr Saint Stephen, who prayed for his murderers to Thee, O blessed Jesus, Who standest at the right hand of God to succour all those that suffer for Thee, our only Mediator and Advocate. Amen.

At Sext.
Antiphon.—My soul cleaveth unto Thee; since for Thee my body has been stoned, my God.

Chapter. Acts vii. 55, 56.
But Stephen, being full of the Holy Ghost, looked up stedfastly into heaven, and saw the glory of God, and Jesus standing on the right hand of God, and said, Behold, I see the heavens opened, and the Son of man standing on the right hand of God.
R. Thou hast set upon his head, O Lord:. Alleluia, Alleluia. V. A crown of pure gold. R. Alleluia, Alleluia. V. Glory be. R. Thou hast set.
V. The righteous shall flourish like a palm tree. R. And shall spread abroad like a cedar in Libanus.

At None.
Antiphon.—Behold, I see the heavens opened: and Jesus standing on the right hand of God.

Chapter. Acts vii. 60.
And he kneeled down, and cried with a loud voice, Lord, lay not this sin to their charge. And when he had said this, he fell asleep.

ST. JOHN THE APOSTLE'S DAY.

R. The righteous shall flourish like a palm tree. Alleluia, Alleluia. V. And shall spread abroad like a cedar in Libanus. R. Alleluia, Alleluia. V. Glory be. R. The righteous.
V. The righteous shall blossom as a lily. R. He shall flourish for ever before the Lord.

All the Hours are said before Mass on these three days.

At Evensong memorials (1) of St. John, (2) of the Nativity, are made, unless there is a Procession of St John, in which case memorial of the Nativity only is made.

ST. JOHN THE APOSTLE'S DAY.
At Mattins memorials (1) of the Nativity, (2) of St. Stephen.

At Prime.

Antiphon.—This is the disciple which did bear testimony: and we know that his testimony is true.

At Terce.

Antiphon.—This is My disciple: so I will that he tarry till I come.

Chapter. Ecclus. xv. 1.

He that feareth the Lord will do good: and he that hath the knowledge of the law shall obtain her; and as an honoured mother shall she meet him.

R. Their sound is gone out into all lands: Alleluia, Alleluia.
V. And their words into the ends of the world. R. Alleluia, Alleluia. V. Glory be. R. Their sound.
V. Thou shalt make them princes in all lands. R. They shall remember Thy Name, O Lord.

Collect.

MERCIFUL Lord, we beseech Thee to cast Thy bright beams of light upon Thy Church, that it being enlightened by the doctrine of Thy blessed Apostle and Evangelist Saint John may so walk in the light of Thy truth, that it may at length attain to the light of everlasting life; through Jesus Christ our Lord. Amen.

At Sext.

Antiphon.—Behold My servant, Mine elect whom I have chosen: I have put My Spirit upon him.

Chapter. Ecclus. xv. 3.

With the bread of life and understanding hath she fed him, and given him the water of saving wisdom to drink: he shall be stayed upon her, and shall not be moved, and shall rely upon her, and shall not be confounded, and she shall exalt him above his neighbours.

R. Thou shalt make them princes in all lands: Alleluia, Alleluia. V. They shall remember Thy Name, O Lord. R. Alleluia, Alleluia. V. Glory be. R. Thou shalt make.
V. Great is the honour of Thy friends, O God. R. Great is the might of their dominion.

At None.

Antiphon.—So I will that he tarry till I come: follow thou Me.

HOLY INNOCENTS' DAY.

Chapter. Ecclus. xv.

In the midst of the congregation he opened his mouth, and the Lord filled him with the spirit of wisdom and understanding: with a robe of glory He clothed him.

R. Great is the honour of Thy friends, O God: Alleluia, Alleluia. *V.* Great is the might of their dominion. *R.* Alleluia, Alleluia. *V.* Great is the honour.

V. They have declared the marvellous acts of God. *R.* They have also told of His greatness.

At Evensong memorial is made (1) *of the Holy Innocents,* (2) *of the Nativity,* (3) *of St. Stephen; unless there be a Procession of the Holy Innocents, in which case memorial is made* (1) *of the Nativity,* (2) *of St. Stephen.*

HOLY INNOCENTS' DAY.

At Mattins memorial (1) *of the Nativity,* (2) *of St. Stephen,* (3) *of St. John.*

At Prime.

Antiphon.—Herod, being exceeding wrath, slew many children: in Bethlehem of Judæa the city of David.

At Terce.

Antiphon.—From two years old and under: did Herod slay many children for the Lord's sake.

Chapter. Revelation xiv. 1.

I looked, and lo, a Lamb stood on the mount Sion, and with Him a hundred forty and four thousand, having His Father's Name written in their foreheads.

R. Be glad, O ye righteous, and rejoice in the Lord. Alleluia, Alleluia. *V.* And be joyful, all ye that are true of heart. *R.* Alleluia, Alleluia. *V.* Glory be. *R.* Be glad.

V. Let the righteous be glad and rejoice before God. *R.* Let them also be merry and joyful.

Collect.

O ALMIGHTY God, Who out of the mouths of babes and sucklings hast ordained strength, and madest infants to glorify Thee by their deaths; Mortify and kill all vices in us, and so strengthen us by Thy grace, that by the innocency of our lives, and constancy of our faith even unto death, we may glorify Thy holy Name; through Jesus Christ our Lord. Amen.

At Sext.

Antiphon.—A voice was heard in Ramah: lamentation and bitter weeping; Rachel weeping for her children.

Chapter. Revelation xiv. 4.

These are they which were not defiled with women; for they are virgins.

R. Let the righteous be glad, and rejoice before God: Alleluia, Alleluia. *V.* Let them also be merry and joyful. *R.* Alleluia, Alleluia. *V.* Glory be. *R.* Let the righteous.

V. The souls of the righteous are in the hand of God. *R.* And there shall no torment touch them.

THE CIRCUMCISION OF THE LORD.

At None.

Antiphon.—From under the altar all the saints of God do cry : Avenge our blood, O our God.

Chapter. Rev. xiv. 4, 5.

These were redeemed from among men, being the first-fruits unto God and to the Lamb, and in their mouth was found no guile.

R. The souls of the righteous are in the hand of God : Alleluia, Alleluia. *V.* And there shall no torment touch them. *R.* Alleluia, Alleluia. *V.* Glory be. *R.* The souls.

V. Wonderful art Thou in Thy saints, O God. *R.* And glorious in Thy majesty.

At Evensong memorial is made (1) *of the Nativity,* (2) *of St. Stephen,* (3) *of St. John. If the Feast of St. Thomas of Canterbury be observed, then memorial of St. Thomas is made before that of the Nativity, unless there be a Procession.*

ON THE FIFTH AND SIXTH DAYS AFTER THE NATIVITY; I.E. DECEMBER 29TH, 30TH

(if the Feast of St. Thomas of Canterbury be not kept)

All as on Christmas Day, except the Antiphon to the Creed of St. Athanasius, which shall be Thee all Thy creatures; *and the Collect at Prime, which shall be as follows :*

Collect.

ALMIGHTY and everlasting God, grant, we pray Thee, that in all our doings we may glorify Thy holy Name; that through the merits of Thy beloved Son we may be made fruitful in all good works; Who liveth and reigneth with Thee in the unity of the Holy Ghost, one God, world without end. Amen.

December 31st.
ST. SILVESTER. POPE AND CONFESSOR.

Feast of nine Lessons. All of the Common of a Bishop and Confessor, except that the Responsories are said with Alleluia, and the alternative Collect is said.

At First Evensong and at Mattins memoria' is made (1) *of the Nativity,* (2) *of St. Stephen,* (3) *of St. John,* (4) *of the Holy Innocents,* (5) *of St. Thomas (if the Feast be kept).*

THE CIRCUMCISION OF THE LORD.

At First Evensong no memorials are made, nor at Mattins.

At Compline.
All as in Compl. iv.

At Prime.

Antiphon.—O marvellous exchange! The Creator of mankind, taking to Himself a living body, hath deigned to be born of a Virgin : and proceeding forth as man by an Immaculate Conception, hath made us co-heirs of His Godhead.

The rest as on Christmas Day.

At Terce.

Antiphon.—When Thou wast born ineffably of a Virgin, then were the Scriptures fulfilled : Thou shalt come down as rain into a fleece of wool, to accomplish the salvation of mankind. We praise Thee, O our God.

EVE OF THE EPIPHANY.

Chapters, RR., VV. as on Christmas Day at all the Hours, with the Collect of the day.

Collect.

ALMIGHTY God, Who madest Thy blessed Son to be circumcised, and obedient to the law for man; Grant us the true Circumcision of the Spirit; that, our hearts, and all our members, being mortified from all worldly and carnal lusts, we may in all things obey Thy blessed will; through the same Thy Son Jesus Christ our Lord. Amen. [1549.]

Or this.

O GOD, by whose grace we celebrate the circumcision of our Saviour; Grant that as we have been renewed by the covenant of His flesh, so we may be defended by His eternal Godhead; Who liveth and reigneth.

At Sext.

Antiphon.—In the bush which Moses beheld burning but unconsumed, we recognise thy glorious virginity: O Mother of God.

At None.

Antiphon.—The root of Jesse hath budded: a star hath risen out of Jacob, a virgin hath borne the Saviour: we praise Thee, O our God.

At Second Evensong memorial is made of St. Stephen only.

OCTAVE OF ST. STEPHEN.

All as on St. Stephen's Day, whether it be Sunday or not.

At Prime Antiphon to Athanasian Creed, Thee all Thy creatures.

At Mattins and Evensong memorials are made (1) of St. John, (2) of the Holy Innocents, (3) of St. Thomas, (4) of holy Mary.

From this day until the Purification memorial is made of holy Mary, whatever be the service, both at Mattins and Evensong, except on the Eve and Feast of the Epiphany.

It is to be noted that when the Octave of St. John falls on Sunday, then Evensong on the preceding Saturday is of St. Stephen with memorial of St. John.

Similarly when the Octave of the Holy Innocents falls on Sunday, Evensong on the preceding Saturday is of St. John, with memorial of the Holy Innocents.

OCTAVE OF ST. JOHN.

All as on St. John's Day.

At Prime Antiphon over Athanasian Creed, Thee all Thy creatures.

At Mattins and Evensong memorials are made (1) of the Holy Innocents, (2) of St. Thomas, (3) of holy Mary.

OCTAVE OF THE HOLY INNOCENTS.

All as on Holy Innocents' Day.

At Prime Antiphon over Athanasian Creed, Thee all Thy creatures.

At Mattins and Evensong memorials are made (1) of St. Thomas, (2) of holy Mary.

EVE OF THE EPIPHANY.

At Mattins Te Deum is not said, unless it be Sunday. Memorials are made of St. Thomas, and, if it be not Sunday, of All Saints. No memorial is made of holy Mary.

At Prime all as on the Feast of the Circumcision with Chapter, Lord, be gracious.

If the Eve fall on Sunday, then at Prime is said Antiphon over Athanasian Creed, Thee duly praise, *and Chapter,* Now unto the King.

At Terce, Sext, and None all as on the Circumcision, with this Collect:

GRANT, we beseech Thee, O Lord, that the glory of this Festival which we are about to celebrate may shine in our hearts: that, being delivered from the darkness of this world, we may come to the brightness of our true home; through.

At Evensong no memorials are made.
At Compline all as in Compl. v.

FEAST OF THE EPIPHANY.

At Prime.

The Hymns at all the Hours are said with this doxology:

All glory, blessed Lord, to Thee
On this Thy glad Epiphany.
Whom with the Father we adore
And Holy Spirit evermore.

Antiphon. — Begotten before the morning star, or ever the worlds were made: the Lord our Saviour hath appeared on earth to-day.

Antiphon.—Thanks be to Thee.

Chapter. 1 Tim. i. 17.
Now unto the King eternal.

R. Jesu Christ, Son of the living God, have mercy upon us. Alleluia, Alleluia. V. Thou Who hast appeared on earth to-day. R. Have mercy upon us. Alleluia, Alleluia. V. Glory be. R. Jesu Christ.

V. O Lord, arise, help us. R. And deliver us for Thy Name's sake.

Petitions, etc., as usual.

At Terce.

Antiphon.—Thy light is come, O Jerusalem: and the glory of the Lord is risen upon thee: and the Gentiles shall walk in thy light. Alleluia.

Chapter. Isaiah lx. i.
Arise, shine, O Jerusalem; for thy light is come, and the glory of the Lord is risen upon thee.

R. All they from Sheba shall come: Alleluia, Alleluia. V. They shall bring gold and incense, and they shall show forth the praises of the Lord. R. Alleluia, Alleluia. V. Glory be. R. All they.

V. The kings of Tharsis and the isles shall give presents. R. The kings of Arabia and Saba shall bring gifts.

Collect.

O GOD, Who by the leading of a star didst manifest Thy only begotten Son to the Gentiles; Mercifully grant, that we which know Thee now by faith, may after this life have the fruition of Thy glorious Godhead; through Jesus Christ our Lord. Amen.

At Sext.

Antiphon. — When they had opened their treasures, the wise men presented unto the Lord gold, and frankincense, and myrrh. Alleluia.

Chapter. Isaiah lx. 2, 3.
But the Lord shall arise upon thee, O Jerusalem, and His glory shall be seen upon thee. And the Gentiles shall come to thy light, and kings to the brightness of thy rising.

OCTAVE OF THE EPIPHANY.

R. The kings of Tharsis and the isles shall give presents: Alleluia, Alleluia. *V.* The kings of Arabia and Saba shall bring gifts. *R.* Alleluia, Alleluia. *V.* Glory be. *R.* The kings.
V. O worship the Lord. *R.* In His holy house.

At None.

Antiphon.—Three are the gifts which the wise men offered to the Lord: gold, frankincense, and myrrh, to the Son of God, the mighty King. Alleluia.

Chapter. Isaiah lx. 6.
All they from Sheba shall come: they shall bring gold and incense; and they shall show forth the praises of the Lord.

R. O worship the Lord. Alleluia, Alleluia. *V.* In His holy house. *R.* Alleluia, Alleluia. *V.* Glory be. *R.* O worship.
V. O worship your God. *R.* All ye angels of His.

And so shall the Hours be said throughout the Octaves, except the Antiphon to the Creed of St. Athanasius, which is, Thee all Thy creatures, and the Chapter at Prime, which is, Lord, be gracious to us.
Memorial is made of holy Mary at Mattins and Evensong throughout the Octaves, but not of All Saints, because the choir is ruled.
On the morrow of the Epiphany memorial of St. Lucian is made at Evensong, and both at Mattins and Evensong on the day following.

OCTAVE OF THE EPIPHANY.

At First Evensong and Mattins memorials are made (1) *of St. Hilary*, (2) *of holy Mary*.

At Prime.

Antiphon.—The Saviour, redeeming mankind, came to be baptized: in order that by water He might restore our fallen nature, clothing us with a garment of immortality.
Antiphon. — Thee all Thy creatures.
Chapter. O Lord, be gracious.

At Terce.

Antiphon.—O Thou, Who with the Holy Ghost and with fire dost purify the corruption of our nature: all Thy people glorify Thee, our God and our Redeemer.
Chapter. Isaiah xxv. 1.
O Lord, Thou art my God; I will exalt Thee, I will praise Thy Name; for Thou hast done wonderful things; Thy counsels of old are faithfulness and truth.

RR., VV. at all the Hours as on the Epiphany with this Collect:

O GOD, Whose only begotten Son hath been manifested in substance of our flesh; Grant, we beseech Thee, that as we know Him to have been made outwardly in the likeness of men, so by His power we may be renewed in the inward man; Who liveth and reigneth.

At Sext.

Antiphon.—The Baptist feared, and dared not to touch the holy Head of God: but in fear he crieth, I have need to be baptized of Thee, O my Saviour.

Chapter. Isa. xxviii. 5 (LXX.).
High is Thine Arm, O Lord: O God of hosts, Thou art a crown of hope adorned with beauty.

At None.

Antiphon. Great is the mysstery which is published abroad to-day: for the Creator of all things purgeth away our guilt in Jordan.

Chapter. Isaiah xii. 3.
With joy shall ye draw water out of the wells of salvation. And in that day shall ye say, Praise the Lord, call upon His Name.

At Second Evensong *memorial is made of holy Mary.*
If the Octave of the Epiphany fall upon a Saturday, then Evensong on that Saturday shall be of the Octave, with solemn memorials (1) *of the Sunday,* (2) *of holy Mary.*
It is to be noted that on the Octaves of Epiphany, the Ascension, Corpus Christi, the Visitation, the Assumption, and the Nativity of blessed Mary, and of the Dedication of the church, second Evensong is always of the Octave, even though on the morrow may fall a Feast of nine Lessons, or commemoration of blessed Mary—except it be that such Feast of nine Lessons cannot have a second Evensong.

SUNDAY WITHIN THE OCTAVE OF EPIPHANY.

At First Evensong *the following Collect is said:*

O LORD, we beseech Thee mercifully to receive the prayers of Thy people which call upon Thee; and grant that they may both perceive and know what things they ought to do, and also may have grace and power faithfully to fulfil the same; through.

Memorial of holy Mary.

At Compline.

All as within the Octaves of Epiphany. Compl. v.
At Mattins *Collect as above; and memorial of holy Mary, and so at Mattins and Evensong until the Purification.*

At Prime.

All as within Octaves.
Antiphon. Begotten before the morning star (*p.* 14).
Antiphon. Thee all Thy creatures.

At Terce, Sext, and None *all as on the Feast of Epiphany, but with the above Collect.*
At Second Evensong *Collect as above, with memorial of holy Mary.*
On the morrow of the Octave of Epiphany, and daily until Septuagesima Sunday, all is said at all the Hours as is noted in the Psalter, except that at Prime, the V., Thou that didst not abhor the Virgin's womb, *is said until the morrow of the Purification, and the Hymns end with the Christmas doxology.*
At Compline *all as in Compl.* vi. *until the First Sunday in Lent.*
At Mattins and Evensong *memorials are made* (1) *of holy Mary, until the Purification,* (2) *of All Saints, until Septuagesima.*

SECOND SUNDAY AFTER EPIPHANY.

Collect.

ALMIGHTY and everlasting God, Who dost govern all things in heaven and earth; Mercifully hear the supplications of Thy people, and grant us Thy peace all the days of our life; through.

THIRD SUNDAY AFTER EPIPHANY.

Collect.

ALMIGHTY and everlasting God, mercifully look upon our infirmities, and in all our dangers and necessities stretch forth Thy right hand to help and defend us; through Jesus Christ our Lord. Amen.

FOURTH SUNDAY AFTER EPIPHANY.

Collect.

O GOD, Who knowest us to be set in the midst of so many and great dangers, that by reason of the frailty of our nature we cannot always stand upright; Grant to us such strength and protection, as may support us in all dangers, and carry us through all temptations; through Jesus Christ our Lord. Amen.

FIFTH SUNDAY AFTER EPIPHANY.

Collect.

O LORD, we beseech Thee to keep Thy Church and household continually in Thy true religion; that they who do lean only upon the hope of Thy heavenly grace may evermore be defended by Thy mighty power; through Jesus Christ our Lord. Amen.

SIXTH SUNDAY AFTER EPIPHANY.

Collect.

O GOD, Whose blessed Son was manifested that He might destroy the works of the devil, and make us the sons of God, and heirs of eternal life; Grant us, we beseech Thee, that, having this hope, we may purify ourselves, even as He is pure; that, when He shall appear again with power and great glory, we may be made like unto Him in His eternal and glorious kingdom; where with Thee, O Father, and Thee, O Holy Ghost, He liveth and reigneth, ever one God, world without end. Amen [1661].

SEPTUAGESIMA SUNDAY.

At First Evensong and from this time till Mass on Easter Eve Alleluia *is not said.*

At First Evensong no memorial is made unless a Feast of three Lessons fall on the Sunday, or a Feast of nine Lessons on the Saturday. If however Septuagesima fall before the Purification, a memorial of St. Mary is made as is aforesaid.

At Mattins from this day until Easter Te Deum *is not said.*

From Septuagesima to Easter no memorials are made on Saturdays or Sundays, unless a Feast of three or nine Lessons fall on the Sunday itself, or on Monday, or if Septuagesima fall before the Purification; for then memorial of St. Mary is made at both Evensongs, at Mattins, and at Mass. If a Feast of three Lessons fall on a Feria between Septuagesima and Lent, the whole service is of the Feast except on Saturdays.

SEPTUAGESIMA SUNDAY.

At Prime.

Antiphon.—And when he had agreed with the labourers for a penny a day: he sent them into his vineyard.

Instead of Psalm cxviii., O give thanks, is said Psalm xciii., The Lord is King. And this is to be observed on all Sundays until Ea.ter. All the other Psalms are said as on Advent Sunday.

At Terce.

Antiphon.—Go ye also into My vineyard: and whatsoever is right I will give you.

Chapter. 1 Cor. ix. 24.

Know ye not that they which run in a race run all, but one receiveth the prize? So run, that ye may obtain.

A clerk begins the R.—Be Thou my helper. *The choir continue*, O Lord: leave me not. *The clerk sings the V.*—Neither forsake me, O God of my salvation. *Choir.—R.* Leave me not. *Clerk.—V.* Glory be. *Choir.— R.* Be Thou my helper, O Lord. Leave me not.

The Clerk says the V.—I said, Lord, be merciful unto me. *R.* Heal my soul, for I have sinned against Thee.

In this manner the Responsories at the Hours are said daily until Maundy Thursday; except only on Ferias before Lent. In Passiontide however they are said without Glory be.

Collect.

O LORD, we beseech Thee favourably to hear the prayers of Thy people; that we, who are justly punished for our offences, may be mercifully delivered by Thy goodness, for the glory of Thy Name; through.

At Sext.

Antiphon.—Why stand ye here all the day idle?: they say unto him, Because no man hath hired us.

Chapter. 1 Cor. ix. 25.

And every man that striveth for the mastery is temperate in all things. Now they do it to obtain a corruptible crown; but we an incorruptible.

R. Thou, O Lord, art my hope: even from my youth. *V.* Through Thee have I been holden up ever since I was born, Thou art my God even from my mother's womb. *R.* Even from my youth. *V.* Glory be to the Father, and to the Son, and to the Holy Ghost. *R.* Thou, O Lord, art my hope even from my youth.

V. The Lord is my shepherd, therefore I can lack nothing. *R.* He shall feed me in a green pasture.

At None.

Antiphon.—The goodman of the house said unto his labourers, Why stand ye here all the day idle? because no man hath hired us: go ye also into my vineyard, and whatsoever is right, I will give you.

Chapter. 1 Cor. x. 1.

I would not that ye should be ignorant, brethren, how that all our fathers were under the cloud, and all passed through the sea; and were all baptized unto Moses in the cloud and in the sea.

SEXAGESIMA SUNDAY.

R. Cleanse me, O Lord, from my secret faults. V. Keep Thy servant also from presumptuous sins. R. From my secret faults. V. Glory be to the Father, and to the Son, and to the Holy Ghost. R. Cleanse me, O Lord, from my secret faults.

V. Thou hast been my succour. R. Leave me not, neither forsake me, O God of my salvation.

If the Feast of the Purification fall on this Sunday, or on Sexagesima or Quinquagesima Sunday, then only a memorial of the Sunday is made. If it fall on Quinquagesima Sunday the Feast of St. Blasius is not observed. If any other Feast fall on this Sunday, or on any other Sunday until Maundy Thursday, it is transferred to the next vacant Feria in the same week, the Feast of the dedication of the church only excepted. In Passiontide double Feasts only are observed.

From Ash Wednesday to the morrow of Low Sunday, Feasts of three Lessons are not observed.

On Ferias, until the First Sunday in Lent, all is said as is noted in the Psalter.

SEXAGESIMA SUNDAY.

At Prime.

Antiphon.—The seed fell on good ground: and bare fruit, some an hundred-fold, some sixty-fold.

At Terce.

Antiphon.—The seed fell on good ground: and brought forth fruit with patience.

Chapter. 2 Cor. xi. 19.

Ye suffer fools gladly, seeing ye yourselves are wise. For ye suffer, if a man bring you into bondage, if a man devour you, if a man take of you, if a man exalt himself, if a man smite you on the face.

RR., VV., *as on Septuagesima Sunday, at Terce, Sext, and None.*

Collect.

O LORD GOD, Who seest that we put not our trust in anything that we do; Mercifully grant that by Thy power we may be defended against all adversity; through.

At Sext.

Antiphon.—When Jesus had said these things, He cried: He that hath ears to hear, let him hear.

Chapter. 2 Cor. xii. 2.

I knew a man in Christ above fourteen years ago, (whether in the body, I cannot tell; or whether out of the body, I cannot tell: God knoweth;) such an one caught up to the third heaven.

At None.

Antiphon.— Unto you it is given to know the mysteries of the kingdom of God: but to others in parables, said Jesus to His disciples.

Chapter. 2 Cor. xii. 3.

I knew such a man, (whether in the body, or out of the body, I cannot tell: God knoweth;) how that he was caught up into paradise, and heard unspeakable words, which it is not lawful for a man to utter.

ASH WEDNESDAY.

QUINQUAGESIMA SUNDAY.

At Prime.

Antiphon.—As Jesus journeyed on the way to Jerusalem: a blind man cried unto Him that he might receive his sight.

At Terce.

Antiphon.—As the Lord passed by, the blind man cried unto Him: Thou Son of David, have mercy upon me.

Chapter. 1 Cor. xiii. 1.

Though I speak with the tongues of men and of angels, and have not charity, I am become as sounding brass, or a tinkling cymbal.

RR., VV., as on Septuagesima Sunday, at Terce, Sext, and None.

Collect.

O LORD, Who hast taught us that all our doings without charity are nothing worth; Send Thy Holy Ghost, and pour into our hearts that most excellent gift of charity, the very bond of peace and of all virtues, without which whosoever liveth is counted dead before Thee; Grant this for Thine only Son Jesus Christ's sake. Amen.

At Sext.

Antiphon —The blind man sat by the wayside, and cried: Have mercy upon me, Thou Son of David.

Chapter. 1 Cor. xiii. 4.

Charity suffereth long, and is kind; charity envieth not; charity vaunteth not itself, is not puffed up, doth not behave itself unseemly, seeketh not her own.

At None.

Antiphon.— The blind man cried so much the more: that the Lord would open his eyes.

Chapter. 1 Cor. xiii. 5.

Charity is not easily provoked, thinketh no evil; rejoiceth not in iniquity, but rejoiceth in the truth.

ASH WEDNESDAY.

At Prime and all the other Hours, all is done as on the preceding days; and so they are said until the First Sunday in Lent, with the proper Collect.

Collect.

ALMIGHTY and everlasting God, Who hatest nothing that Thou hast made, and dost forgive the sins of all them that are penitent; Create and make in us new and contrite hearts, that we worthily lamenting our sins, and acknowledging our wretchedness, may obtain of Thee, the God of all mercy, perfect remission and forgiveness; through Jesus Christ our Lord. Amen. [1549]

This Collect shall be said daily, as a memorial for Penitents, at Mattins and Evensong from this day until Maundy Thursday, whenever the service is of the Feria.

Or this Collect may be said at the Hours on this day:

GRANT, O Lord, to Thy faithful people grace to enter upon the solemnities of the holy fast with true intention, that being free from all adversities they may accomplish it with gladness; through.

Whatever Feast may fall on this day, it is always transferred. On any Feast of nine Lessons that is celebrated between this day and Maundy Thursday, a solemn memorial is always made of the Fast at Mattins and at both Evensongs, but not at Mass. For after the Mass of the Feast the Mass of the Fast is said, both at the principal altar.

Thursday.

The Collect at Terce, Sext, and None changes daily throughout Lent.

Collect.

O GOD, Who hast revealed Thy wrath upon sin, but art gracious to those that repent, mercifully hear the supplications of Thy humble servants: and of Thy bountiful goodness turn from us the fierceness of Thine anger which for our sins we have deserved; through.

Friday.
Collect.

ASSIST us mercifully, O Lord, in the fast which we have begun: that the outward mortifying of our bodies may avail to the health of our souls; through.

Saturday.
Collect.

HEAR our prayers, O Lord, we beseech Thee; and grant us so worthily to celebrate this holy fast, that of Thy mercy we may obtain that health of body and soul for which its solemnities were ordained; through.

FIRST SUNDAY IN LENT.

At Compline.

All as in Compl. vii.: and so Compline is said until the Third Sunday in Lent.

At Prime.

Antiphon.—And when Jesus had fasted forty days and forty nights: He was afterwards an hungred.

At Terce.

Antiphon.—Man shall not live by bread alone: but by every word that proceedeth out of the mouth of God.

Chapter. 2 Cor. vi. 1.

We beseech you that ye receive not the grace of God in vain. For He saith, I have heard thee in a time accepted, and in the day of salvation have I succoured thee.

R. Make me a companion: O God, of all them that fear Thee, and keep Thy commandments. *V.* O look Thou upon me, and be merciful unto me: as Thou usest to do unto those that love Thy Name. *R.* And keep Thy commandments. *V.* Glory be. *R.* Make me.

V. He shall say unto the Lord. *R.* Thou art my hope and my stronghold, my God.

Collect.

O LORD, Who for our sake didst fast forty days and forty nights: Give us grace to use such abstinence, that, our flesh being subdued to the Spirit, we may ever obey Thy godly motions in righteousness, and true holiness, to Thy honour and glory, Who livest and reignest. [1549]

Or this.

O GOD, Who by the forty days' fast dost cleanse Thy Church year by year; Mercifully behold this Thy family, and grant to us who approach Thee with holy abstinence grace to live according to Thy will; through.

At Sext.

Antiphon.—Then the devil taketh Him up into the holy city: and setteth Him on a pinnacle of the Temple: and saith unto Him, If Thou be the Son of God, cast Thyself down.

Chapter. 2 Cor. vi. 2.

Behold, now is the accepted time; behold, now is the day of salvation. Giving no offence in anything, that the ministry be not blamed.

R. Refrain: my feet from every evil way, that I may keep Thy word, O Lord. *V.* I have not shrunk from Thy judgments; for Thou teachest me Thy law. *R.* That I may keep Thy word, O Lord. *V.* Glory be. *R.* Refrain my feet.

V. He hath delivered me. *R.* From the snare of the hunter and from the noisome pestilence.

At None.

Antiphon.—Get thee hence, Satan: thou shalt not tempt the Lord thy God.

Chapter. 2 Cor. vi. 4.

In all things approving ourselves as the ministers of God, in much patience.

R. Show: us, O God, Thy mercy. *V.* When Thy word goeth forth it giveth understanding, O Lord. *R.* Thy mercy. *V.* Glory be. *R.* Show us.

V. He shall defend thee under His wings. *R.* And thou shalt be safe under His feathers.

MONDAY OF THE FIRST WEEK IN LENT.

*Here it is to be noted that at Mattins and Evensong, and at all the Hours during the whole of Lent, whenever the service is of the Feria, one of the seven penitential Psalms, according to their order, is said after Psalm li., Have mercy, except at Sext: for then is said Psalm lxvii., God be merciful unto us, in place of Psalm li.
And if a Feast of nine Lessons follow on the morrow, then the three last of these Psalms are said at None. The same is done on Saturdays.*

At Prime.

Antiphon.—As I live, saith the Lord, I have no pleasure in the death of a sinner: but rather that he be converted and live.

Every day throughout Lent until Maundy Thursday, whenever the service is of the Feria, immediately after Prime, before the Chapter Mass, is said the Commendation of Souls, except on the morrow of a Double Feast.

At Terce.

Antiphon.— Let us chasten ourselves in much patience: by the armour of the righteousness of God.

Chapter. Joel ii. 13.

Turn unto the Lord your God: for He is gracious and merciful,

FIRST SUNDAY IN LENT.

slow to anger, and of great kindness, and repenteth Him of the evil.
R. Make me a companion: O God, of all them that fear Thee, and keep Thy commandments.
V. O look Thou upon me, and be merciful unto me: as Thou usest to do unto those that love Thy Name. *R.* And keep Thy commandments. *V.* Glory be. *R.* Make me.
V. He shall say unto the Lord. *R.* Thou art my hope and my stronghold, my God.

From this day until Wednesday before Easter, whenever the service is of the Feria, are said, after Terce, the fifteen Gradual Psalms for all the people of God.
And here it should be noted that on every Feria is said the Litany, as is directed in this book, and all is said kneeling and without note.

At Sext.

Antiphon. — Let us chasten ourselves in much patience: and fastings by the armour of righteousness.

Chapter. Isaiah lv. 7.
Let the wicked forsake his way, and the unrighteous man his thoughts: and let him return unto the Lord, and He will have mercy upon him; and to our God, for He will abundantly pardon.

R. Refrain: my feet from every evil way, that I may keep Thy word, O Lord. *V.* I have not shrunk from Thy judgments; for Thou teachest me Thy law. *R.* That I may keep Thy word, O Lord. *V.* Glory be. *R.* Refrain my feet.

V. He hath delivered me. *R.* From the snare of the hunter and from the noisome pestilence.

And here it is to be noted that on every day throughout Lent, i.e. on Ferias, all the Hours should be said before Mass.

At None.

Antiphon.—The days of repentance are come upon us: for the redemption of sins and our souls' salvation.

Chapter. Isaiah lviii. 7.
Deal thy bread to the hungry, and bring the poor that are cast out to thy house: when thou seest the naked, cover thou him; and hide not thyself from thine own flesh, saith the Lord Almighty.

R. Show: us, O God, Thy mercy. *V.* When Thy word goeth forth, it giveth understanding, O Lord. *R.* Thy mercy. *V.* Glory be. *R.* Show us.
V. He shall defend thee under His wings. *R.* And thou shalt be safe under His feathers.

And the Hours are said thus until the Third Sunday in Lent.
And every day throughout Lent, whatever be the service, Evensong should be said after Mass before the meal of the day, Sundays only excepted.
On all Ferias in Lent until Wednesday before Easter, after Mass and before Evensong, is said Evensong of the Dead, unless on the next day a Feast of nine Lessons occur, or when a body is to be buried on the morrow. If there be such a body, then Evensong and Mattins of the Dead are said after the meal before Compline, in the usual manner, as far as to Lauds.

SECOND SUNDAY IN LENT.

Collects.

MONDAY.—Turn us, O God our Saviour: and store our minds, we pray Thee, with Thy heavenly precepts, that the forty days of our fast may be unto us for spiritual refreshing; through.

TUESDAY.—O Lord, we beseech Thee mercifully to behold Thy family: and grant, that as we chasten our bodies with fasting, so our souls may ever shine in Thy sight with exceeding desire and longing after Thee; through.

WEDNESDAY.—We pray Thee, O Lord, mercifully to hearken to our prayers: and stretch out the right hand of Thy majesty to shield and defend us from all adversity; through.

THURSDAY.—O Almighty and everlasting God, Who in Thy providence hast appointed fasting and almsdeeds to be remedies for sin; Grant that we, being ready both in body and soul, may serve Thee devoutly all the days of our life; through.

FRIDAY.—Be merciful, we beseech Thee, O Lord, to Thy people: and that they may perfectly serve Thee, strengthen and refresh them evermore by Thy most gracious and ready help; through.

SATURDAY.—We beseech Thee, O Lord, look graciously upon Thy people: and of Thy tender mercy turn from them the fierceness of Thy fiery indignation and wrath; through.

SECOND SUNDAY IN LENT.

At Prime.

Antiphon. — Jesus' disciples came and besought Him, saying: Send her away, for she crieth after us.

At Terce.

Antiphon.—I am not sent: but unto the lost sheep of the house of Israel, saith the Lord.

Chapter. 1 Thess. iv. 1.

We beseech you and exhort you by the Lord Jesus, that as ye have received of us how ye ought to walk and to please God, so ye would abound more and more.

RR., VV. *as in the preceding week at all the Hours.*

Collect.

ALMIGHTY God, Who seest that we have no power of ourselves to help ourselves; Keep us both outwardly in our bodies, and inwardly in our souls; that we may be defended from all adversities which may happen to the body, and from all evil thoughts which may assault and hurt the soul; through.

At Sext.

Antiphon.—O woman, great is thy faith: be it unto thee even as thou wilt.

Chapter. 1 Thess. iv. 3.

This is the will of God, even your sanctification, that ye should abstain from fornication: that every one of you should know how to possess his vessel in sanctification and honour.

At None.

Antiphon.—Woman, depart, I have already said unto thee: If thou wilt believe, thou shalt see marvellous things.

Chapter. 1 Thess. iv. 6.

It is the will of God, that no man go beyond and defraud his brother in any matter: because that the Lord is the avenger of all such, as we also have forewarned you and testified.

The Second Week in Lent.

All as in the first week except the Collects.

Collects.

Monday.—Grant, we beseech Thee, Almighty God, to us Thy humble servants: that as to the afflicting our flesh we mortify ourselves by abstinence, so pursuing after holiness we may ever abstain from sin; through.

Tuesday.—Mercifully grant, we beseech Thee, O Lord, that we may so perfectly observe the discipline of our holy fast: that, according as we have learnt at Thy mouth, so by Thy mighty aid we may accomplish those things that Thou wouldest have done; through.

Wednesday.—Look graciously, O Lord, on us Thy servants: and as Thou dost enjoin upon us to abstain from pleasant meat, so give us grace to flee from sin and from all things that may do hurt; through.

Thursday.—Grant us, we beseech Thee, O Lord, the assistance of Thy grace: that, giving ourselves to prayer and fasting at this holy season, we may be delivered from all adversities that may happen to the body, and from all enemies that may assault and hurt the soul; through.

Friday.—Grant, we beseech Thee, Almighty God: that, being cleansed by this holy fast, we may with pure hearts and minds approach the blessed feast for which we wait; through.

Saturday.—O Lord, we beseech Thee, make this our fast to be both pleasing unto Thee and for salvation unto us Thy servants: that the mortifying of our flesh may be for our spiritual advancement in the heavenly life; through.

THIRD SUNDAY IN LENT.

At Compline.

All as in Compl. ix. And Compline is said thus until Passion Sunday.

At Prime.

Antiphon.—If I, by the finger of God, cast out devils: no doubt the kingdom of God is come upon you.

At Terce.

Antiphon.—When a strong man armed keepeth his palace: his goods are in peace.

Chapter. Ephesians v. 1.

Be ye followers of God as dear children; and walk in love, as Christ also hath loved us, and hath given Himself for us an offering and a sacrifice to God for a sweetsmelling savour.

R. It is good for me, Lord: that I have been in trouble. The

THIRD SUNDAY IN LENT.

law of Thy mouth is dearer to me than thousands of gold and silver. *V.* Thy hands have made me and fashioned me: O give me understanding, that I may learn Thy commandments. *R.* The law of Thy mouth is dearer unto me than thousands of gold and silver. *V.* Glory be. *R.* It is good for me.

V. He shall say unto the Lord. *R.* Thou art my hope and my stronghold, my God.

Collect.

WE beseech Thee, Almighty God, look upon the hearty desires of Thy humble servants, and stretch forth the right hand of Thy Majesty, to be our defence against all our enemies; through.

At Sext.

Antiphon.—He that gathereth not with Me scattereth: and he that is not with Me is against Me.

Chapter. Ephesians v. 3.

But fornication, and all uncleanness, or covetousness, let it not be once named among you, as becometh saints.

R. I am Thy servant: grant me understanding, O Lord. *V.* That I may know Thy testimonies. *R.* Grant me understanding, O Lord. *V.* Glory be. *R.* I am.

V. He hath delivered me. *R.* From the snare of the hunter and from the noisome pestilence.

At None.

Antiphon.—When the unclean spirit is gone out of a man: he walketh through dry places, seeking rest, and finding none.

Chapter. Ephesians v. 5.

Know this, brethren, that no whoremonger, nor unclean person, nor covetous man, who is an idolater, hath any inheritance in the kingdom of Christ and of God.

R. Seven times a day: do I praise Thee, O Lord. My God, cast me not away. *V.* I have gone astray like a sheep that is lost; O seek Thy servant, for I do not forget Thy commandments. *R.* My God, cast me not away. *V.* Glory be. *R.* Seven times.

V. He shall defend thee under His wings. *R.* And thou shalt be safe under His feathers.

MONDAY OF THE THIRD WEEK IN LENT.

At Prime.

Antiphon.—As I live, saith the Lord, I have no pleasure in the death of a sinner: but rather that he be converted and live.

At Terce.

Antiphon. — Let us chasten ourselves in much patience: by the armour of the righteousness of God.

Chapter. Isaiah i. 16.

Wash you, make you clean; put away the evil of your doings from before Mine eyes; cease to do evil; learn to do well.

R. It is good for me, O Lord: that I have been in trouble. The law of Thy mouth is dearer unto me than thousands of gold and

THIRD SUNDAY IN LENT.

silver. *V.* Thy hands have made me and fashioned me: O give me understanding, that I may learn Thy commandments. *R.* The law of Thy mouth is dearer unto me than thousands of gold and silver. *V.* Glory be. *R.* It is good for me.
V. He shall say unto the Lord. *R.* Thou art my hope and my stronghold, my God.

At Sext.

Antiphon.—Let us chasten ourselves in much patience: and fastings, by the armour of righteousness.

Chapter. Isaiah i. 17.

Seek judgment, relieve the oppressed, judge the fatherless, plead for the widow. And come, and let us reason together, saith the Lord.

R. I am Thy servant: grant me understanding, O Lord. *V.* That I may know Thy testimonies. *R.* Grant me understanding, O Lord. *V.* Glory be. *R.* I am.
V. He hath delivered me. *R.* From the snare of the hunter and from the noisome pestilence.

At None.

Antiphon.—The days of repentance are come upon us: for the redemption of sins and our souls' salvation.

Chapter. Isaiah i. 18.

Though your sins be as scarlet, they shall be as white as snow; though they be red like crimson, they shall be as wool.

R. Seven times a day: do I praise Thee, O Lord. My God, cast me not away. *V.* I have gone astray like a sheep that is lost; O seek Thy servant, for I do not forget Thy commandments. *R.* My God, cast me not away. *V.* Glory be. *R.* Seven times.
V. He shall defend thee under His wings. *R.* And thou shalt be safe under His feathers.

And so shall the Hours be said on Ferias until Passion Sunday, with the Collect of the day.

Collects.

MONDAY.—We beseech Thee, O Lord, pour Thy grace into our hearts: that as we abstain from pleasant meat, so all carnal affections may die in us Thy servants; through.

TUESDAY.—Hear us, Almighty and merciful Lord; and of Thy tender mercy bestow on us the saving grace of chastity; through.

WEDNESDAY.—Grant, we beseech Thee, O Lord, that, taught by these saving fasts, we may be set free from all sin and evil, and draw down the abundance of Thy mercy on our souls; through.

THURSDAY. — Grant, we beseech Thee, Almighty Lord: that we, who obediently keep these holy fasts, may be cleansed from all sin and made worthy to stand in the presence of Thy Divine majesty; through.

FRIDAY. — Assist us mercifully, O Lord, in these our days of fasting: that as by abstinence from food we mortify the body, so by cutting off all occasion of sin we may render to Thee our reasonable service; through.

SATURDAY. — Grant, we beseech Thee, Almighty God, to us Thy humble servants: that as, to the afflicting of our flesh, we mortify ourselves by abstinence, so in pursuing after holiness we may ever abstain from sin; through.

FOURTH SUNDAY IN LENT.

At Prime.

Antiphon. — Jesus therefore went up into a mountain, and there He sat with His disciples: and the Passover, a feast of the Jews, was nigh.

At Terce.

Antiphon. — Jesus therefore took the loaves, and when He had given thanks He distributed to them that were set down: and likewise of the fishes as much as they would.

Chapter. Galatians iv. 22.

It is written, that Abraham had two sons, the one by a bondmaid, the other by a freewoman. But he who was of the bondwoman was born after the flesh; but he of the freewoman was by promise.

RR., VV. *at all the Hours, as in the preceding week.*

Collect.

GRANT, we beseech Thee, Almighty God, that we, who for our evil deeds do worthily deserve to be punished, by the comfort of Thy grace may mercifully be relieved; through.

At Sext.

Antiphon.—With five loaves and two fishes: did the Lord satisfy five thousand men.

Chapter. Galatians iv. 27.

Rejoice, thou barren that bearest not; break forth and cry, thou that travailest not: for the desolate hath many more children than she which hath an husband.

At None.

Antiphon.—The Lord fed five thousand men: with five loaves and two fishes.

Chapter. Galatians iv. 28.

Now we, brethren, as Isaac was, are the children of promise. But as then he that was born after the flesh persecuted him that was born after the Spirit, even so it is now. Nevertheless what saith the Scripture? Cast out the bondwoman and her son.

FOURTH WEEK IN LENT.

All as in the third week, except the Collects.

Collects.

MONDAY.—Grant, we beseech Thee, Almighty God, that as we chasten ourselves with the yearly observance of our holy fast, so we may please Thee, both in body and soul; through.

TUESDAY.— Assist us mercifully, O Lord, in these our days of abstinence: and grant that, advancing in holiness of life, we may be protected by Thy continual help and mercy; through.

WEDNESDAY.— O God, who

rewardest the righteous after their works, and grantest pardon to all sinners who turn to Thee with weeping and fasting: have mercy on us Thy servants, and spare all those who acknowledge their guilt unto Thee; through.

THURSDAY. — Grant, we beseech Thee, Almighty God, that as we chasten our bodies with fasting, so our souls may be gladdened with the joy of true devotion: and all carnal lusts being dead in us, we may with readier mind lay hold of heavenly things; through.

FRIDAY. — O God, Who renewest the face of the earth with Thine ineffable Sacraments: grant that Thy Church may ever profit by the eternal gifts, nor yet be left destitute of temporal blessings; through.

SATURDAY.—O Lord, Who hast promised to reward all those who please Thee in their fasting: grant that, by the power of Thy grace, these exercises of our devotion may bring forth in us the fruit of good works; through.

From Saturday in this week until the morrow of Low Sunday only Double Feasts are observed, and they only until Maundy Thursday. If a Double fall on this Saturday, or on the Saturday following, Evensong is of the Sunday, and a solemn memorial of the Feast is made.

PASSION SUNDAY.

At Compline.

All as in Compl. ix.; and Compline is said thus until Maundy Thursday, what ve be the service.

At Prime.

Antiphon.—I have not a devil: but I honour My Father, saith the Lord.

From this day until Low Sunday the Responsory Jesus Christ is not said, but immediately after the chapter is said the verse.

V. O Lord, arise, help us.
R. And deliver us for Thy Name's sake.

And in this way it is said daily until Maundy Thursday, whenever the service is of the season.

At Terce.

Antiphon.— I seek not Mine own glory: there is One that seeketh and judgeth.

Chapter. Hebrews ix. 11.

Christ being come an High Priest of good things to come, by a greater and more perfect tabernacle, not made with hands, that is to say, not of this building; neither by the blood of goats and calves, but by His own blood He entered in once into the holy place, having obtained eternal redemption.

R. Deliver my soul, O God, from the sword, and my darling from the power of the dog. V. Deliver me, O Lord, from the evil man: and preserve me from the wicked man. R. And my darling from the power of the dog.

V. Save me from the lion's mouth, O Lord. R. And my lowliness from the horns of the unicorn.

PASSION SUNDAY.

Collect.

WE beseech Thee, Almighty God, mercifully to look upon Thy people; that by Thy great goodness they may be governed and preserved evermore, both in body and soul; through.

At Sext.

Antiphon.— Verily, verily, I say unto you: If a man keep My saying, he shall never see death.

Chapter. Hebrews ix. 14.

The blood of Christ, Who through the eternal Spirit offered Himself without spot to God, shall purge your conscience from dead works to serve the living God.

R. Save me: from the lion's mouth, O Lord, and my lowliness from the horns of the unicorn. V. Deliver my soul, O God, from the sword: and my darling from the power of the dog. R. And my lowliness from the horns of the unicorns. V. O shut not up my soul, O God, with the sinners. R. Nor my life with the bloodthirsty men.

At None.

Antiphon.—Your father Abraham rejoiced to see My day: and he saw it, and was glad.

Chapter. Hebrews ix. 15.

For this cause, brethren, Christ is the Mediator of the New Testament, that by means of death, for the redemption of the transgressions, they which were called might receive the promise of eternal inheritance.

R. Princes have persecuted me without a cause: but my heart standeth in awe of Thy word. I am glad of Thy word. V. As one that findeth great spoils. R. I am glad of Thy word.

V. Deliver me, O Lord, from the evil man. R. And preserve me from the wicked man.

MONDAY IN PASSION WEEK.

At Prime.

Antiphon.—The souls of the wicked are mad against me: and my heart is disquieted because of them.

At Terce.

Antiphon.—O Lord, Thou hast pleaded the causes of my soul: Thou hast redeemed my life, O Lord my God.

Chapter. Isaiah l. 6.

I hid not my face from shame and spitting. For the Lord God will help me; therefore shall I not be confounded.

RR., VV. at all the Hours as on Sunday with the Collect of the day.

At Sext.

Antiphon.—O My people, what have I done unto thee? and wherein have I wearied thee? answer me.

Chapter. Isaiah l. 7.

The Lord God will help me; therefore shall I not be confounded: therefore have I set my face like a flint, and I know that I shall not be ashamed.

R.R., V.V., and Collect as is noted above.

At None.

Antiphon.—Shall evil be recompensed for good? : for they have digged a pit for my soul.

Chapter. Jeremiah xvii. 18.

Let them be confounded that persecute me, but let not me be confounded: let them be dismayed, but let not me be dismayed: bring upon them the day of evil, and destroy them with double destruction, O Lord our God.

RR., VV., *and Collect, as noted above.*

Collects.

MONDAY.— Sanctify our fast, we beseech Thee, O Lord: and of Thy great mercy grant us pardon for all our sins; through.

TUESDAY.—Accept, we beseech Thee, O Lord, our fast: that winning pardon for our sins, we may be made worthy of Thy grace, and attain to everlasting life; through.

WEDNESDAY.— O most merciful God, look graciously upon this our fast, and lighten the hearts of Thy faithful people; and as Thou hast given us an hearty desire to pray, turn a gracious ear to our supplications; through.

THURSDAY.—Grant, we beseech Thee, Almighty God, that as by the lusts of the flesh we have fallen from the true dignity of man, so by continual mortifying of our corrupt affections we may be mercifully restored; through.

FRIDAY.— We beseech Thee, O Lord, pour Thy grace into our hearts: that, chastening ourselves for sin with a ready will, we may endure heaviness for a season, and escape eternity of woe; through.

SATURDAY. — Strengthen, we beseech Thee, O Lord, Thy faithful people with the spirit of true devotion; that, brought up in the nurture of the Lord, they may ever more and more set forth Thy glory and set forward their own salvation; through.

PALM SUNDAY.

At Prime.

Antiphon.—Hosanna to the Son of David, blessed is He that cometh in the Name of the Lord, the King of Israel: Hosanna in the highest.

At Terce.

Antiphon.—The children of the Hebrews strewed their garments in the way: and cried, saying, Hosanna to the Son of David, blessed is He that cometh in the Name of the Lord.

Chapter. Philippians ii. 5.

Brethren, let this mind be in you, which was also in Christ Jesus : Who, being in the form of God, thought it not robbery to be equal with God: but made Himself of no reputation, and took upon Him the form of a servant.

R. My brethren : stood afar off, and mine acquaintances conveyed themselves from me as though they were strangers. V. My lovers and my neighbours. R.

Conveyed themselves from me as though they were strangers. *Repeat the Responsory.* My brethren: stood afar off, and mine acquaintances conveyed themselves from me as though they were strangers.

V. Deliver my soul, O God, from the sword. *R.* And my darling from the power of the dog.

Collect.

ALMIGHTY and everlasting God, Who, of Thy tender love towards mankind, hast sent Thy Son, our Saviour Jesus Christ, to take upon Him our flesh, and to suffer death upon the cross, that all mankind should follow the example of His great humility; Mercifully grant, that we may both follow the example of His patience, and also be made partakers of His resurrection; through the same.

At Sext.

Antiphon.—The children of the Hebrews went forth with olive branches to meet the Lord: crying out and saying, Hosanna in the highest.

Chapter. Philippians ii. 8.

Christ humbled Himself for our sakes, and became obedient unto death, even the death of the cross.

R. Give heed: to me, O Lord, and hearken to the voice of them that contend with me: shall evil be recompensed for good? for they have digged a pit for my soul. *V.* Remember that I stood before Thee to speak good for them, and to turn away Thy wrath from them. *R.* Shall evil be recompensed for good? for they have digged a pit for my soul. *Repeat the Responsory.* Give heed: to me, O Lord, and hearken to the voice of them that contend with me: shall evil be recompensed for good? for they have digged a pit for my soul.

V. Save me from the lion's mouth, O Lord. *R.* And my lowliness from the horns of the unicorns.

At None.

Antiphon.—All men highly exalt Thy Name, and say, Blessed is He that cometh in the Name of the Lord: Hosanna in the highest.

Chapter. Philippians ii. 9.

God the Father hath highly exalted His Christ, and given Him a name which is above every Name: that at the Name of Jesus every knee should bow, of things in heaven, and things in earth, and things under the earth.

R. Save me: O God, for the waters are come in even unto my soul: hide not Thy face from Thy servant. Since I am in trouble, O haste Thee and hear me, my God. *V.* Draw nigh unto my soul and save it: O deliver me because of mine enemies. *R.* Since I am in trouble, O haste Thee and hear me, my God. *Repeat the Responsory.* Save me: O God, for the waters are come in even unto my soul: hide not Thy face from Thy servant. Since I am in trouble, O haste Thee and hear me, my God.

PALM SUNDAY. 33

V. O shut not up my soul, O God, with the sinners. *R.* Nor my life with the bloodthirsty men.

MONDAY IN HOLY WEEK.

At Prime.

Antiphon.—The souls of the wicked are mad against me: and my heart is disquieted because of them.

At Terce.

Antiphon.—O Lord, Thou hast pleaded the causes of my soul: Thou hast redeemed my life, O Lord my God.

Chapter. Isaiah l. 6.

I hid not my face from shame and spitting. For the Lord God will help me; therefore shall I not be confounded.

RR., VV. as on Palm Sunday, at all the Hours.

At Sext.

Antiphon.—O My people, what have I done unto thee: and wherein have I wearied thee? answer Me.

Chapter. Isaiah i. 7.

The Lord God will help me; therefore shall I not be confounded: therefore have I set my face like a flint, and I know that I shall not be ashamed.

RR., VV. as above.

At None.

Antiphon.—Shall evil be recompensed for good: for they have digged a pit for my soul.

Chapter. Jeremiah xvii. 18.

Let them be confounded that persecute me, but let not me be confounded: let them be dismayed, but let not me be dismayed: bring upon them the day of evil, and destroy them with double destruction, O Lord our God.

RR., VV. as above.

Collects.

MONDAY.—Grant, we beseech Thee, Almighty God, that whereas through the weakness of our mortal nature we faint oftentimes in the midst of so many and great adversities, yet through the prevailing merit of the Passion of Thine only begotten Son, we may be strengthened and refreshed evermore; Who liveth and reigneth with Thee.

TUESDAY.—O almighty and everlasting God, grant us so worthily to celebrate the mysteries of the Lord's Passion, that we may not fail of Thy mercy; through the same.

WEDNESDAY.—Hear us, we beseech Thee, Almighty God, and grant that we, who for our evil deeds are in continual affliction, by the Passion of Thine only begotten Son may be mercifully delivered; Who liveth and reigneth.

ON TUESDAY, *after Evensong is said the Watches of the Dead with nine Lessons solemnly, and with Mass on the morrow: unless a Double Feast, falling on Wednesday, prevent it; and then the aforesaid service is performed on any preceding day of this week, viz. Sunday or Monday. And so is finished the Service of the Dead until the Octaves of Easter; unless a body be present.*

D

GOOD FRIDAY.

ON WEDNESDAY *the Altar is not censed at Evensong; nor is any memorial made, on account of the morrow's solemnity: unless a Double Feast is being celebrated that day, the Priest does not wear a cope: there are no candle-bearers, but only the Boy ministering the book with a light in the ordinary manner, because the Choir is not ruled.*

If the Feast of the Annunciation or any other Double Feast fall on this day, be it the Feast of the place or of the Dedication of the Church, it shall be solemnly observed; yet Evensong of the Feria is said, with a solemn memorial of the Feast. But if any Double Feast fall between this day and Low Sunday, it is transferred until after the Easter Octaves, and is celebrated on the first day on which it can have two Evensongs.

Compline ix. is said with the verses after Nunc Dimittis.

The Petitions, etc., are said in the usual manner, without kneeling, and without Psalm li., Have mercy upon me, O God. On account of the solemnity of the morrow, To Thee lift I up mine eyes, is not said, nor from this day until the morrow of the first Sunday after Trinity.

MAUNDY THURSDAY.

At Mattins and until Evensong on Easter Eve, Glory be to the Father is wholly omitted, except after the Penitential Psalms on Maundy Thursday, and after the Office at Mass on that day if the Bishop celebrate.

At Prime.

Immediately after Our Father, *etc., the Antiphon is begun.*

Antiphon.—Christ for our sakes became obedient unto death: even the death of the cross.

Psalm liv. Save me, O God.
Psalm cxix. Blessed are those.
Psalm cxix. O do well.

The Psalms end without Glory be to the Father, *and the whole Antiphon is said. Then let the Priest say,*

V. The Lord be with you.
R. And with thy spirit.
Let us pray.

- Collect.

ALMIGHTY GOD, we beseech Thee graciously to behold this Thy family, for which our Lord Jesus Christ was contented to be betrayed, and given up into the hands of wicked men, and to suffer death upon the cross, Who now liveth and reigneth with Thee and the Holy Ghost, ever one God, world without end. Amen.

V. The Lord be with you.
R. And with thy spirit.
V. Bless we the Lord.
R. Thanks be to God.

In this manner all the Hours *are said on this day with their own Psalms.*

On this day, Terce, Sext, *and* None *are said before Mass.*

Compline *is said without note secretly.*

GOOD FRIDAY.

The Hours are said in a low voice.

At Prime.

The Priest begins the Antiphon, Christ for our sakes; *and at these words let all genuflect.*

The Psalms are said as on Maundy Thursday, and after the repetition of the Antiphon follows Our Father *and* Hail, Mary, *kneeling, Ps. li.,* Have mercy, *without* Glory be to the Father; *and then immediately is said the Collect kneeling, without* The Lord be with you, *and without* Let us pray, *as follows:*

EASTER DAY.

ALMIGHTY GOD, we beseech Thee graciously to behold this Thy family, for which our Lord Jesus was contented to be betrayed, and given up into the hands of wicked men, and to suffer death upon the cross. Amen.

And so the service ends.
In this manner are said Prime, Terce, Sext, and None on this day and on Easter Eve. At the beginning of each Hour is said Our Father, etc., as usual. After the Psalms all kneel until after the Collect. In like manner is said Compline on this day.

Evensong on this day is not sung, but said in a low voice, antiphonally, the Choir standing before the altar.

EASTER EVE.

On this day let the church be decorated solemnly in all respects as on principal Feasts, except the images and crosses, which are not uncovered until after the Lord's Resurrection on Easter Day, because all the Saints arose with Christ.

All the Hours are said in a low voice as on Good Friday.

Let Mass be said after None. O Lamb of God is not said, nor is the Peace given. Evensong is said in a loud voice without rulers of the Choir, with Alleluia. The Psalms at Evensong end with Glory be to the Father.

At Compline all as in Compl. xii.
The Paschal candle, from the time when it is lighted, shall burn continuously until after Compline on Easter Day. Also it shall burn on the three following days at Mattins, Masses, Evensong, and Compline. Also on Saturday and Sunday within the Octaves of Easter, as on the aforesaid three days. Also on the Feast of the Annunciation of blessed Mary, if it be celebrated in Eastertide; and on the Feast of the Invention of the Holy Cross, as on the aforesaid three days.

Also on the Feast of the Ascension at Mattins, Mass, and both Evensongs, and at Compline. Also on the Feast of St. Philip and St. James, Apostles, and of St. Mark the Evangelist, and on all Sundays at Mass only. And on the morrow of the Ascension, the said Paschal Candle shall be removed in the morning.

EASTER DAY.

At Mattins Te Deum is sung.

At Prime.

Prime begins as usual, but the Hymn is not said. And in like manner at all the Hours of this day and of the whole week.

Antiphon.—And the angel of the Lord descended from heaven: and came and rolled back the stone, and sat upon it. Alleluia, Alleluia.

Ps. liv. Save me, O God.
Ps. cxviii. O give thanks (*on this day only*).
Ps. cxix. Blessed are those.
Ps. cxix. O do well.

The Athanasian Creed is not said throughout the week, but after the Psalms and Antiphon immediately is begun the Graile, as follows:

This is the day which the Lord hath made: we will rejoice and be glad in it.

And so is done at all the Hours throughout the week until Saturday. Then is said—

V. The Lord is risen.
R. As He said. Alleluia.
V. The Lord be with you.
R. And with thy spirit.
Let us pray.

EASTER DAY.

Collect.

ALMIGHTY GOD, Who through Thine only begotten Son Jesus Christ hast overcome death, and opened unto us the gate of everlasting life; We humbly beseech Thee, that, as by Thy special grace preventing us Thou dost put into our minds good desires, so by Thy continual help we may bring the same to good effect; through the same Jesus Christ our Lord, Who liveth and reigneth with Thee and the Holy Ghost, ever one God, world without end. Amen.

V. The Lord be with you.
R. And with thy spirit.
V. Bless we the Lord.
R. Thanks be to God.

In this manner, but omitting Ps. cxviii., Prime is said throughout the week, except on Saturday.

At Terce.

The Hymn is not said.

Antiphon.—And, behold, there was a great earthquake: for the angel of the Lord descended from heaven. Alleluia.

Graile.—This is the day which the Lord hath made: we will rejoice and be glad in it.

V. The Lord is risen indeed.
R. And hath appeared unto Symon. Alleluia.
V. The Lord be with you.
R. And with thy spirit.

Let us pray.

Collect.

Almighty God, Who through.

At Sext.

The Hymn is not said.

Antiphon.— His countenance was like lightning: and his raiment white as snow. Alleluia, Alleluia.

Graile.—This is the day which the Lord hath made: we will rejoice and be glad in it.

V. The Lord is risen from the tomb.
R. Who for our sakes hung upon the tree. Alleluia.
V. The Lord be with you.
R. And with thy spirit.

Let us pray.

Collect.

Almighty God, Who through.

At None.

The Hymn is not said.

Antiphon.—For fear of him the keepers did shake: and became as dead men. Alleluia.

Graile.—This is the day which the Lord hath made: we will rejoice and be glad in it.

V. In Thy Resurrection, O Christ.
R. Let heaven and earth rejoice.
V. The Lord be with you.
R. And with thy spirit.

Let us pray.

Collect.

Almighty God, who through.

At Compline.

All as in Compl. xiii.

And so shall the Hours be said throughout the week, with the Collect of the day; except that on Saturday the Graile is not said at the Hours, but in its place is said by the whole Choir, the Cantor beginning—

Alleluia. *V.* This is the day which the Lord hath made: we

LOW SUNDAY.

will rejoice and be glad in it. Alleluia.

And here it is to be noted, that if any Feast fall within Easter week, it shall not be observed that year; because all the Saints have risen with Christ and are restored to life in Him, and the Feast of the Resurrection is common to all the Saints. Yet if it be a double Feast that so falls, it is transferred to the first day after the Octave on which it can have two Evensongs. This same rule applies to Whitsun Eve and the week following the same.

Collects.

MONDAY.—O God, Who by the Paschal victory hast regenerated mankind; We beseech Thee to grant unto Thy people such a measure of the heavenly gift, that all their life long they may walk at perfect liberty, and at length attain unto Thine eternal kingdom; through.

TUESDAY.—O God, by Whose power Thy Church is ever multiplied with new-born offspring; Grant unto Thy family such grace, that they may alway hold the mystery of the faith in a pure conscience; through.

WEDNESDAY.—O God, Who makest us glad with the yearly remembrance of the Resurrection of our Lord and Saviour Jesus Christ; Mercifully grant that we who share in the Easter joy on earth may hereafter attain unto the joy of everlasting life; through.

THURSDAY.—O God, Who hast knit into one all the nations of the earth in the glorious confession of Thy holy Name; Grant that all they who are newborn in the saving waters of Baptism may be ever one in the faith of Thy holy Church, and in all manner of godly conversation; through.

FRIDAY. — O Almighty and everlasting God, Who hast made the Paschal mystery to be the new bond of human brotherhood; Grant us, we beseech Thee, such fervent charity toward all men, that, both outwardly in our actions and inwardly in our thoughts, we may be ever worthy of our Christian profession; through.

SATURDAY. — Grant, we beseech Thee, Almighty God, that we who reverently celebrate the Paschal Feast may attain in the power of our risen Lord to the joys of eternal life; through.

Instead of the Graile on Saturday, is said,

Alleluia.
V. This is the day which the Lord hath made: we will rejoice and be glad in it. Alleluia.

LOW SUNDAY.
LESSER DOUBLE.

Memorial of St. Mary is made at First Evensong of all Sundays until Ascension Day, except that it is not made at either Evensong of the Invention of the Holy Cross, supposing it fall on a Saturday.

At Compline.
All as in Compl. xiv.

The two following verses are said at the end of all Hymns of the same metre, until Ascension-tide:

LOW SUNDAY.

O Lord of life, to Thee we pray,
Triumphant o'er the grave to-day,
In this our Easter joy protect
From death and hell Thine own elect.
ToThee be sung Thy people's praise,
O risen Lord, through endless days:
Whom with the Father we adore
And Holy Spirit evermore.

Whatever Feast may happen to fall on this Sunday, even if it be the Feast of the place or of the Dedication of the church, it is invariably transferred to the next vacant Feria. Simple Feasts with rulers of the choir falling on the Sunday next before Ascension Day are always transferred; double Feasts falling on that day are observed, and solemn memorials of the Sunday and of the Resurrection are made. Simple Feasts with rulers of the Choir falling on any of the intermediate Sundays are not transferred.

At Mattins is made a memorial of the Resurrection.

At Prime.

V. O God, make speed, etc.

Hymn. Now that the lights of morn.

Antiphon.—The angel of the Lord descended from heaven: and came and rolled back the stone, and sat upon it. Alleluia.

Psalm. Save me, O God.
Psalm. Blessed are those.
Psalm. O do well.

Antiphon. — Thanks be to Thee.

Chapter.—Now unto the King eternal.

R. Jesus Christ, Son of the living God, have mercy upon us. Alleluia, Alleluia. *V.* Thou Who hast risen from the dead. *R.* Have mercy upon us. Alleluia, Alleluia. *V.* Glory be. *R.* Jesus Christ.

This R. is used daily till Ascensiontide.
All the rest as usual.

At Terce.

Hymn.—Come, Holy Ghost.

Antiphon.—And, behold, there was a great earthquake: for the angel of the Lord descended from heaven. Alleluia.

Chapter. 1 *John* v. 4.

Whatsoever is born of God overcometh the world: and this is the victory that overcometh the world, even our faith.

R. The Lord is risen. Alleluia, Alleluia. *V.* As He said unto you. *R.* Alleluia, Alleluia. *V.* Glory be. *R.* The Lord.

V. The Lord is risen indeed. *R.* And hath appeared unto Symon. Alleluia.

Collect.

ALMIGHTY FATHER, Who hast given Thine only Son to die for our sins, and to rise again for our justification; Grant us so to put away the leaven of malice and wickedness, that we may alway serve Thee in pureness of living and truth; through the merits of the same Thy Son Jesus Christ. *Amen.* [1549.]

Or this.

O ALMIGHTY GOD, of Whose only gift it cometh that Thy faithful people do unto Thee true and laudable service; Mercifully grant, that we who have now accomplished the Paschal Feast, may ever hold fast its blessed lessons and walk by its quickening power; through.

LOW SUNDAY.

At Sext.

Hymn. — Almighty God of truth and power.

Antiphon.— His countenance was like lightning: and His raiment white as snow. Alleluia.

Chapter. 1 John v. 5.
Brethren, who is he that overcometh the world, but he that believeth that Jesus is the Son of God? This is He that came by water and blood, even Jesus Christ.

R. The Lord is risen indeed. Alleluia, Alleluia. V. And hath appeared unto Symon. R. Alleluia, Alleluia. V. Glory be. R. The Lord.
V. The Lord is risen from the tomb. R. Who for our sakes hung upon the tree. Alleluia.

At None.

Hymn. — O God, creation's strength and stay.

Antiphon. — For fear of him the keepers did shake: and became as dead men. Alleluia.

Chapter. 1 John v. 8.
There are three that bear witness in earth, the spirit, and the water, and the blood.

R. The Lord is risen from the tomb. Alleluia, Alleluia. V. Who for our sakes hung upon the tree. R. Alleluia, Alleluia.
V. Glory be. R. The Lord.
V. In Thy resurrection, O Christ. R. Let heaven and earth rejoice. Alleluia.

At second Evensong of all Sundays until Ascensiontide a memorial of the Resurrection is made, except only when the Feast of the Invention of the Holy Cross fall on a Sunday. No memorial is made at this Evensong of any Feast without rulers of the Choir which may fall on the morrow of Low Sunday. But if a double Feast fall on that day. Second Evensong on the Sunday shall be of the Feast, with a solemn memorial of the Sunday, and afterwards of the Resurrection.

ON FERIAS IN EASTERTIDE.

Whenever the Service is of the Feria, all is said as on the next preceeding Sunday, except as follows:

At Prime.

Antiphon.—Alleluia, Alleluia, Alleluia, Alleluia, Alleluia, Alleluia.

Antiphon. — Glory to Thee, Coequal Trinity.

Chapter.—Lord, be gracious to us.

Petitions, etc., said standing.

At Terce.

Antiphon.—Alleluia, Alleluia, Alleluia, Alleluia, Alleluia, Alleluia.

At Sext.

Antiphon.—Alleluia, Alleluia, Alleluia.

At None.

Antiphon.—Alleluia, Alleluia.

And here it is to be noted that between Easter and the First Sunday after Trinity, the Petitions are not said at Terce, Sext, or None; at Prime and Compline the usual Petitions are said standing.
At Evensong and Mattins on all Ferias until Ascensiontide, Memorials are made (1) of the Holy Cross; (2) of St. Mary; (3) of All Saints.

No memorial of the Feria is made on any Festival in Eastertide, except only at Mattins on Rogation Monday and Ascension Eve. If a Festival fall on either of those days, a solemn memorial is made of the Fast, even though it be the feast of the Dedication of the Church.

SECOND SUNDAY AFTER EASTER.

At Prime.

All as on Low Sunday, except the Antiphon to the Creed of St. Athanasius, which is Thee all Thy creatures. At the other Hours all as on Low Sunday except the Chapters. And so on all Sundays till Ascensiontide, whenever the service is of the Sunday.

AT TERCE.—*Chapter.* 1 Peter ii. 21. Christ suffered for us, leaving us an example, that ye should follow His steps: who did no sin, neither was guile found in His mouth.

AT SEXT.—*Chapter.* 1 Peter ii. 23. But He committed Himself to Him that judgeth righteously: Who His own self bare our sins in His own body on the tree: by Whose stripes we were healed.

AT NONE.—*Chapter.* 1 Peter ii. 25. Ye were as sheep going astray; but are now returned unto the Shepherd and Bishop of your souls.

Collect.

ALMIGHTY GOD, Who hast given Thine only Son to be unto us both a sacrifice for sin, and also an ensample of godly life; Give us grace that we may always most thankfully receive that His inestimable benefit, and also daily endeavour ourselves to follow the blessed steps of His most holy life; through the same. [1549.]

Or this.

O GOD, Who didst humble Thine only Son unto the death of the cross, that Thou mightest thereby raise a fallen world; Look down with the eyes of Thy mercy upon us Thy faithful people, and grant, that we, whom Thou hast delivered out of the jaws of hell, may be brought unto everlasting bliss and glory; through the same.

THIRD SUNDAY AFTER EASTER.

AT TERCE.—*Chapter.* 1 Peter ii. 11. I beseech you as strangers and pilgrims, abstain from fleshly lusts, which war against the soul.

AT SEXT.—*Chapter.* 1 Peter ii. 13. Submit yourselves to every ordinance of man for the Lord's sake: whether it be to the king, as supreme; or unto governors, as unto them that are sent by him for the punishment of evildoers, and for the praise of them that do well.

AT NONE.—*Chapter.* 1 Peter ii. 15. So is the will of God, that with well doing ye may put to silence the ignorance of foolish men.

Collect.

ALMIGHTY GOD, Who showest to them that be in error the light of Thy truth, to the intent that they may return into the way of righteousness;

Grant unto all them that are admitted into the fellowship of Christ's Religion, that they may eschew those things that are contrary to their profession, and follow all such things as are agreeable to the same; through.

FOURTH SUNDAY AFTER EASTER.

At Terce.—*Chapter. James* i. 17. Every good gift and every perfect gift is from above, and cometh down from the Father of lights, with Whom is no variableness, neither shadow of turning.

At Sext.—*Chapter. James* i. 19. Wherefore let every man be swift to hear, slow to speak, slow to wrath.

At None.—*Chapter. James* i. 21. Lay apart all filthiness and superfluity of naughtiness, and receive with meekness the engrafted word, which is able to save your souls.

Collect.

O ALMIGHTY GOD, Who alone canst order the unruly wills and affections of sinful men; Grant unto Thy people, that they may love the thing which Thou commandest, and desire that which Thou dost promise; that so, among the sundry and manifold changes of the world, our hearts may surely there be fixed, where true joys are to be found; through.

FIFTH SUNDAY AFTER EASTER.

At Terce.—*Chapter. James* i. 22. Be ye doers of the word, and not hearers only, deceiving your own selves. For if any be a hearer of the word, and not a doer, he is like unto a man beholding his natural face in a glass.

At Sext.—*Chapter. James* i. 25. But whoso looketh into the perfect law of liberty, and continueth therein, he being not a forgetful hearer, but a doer of the work, this man shall be blessed in his deed.

At None.—*Chapter. James* i. 27. Pure religion and undefiled before God and the Father is this, To visit the fatherless and widows in their affliction, and to keep himself unspotted from the world.

Collect.

O LORD, from Whom all good things do come; Grant to us Thy humble servants, that by Thy holy inspiration we may think those things that be good, and by Thy merciful guiding may perform the same; through.

On Monday and Tuesday in this week (Rogation Days) everything at the Hours as on Sunday.

If a Feast without rulers fall on Monday or Wednesday it is not observed. And in this week there is no Commemoration of the Feast of the place unless it be St. Mary.

But if a Feast with rulers fall on Monday, the whole Service is of the Feast, with a memorial of the Fast at Mattins only; and after Sext the Mass of the Feast is said in Choir with rulers. The Mass of the Fast and the Procession are said after None in the usual manner.

THE EVE OF THE ASCENSION OF THE LORD.

No memorial of the Holy Cross is made at Mattins, nor again until the First Sunday after Trinity.

At Terce.

All as on Sunday, except the Chapter; and so is done at Sext and None.

Chapter. Acts iv. 32.

The multitude of them that believed were of one heart and of one soul: neither said any of them that ought of the things which he possessed was his own, but they had all things in common.

At Sext.

Chapter. Acts iv. 33.

With great power gave the apostles witness of the resurrection of the Lord Jesus: and great grace was upon them all.

At None.

Chapter. Acts iv. 34.

As many as were possessors of lands or houses sold them, and brought the prices of the things that were sold. And they laid them down at the apostles' feet: and distribution was made unto every man according as he had need.

Collect.

GRANT, we beseech Thee, Almighty God, that we may in heart and mind ascend whither Thine only begotten Son our Lord hath entered in, the great High Priest of our profession; that following His Ascension in faith we may with Him continually dwell; through the same.

If a Feast with rulers fall on this day it is not transferred: but a memorial of the Eve is made at Mattins only, and not at First Evensong. The Mass of the Feast is said after Sext in Choir; and the Mass of the Eve at the Procession, where the Station is made.

At Compline.

All as in Compl. xv.

THE ASCENSION OF OUR LORD JESUS CHRIST.

PRINCIPAL FEAST.

The two following verses are said at the end of all Hymns of the same metre until Whitsuntide:

In Thee be all our joy, O Lord,
As Thou wilt be our high reward;
Be all our glory now in Thee,
And to a glad eternity.

To Thee be sung Thy people's praise,
Ascended Lord, through endless days:
Whom with the Father we adore
And Holy Spirit evermore.

At Prime.

Antiphon.—Ye men of Galilee, why stand ye gazing up into heaven? This same Jesus which is taken up from you into heaven: shall so come. Alleluia.

Antiphon.—Thanks be to Thee.

R. Jesus Christ, Son of the living God, have mercy upon us. Alleluia, Alleluia. V. Thou that sittest at the right hand of the Father. R. Have mercy upon us. Alleluia, Alleluia. V. Glory be. R. Jesus Christ.

The rest as usual.

At Terce.

Antiphon.—And while they looked stedfastly toward heaven as He went up: they said Alleluia.

Chapter. Acts i. 1.

The former treatise have I made, O Theophilus, of all that Jesus began both to do and teach, until the day in which He was taken up, after that He through the Holy Ghost had given commandment to the apostles whom He had chosen.

R. Thou hast set Thy glory. Alleluia, Alleluia. V. Above the heavens, O God. R. Alleluia, Alleluia. V. Glory be. R. Thou hast set.

V. God is gone up with a merry noise. R. And the Lord with the sound of the trump. Alleluia.

Collect.

GRANT, we beseech Thee, Almighty God, that like as we do believe Thy only begotten Son our Lord Jesus Christ to have ascended into the heavens; so we may also in heart and mind thither ascend, and with Him continually dwell, Who liveth and reigneth.

At Sext.

Antiphon.—While He lifted up His hands He was carried up into heaven: and He blessed them. Alleluia.

Chapter. Acts i. 4.

While eating together with them, He commanded them that they should not depart from Jerusalem, but wait for the promise of the Father, which, saith He, ye have heard of Me.

R. God is gone up with a merry noise. Alleluia, Alleluia. V. And the Lord with the sound of the trump. R. Alleluia, Alleluia. V. Glory be. R. God is gone up.

V. Christ ascending up on high. R. Led captivity captive. Alleluia.

At None.

Antiphon.—While they beheld He was taken up: and a cloud received Him in the sky. Alleluia.

Chapter. Acts i. 5.

John truly baptized with water; but ye shall be baptized with the Holy Ghost not many days hence.

R. Christ ascending up on high. Alleluia, Alleluia. V. Led captivity captive. R. Alleluia, Alleluia. V. Glory be. R. Christ ascending.

V. I ascend to My Father and your Father. R. To My God and your God. Alleluia.

The Hours are said thus throughout the Octaves, whenever the service is of the Ascension, except on the following Sunday.

At Compline. *All as in Compl. xv.*
On no day throughout the Octaves is a memorial made of the Cross, or of St. Mary, or of All Saints, because the Choir is ruled.

If any Feast without rulers fall within the Octaves, a memorial only is made of it at Evensong, and at Mattins, and at the Mass of the day. But if a Feast with rulers occur, the whole service is of that Feast with memorial of the Ascension at both Evensongs, Mattins, and Mass. If such a Feast fall on the Sunday, then only a memorial of the Sunday is made before the memorial of the Ascension. If such a Feast fall on the Octave day, it is transferred to the morrow, unless a Feast with rulers fall on that day; in which case the former Feast is not kept that year. If however it be a double Feast that so falls on the Octave day, the whole service is of the Feast with a solemn memorial only of the Octave.

SUNDAY WITHIN THE OCTAVES OF THE ASCENSION.

At First Evensong all the service is of the Ascension: no memorial of the Sunday.

If a Feast with rulers fall on this Sunday, then First Evensong is of that Feast, with a solemn memorial of the Ascension.

At Mattins and Second Evensong a memorial is made of the Ascension.

At Prime all as on Ascension Day, except the Antiphon to the Creed of St. Athanasius, as follows, Thee all Thy creatures.

At Terce and the other Hours all as on Ascension Day, except the following:

AT TERCE. *Chapter.* 1 Peter iv. 7. Be ye sober, and watch unto prayer. And above all things have fervent charity among yourselves: for charity shall cover the multitude of sins.

AT SEXT. *Chapter.* 1 Peter iv. 9. Use hospitality one to another without grudging. As every man hath received the gift, even so minister the same one to another, as good stewards of the manifold grace of God.

AT NONE. *Chapter.* 1 Peter iv. 11. If any man minister, let him do it as of the ability which God giveth: that God in all things may be glorified through Jesus Christ.

Collect.

O GOD the King of glory, Who hast exalted Thine only Son Jesus Christ with great triumph unto Thy kingdom in heaven; We beseech thee, leave us not comfortless, but send to us Thine Holy Ghost to comfort us, and exalt us unto the same place whither our Saviour Christ is gone before, Who liveth and reigneth with Thee and the Holy Ghost, one God, world without end. Amen. [*Ascension Day Antiphon to Magnificat.*]

Or this.

O ALMIGHTY and everlasting God, by Whom alone we are enabled both to will and to do of Thy good pleasure; Grant us, we beseech Thee, such a measure of Thy grace, that we may ever serve Thee with gladness and devotion, and adore Thy majesty out of a pure heart; through.

If any Feast with rulers fall on this day, the whole service is of the Feast. If the patronal Feast or Dedication of the church fall within the Octaves of the Ascension, always a solemn memorial of the Ascension is made. The same is done in other Octaves with rulers.

OCTAVE OF THE ASCENSION.

At Prime and the other Hours all as on Ascension Day. Antiphon to Creed of St. Athanasius is Thee all Thy creatures, and the Collect, O Lord our heavenly Father.

At First and Second Evensong and at

WHITSUN DAY.

Mattins, all is done as on Ascension Day.

On this day at Second Evensong is made a solemn memorial of holy Mary with full service on the morrow, if no Feast with rulers fall on that day.

If however the service of the Feria be performed on the morrow of the Octave of Ascension, then the Eastertide Antiphons are said at the Hours, and all the rest is as on the preceding Sunday.

At Evensong on that day memorial is made (1) of holy Mary, (2) of All Saints.

WHITSUN EVE.

All as on the preceding day, except as follows:

At Mattins memorial is made (1) of holy Mary, (2) of All Saints.

AT TERCE. *Chapter. Acts* xix. 1. And it came to pass, that, while Apollos was at Corinth, Paul having passed through the upper coasts came to Ephesus: and finding certain disciples, he said unto them, Have ye received the Holy Ghost since ye believed? And they said unto him, We have not so much as heard whether there be any Holy Ghost.

AT SEXT. *Chapter. Acts* xix. 4. John verily baptized with the baptism of repentance, saying unto the people, that they should believe on Him which should come after him, that is, on Jesus Christ.

AT NONE. *Chapter. Acts* xix. 8. Paul went into the synagogue, and spake boldly for the space of three months, disputing and persuading the things concerning the kingdom of God.

Collect.

GRANT, we beseech Thee, Almighty God, that the bright beams of Thy glory may shine upon us, and the brilliancy of Thy light strengthen and illume with Thy Holy Spirit the hearts of those who by Thy grace have been born again; through.

All the Hours are said before Mass.

If any Feast fall on this day it has no service or memorial; unless it be a Double Feast, in which case it is transferred to the first day after Trinity Sunday on which it can have two Evensongs.

WHITSUN DAY.
PRINCIPAL FEAST.

At First Evensong no memorials are made.

At Compline.

All as in Compl. xvi.

At Prime.

Antiphon.—When the day of Pentecost was fully come: they were all of one accord, saying Alleluia.

Antiphon.—Thanks be to Thee.

All the rest as on Ascension Day.

At Terce.

After the sprinkling of holy water, and after the return of the procession into choir, the Choir standing in silk copes, let seven seniors go to the step of the Quire in silk copes, and there let O God, make speed be begun by a Priest standing in the midst. Then let the aforesaid seven seniors proceed to the step of the altar, the candle-

WHITSUN DAY.

bearers preceding, and seven thuribles having been previously filled with incense at the step of the Quire; and before the highest step of the altar let all together begin this Hymn, Come, Holy Ghost, *genuflecting and kissing the altar step. Let the Choir, genuflecting with them and kissing the benches, then rising, stand and finish the whole verse all together; and meanwhile let the aforesaid seniors cense the altar, all at the same moment kissing the altar.*

Hymn.

Come, Holy Ghost, our souls inspire,
And lighten with celestial fire.
Thou the anointing Spirit art,
Who dost Thy sevenfold gifts impart.

Thy blessèd Unction from above
Is comfort, life, and fire of love.
Enable with perpetual light
The dulness of our blinded sight.

Anoint and cheer our soilèd face
With the abundance of Thy grace.
Keep far our foes, give peace at home:
Where Thou art guide, no ill can come.

Teach us to know the Father, Son,
And Thee, of Both, to be but One.
That, through the ages all along,
This may be our endless song;
 Praise to Thy eternal merit,
Father, Son, and Holy Spirit.
      Amen.

Let this order be observed through all the verses of the whole Hymn on this day only. On Monday, Tuesday, and Wednesday, the Hymn, Come, Holy Ghost, *is said at Terce in the ordinary manner. On the remaining days of the week is said the usual Terce hymn.*

And here it is to be noted that on this day Terce is to be sung by the whole Choir in silk copes with the Hymn, Come, Holy Ghost, *and on no other day throughout the year.*

The hymn being finished, the seven aforesaid seniors, bowing together to the altar, return into the Quire in their copes.

Antiphon.—The Spirit of the Lord filleth the world. Alleluia.

Chapter. Acts ii. 1.

When the day of Pentecost was fully come, the disciples were all with one accord in one place.

R. They were all filled with the Holy Ghost. Alleluia, Alleluia. *V.* And began to speak. *R.* Alleluia, Alleluia. *V.* Glory be. *R.* They were all.

V. The apostles did speak with other tongues. *R.* The wonderful works of God. Alleluia.

Collect.

GOD, Who as at this time didst teach the hearts of Thy faithful people, by the sending to them the light of Thy Holy Spirit; Grant us by the same Spirit to have a right judgment in all things, and evermore to rejoice in His holy comfort; through the merits of Christ Jesus our Saviour, Who liveth and reigneth with Thee, in the unity of the same Spirit, one God, world without end. Amen.

At Sext.

Antiphon. — They were all filled with the Holy Ghost: and began to speak. Alleluia.

Chapter. Acts ii. 2.

And suddenly there came a sound from heaven as of a rushing mighty wind, and it filled all the house where the apostles were sitting.

R. The apostles did speak with other tongues. Alleluia, Alleluia. *V.* The wonderful works of God. R. Alleluia, Alleluia. V. Glory be. R. The apostles. V. The Spirit of the Lord filleth the world. R. And that which containeth all things hath knowledge of the voice. Alleluia.

At None.

Antiphon.—The apostles did speak in other tongues: the wonderful works of God. Alleluia, Alleluia, Alleluia.

Chapter. Acts ii. 3.

There appeared unto the apostles cloven tongues like as of fire, and the Holy Spirit sat upon each of them.

R. The Spirit of the Lord filleth the world. Alleluia, Alleluia. V. And that which containeth all things hath knowledge of the voice. R. Alleluia, Alleluia. V. Glory be. R. The Spirit.

V. Send forth Thy Spirit, and they shall be made. R. And Thou shalt renew the face of the earth. Alleluia.

At Compline.

All as in Compl. xvii.

MONDAY IN WHITSUN WEEK, and the two following days.

LESSER DOUBLE FEASTS.

At Prime.

All as on Whitsun Day.

At Terce and at the other Hours, all as on Whitsun Day, except as follows:

AT TERCE. *Chapter.* Acts ii. 2. Suddenly there came a sound from heaven as of a rushing mighty wind, and it filled all the house where the apostles were sitting.

AT SEXT. *Chapter.* Acts ii. 3. There appeared unto the apostles cloven tongues like as of fire, and the Holy Spirit sat upon each of them.

AT NONE. *Chapter.* Acts ii. 4. They were all filled with the Holy Ghost, and began to speak with other tongues, as the Spirit gave them utterance.

Collects.

MONDAY. — God, Who didst pour out the Holy Spirit on Thine apostles, mercifully listen to the dutiful prayers of Thy people, and grant Thy peace to those on whom Thou hast bestowed grace to believe; through Jesus Christ our Lord, Who liveth and reigneth with Thee in the unity of the same Spirit, one God, world without end. Amen.

TUESDAY.—O Lord, we beseech Thee, may the power of the Holy Ghost be with us; and both mercifully cleanse and purge our hearts, and defend us from all adversities; through. In the unity of the same.

WEDNESDAY.— Grant, we beseech Thee, O Lord, that the Holy Ghost the Comforter, Who proceedeth from Thee, may illuminate our minds, and lead us, as Thy Son has promised, into all truth; who liveth and reigneth. In the unity of the same.

TRINITY SUNDAY.

THURSDAY IN WHITSUN WEEK, and the two following days.

At Prime.

Antiphon to Athanasian Creed, Thee all Thy creatures.

Chapter. O Lord, be gracious.

The rest as on Whitsun Day.

At Terce.

Hymn. Come, Holy Ghost, with God the Son.

All the rest as on Monday, except the Collects; and so at Sext and None.

Collects.

THURSDAY.—Grant, we beseech Thee, almighty and merciful Lord, that the Holy Ghost may dwell in our hearts, and make them a temple worthy of His glory; through.

FRIDAY.—Grant, we beseech Thee, almighty and merciful Lord, that Thy Church, being assembled in the unity of the Spirit, may in no wise be vexed by attack of the enemy; through.

SATURDAY. — Mercifully send Thy Holy Spirit into our hearts, O Lord, that we, who have been created by His wisdom, may be guided and governed evermore by His providence; through.

If any Feast fall within this week, it is not observed: if however a Double Feast occur, it is transferred to the first day after Trinity Sunday on which it can have two Evensongs.

And so the septiform Feast of Pentecost being fulfilled in seven days, on the Octave Day, i.e. the next Sunday after Pentecost, let the Feast of the Holy Trinity be observed.

TRINITY SUNDAY.
GREATER DOUBLE.

At Compline.

All as in Compl. xviii.

And here it is to be noted that the following are the Feasts on which, according to the use of the Church of Sarum, Mattins are said at the hour of Evensong; viz. Trinity Sunday, Corpus Christi, Nativity of St. John the Baptist, the Feast of St. Peter and St. Paul, the Translation of St. Thomas the Martyr, the Feast of Relics, and on the Feast of the place and of the Dedication of the church if it happen to fall between Trinity Sunday and the Feast of Relics.

At Prime.

Antiphon.—O holy, blessed, and glorious Trinity: Father, Son, and Holy Ghost.

Psalm liv. Save me, O God.
Psalm cxix. Blessed are those.
Psalm cxix. O do well.
Creed. Whosoever will be saved.

All said under the above Antiphon; and so is done throughout the week, whenever the service is of the Holy Trinity. But when the service is of any Saint, whether the Choir is ruled or not, then the Creed of St. Athanasius only is said under this Antiphon.

All the rest as on Whitsun Day.

At Terce.

Antiphon.—O holy, blessed, and glorious Trinity: Father, Son, and Holy Ghost.

Chapter. Romans xi. 33.

Oh the depth of the riches both of the wisdom and knowledge of God! for of Him, and through Him, and in Him are all things:

TRINITY SUNDAY.

to Whom be glory for ever. Amen.

R. Let us bless the Father, the Son, and the Holy Ghost. Alleluia, Alleluia. V. Let us praise and highly exalt Him for ever. R. Alleluia, Alleluia. V. Glory be. R. Let us bless.

V. Blessed be Thou, O Lord, in the firmament of heaven. R. Glorious in praise and highly to be exalted for ever.

Collect.

ALMIGHTY and everlasting God, Who hast given unto us Thy servants grace by the confession of a true faith to acknowledge the glory of the eternal Trinity, and in the power of the Divine Majesty to worship the Unity; We beseech Thee that Thou wouldest keep us stedfast in this faith, and evermore defend us from all adversities, Who livest and reignest, one God, world without end. Amen.

At Sext.

Antiphon. — O most high, eternal, very Trinity: Father, Son, and Holy Ghost.

Chapter. 1 John v. 7.

There are Three that bear record in heaven, the Father, the Word, and the Holy Ghost: and these Three are One.

R. Blessed art Thou, O Lord, in the firmament of heaven. Alleluia, Alleluia. V. Glorious in praise and highly to be exalted for ever. R. Alleluia, Alleluia. V. Glory be. R. Blessed.

V. By the word of the Lord were the heavens made. R. And all the host of them by the breath of His mouth.

At None.

Antiphon. — Thee all Thy creatures meetly praise, Thee they worship, Thee they glorify: O blessed Trinity.

Chapter. Ephesians iv. 5.

One Lord, one faith, one baptism, one God and Father of all, Who is above all, and through all, and in us all: Who is blessed for ever.

R. By the word of the Lord were the heavens made. Alleluia, Alleluia. V. And all the host of them by the breath of His mouth. R. Alleluia, Alleluia. V. Glory be. R. By the word.

V. Blessed be the Name of the Lord. R. From this time forth for evermore.

Let any Feast that falls on this day be transferred to the morrow if it be not occupied with a Feast of nine Lessons, even if it be the Feast of the place or of the Dedication of the Church; and then Evensong shall be of the Feast with a solemn memorial of the Holy Trinity. But if the Feast of St. Augustine fall on this day, let it be transferred to the morrow, and at Second Evensong of Trinity Sunday let a solemn memorial be made of St. Augustine. At this Evensong it is not customary to make memorial of a Feast of three Lessons without rulers falling on the morrow, unless a Feast of nine Lessons fall on the same day: in that case solemn memorial is made of each of them.

During the three following days the service is of the Holy Trinity without rulers, until the Feast of Corpus Christi: unless some Feast of nine

E

TRINITY-TIDE.

or three *Lessons intervene, or Commemoration of Blessed Mary be made or of the Feast of the place. Memorials are made throughout this week* (1) *of blessed Mary,* (2) *of All Saints.*

𝔄t 𝔓rime anb the other 𝔒ours *all is done as on the first day, except the Chapter and Collect at Prime.*

𝔄t 𝔈ompline *all is said as on the morrow of the Octave of Epiphany* [*Compl.* vi.], *except the doxology to the Hymn: unless it be the Feast of the place or of the Dedication of the Church, for then the Octaves shall have rulers of the Choir. But when the service of any Saint is performed within the Octaves, then at all the Hours the Responsories and Versicles are said without Alleluia.*

SUNDAYS AFTER TRINITY.

𝔄t 𝔉irst 𝔈bensong *of all Sundays until Advent, when the service is of the Sunday, or a memorial of the Sunday is made, a memorial of the Trinity is made: also at Mattins.*

𝔄t 𝔓rime anb the other 𝔒ours *all is done as on Sundays after Epiphany.*

𝔄t 𝔖econb 𝔈bensong *on Sundays after Trinity no common memorials are made.*

WEEKDAYS IN TRINITY-TIDE.

𝔄t 𝔓rime anb the other 𝔒ours *all as on Ferias after the Octave of Epiphany.*

𝔄t 𝔐attins anb 𝔈bensong *memorials are made* (1) *of the Cross,* (2) *of St. Mary,* (3) *of All Saints. If the memorial of a Festival is made, it precedes the memorial of the Cross.*

COLLECTS.

First Sunday after Trinity.

O GOD, the strength of all them that put their trust in Thee, mercifully accept our prayers; and because through the weakness of our mortal nature we can do no good thing without Thee, grant us the help of Thy grace, that in keeping of Thy commandments we may please Thee, both in will and deed; through Jesus Christ our Lord. Amen.

Second Sunday after Trinity.

O LORD, Who never failest to help and govern them whom Thou dost bring up in Thy stedfast fear and love; Keep us, we beseech Thee, under the protection of Thy good providence, and make us to have a perpetual fear and love of Thy holy Name; through Jesus Christ our Lord. Amen.

Third Sunday after Trinity.

O LORD, we beseech Thee mercifully to hear us; and grant that we, to whom Thou hast given an hearty desire to pray, may by Thy mighty aid be defended and comforted in all dangers and adversities; through Jesus Christ our Lord. Amen.

Fourth Sunday after Trinity.

O GOD, the protector of all that trust in Thee, without Whom nothing is strong, nothing is holy; Increase and multiply upon us Thy mercy; that, Thou being our ruler and guide, we may so pass through things temporal, that we finally lose not the things eternal: Grant this, O heavenly Father, for Jesus Christ's sake our Lord. Amen.

Fifth Sunday after Trinity.

GRANT, O Lord, we beseech Thee, that the course of

this world may be so peaceably ordered by Thy governance, that Thy Church may joyfully serve Thee in all godly quietness; through Jesus Christ our Lord. Amen.

Sixth Sunday after Trinity.

O GOD, Who hast prepared for them that love Thee such good things as pass man's understanding; Pour into our hearts such love toward Thee, that we, loving Thee above all things, may obtain Thy promises, which exceed all that we can desire; through Jesus Christ our Lord. Amen.

Seventh Sunday after Trinity.

LORD of all power and might, Who art the author and giver of all good things; Graft in our hearts the love of Thy Name, increase in us true religion, nourish us with all goodness, and of Thy great mercy keep us in the same; through Jesus Christ our Lord. Amen.

Eighth Sunday after Trinity.

O GOD, Whose never-failing providence ordereth all things both in heaven and earth; We humbly beseech Thee to put away from us all hurtful things, and to give us those things which be profitable for us; through Jesus Christ our Lord. Amen.

Ninth Sunday after Trinity.

GRANT to us, Lord, we beseech Thee, the spirit to think and do always such things as be rightful; that we, who cannot do anything that is good without Thee, may by Thee be enabled to live according to Thy will; through Jesus Christ our Lord. Amen.

Tenth Sunday after Trinity.

LET Thy merciful ears, O Lord, be open to the prayers of Thy humble servants; and that they may obtain their petitions make them to ask such things as shall please Thee; through Jesus Christ our Lord. Amen.

Eleventh Sunday after Trinity.

O GOD, Who declarest Thy almighty power most chiefly in showing mercy and pity; Mercifully grant unto us such a measure of Thy grace, that we, running the way of Thy commandments, may obtain Thy gracious promises, and be made partakers of Thy heavenly treasure; through Jesus Christ our Lord. Amen.

Twelfth Sunday after Trinity.

ALMIGHTY and everlasting God, Who art always more ready to hear than we to pray, and art wont to give more than either we desire, or deserve; Pour down upon us the abundance of Thy mercy; forgiving us those things whereof our conscience is afraid, and giving us those good things which we are not worthy to ask, but through the merits and mediation of Jesus Christ, Thy Son, our Lord. Amen.

Thirteenth Sunday after Trinity.

ALMIGHTY and merciful God, of Whose only gift it cometh that Thy faithful people do unto Thee true and laudable service; Grant, we beseech Thee, that we may so faithfully serve Thee in this life, that we fail not finally to attain Thy heavenly promises; through the merits of Jesus Christ our Lord. Amen.

Fourteenth Sunday after Trinity.

ALMIGHTY and everlasting God, give unto us the increase of faith, hope, and charity; and, that we may obtain that which Thou dost promise, make us to love that which Thou dost command; through Jesus Christ our Lord. Amen.

Fifteenth Sunday after Trinity.

KEEP, we beseech thee, O Lord, Thy Church with Thy perpetual mercy: and, because the frailty of man without Thee cannot but fall, keep us ever by Thy help from all things hurtful, and lead us to all things profitable to our salvation; through Jesus Christ our Lord. Amen.

Sixteenth Sunday after Trinity.

O LORD, we beseech Thee, let Thy continual pity cleanse and defend Thy Church; and, because it cannot continue in safety without Thy succour, preserve it evermore by Thy help and goodness; through Jesus Christ our Lord. Amen.

Seventeenth Sunday after Trinity.

LORD, we pray Thee that Thy grace may always prevent and follow us, and make us continually to be given to all good works; through Jesus Christ our Lord. Amen.

Eighteenth Sunday after Trinity.

LORD, we beseech Thee, grant Thy people grace to withstand the temptations of the world, the flesh, and the devil, and with pure hearts and minds to follow Thee the only God; through Jesus Christ our Lord. Amen.

Nineteenth Sunday after Trinity.

O GOD, forasmuch as without Thee we are not able to please Thee; Mercifully grant, that Thy Holy Spirit may in all things direct and rule our hearts; through Jesus Christ our Lord. Amen.

Twentieth Sunday after Trinity.

O ALMIGHTY and most merciful God, of Thy bountiful goodness keep us, we beseech Thee, from all things that may hurt us; that we, being ready both in body and soul, may cheerfully accomplish those things that Thou wouldest have done; through Jesus Christ our Lord. Amen.

One and Twentieth Sunday after Trinity.

GRANT, we beseech Thee, merciful Lord, to Thy faithful people pardon and peace, that they may be cleansed from all their sins, and serve Thee with a quiet mind; through Jesus Christ our Lord. Amen.

Two and Twentieth Sunday after Trinity.

LORD, we beseech Thee to keep Thy household the Church in continual godliness; that through

FEAST OF THE DEDICATION OF THE CHURCH. 53

Thy protection it may be free from all adversities, and devoutly given to serve Thee in good works, to the glory of Thy Name; through Jesus Christ our Lord. Amen.

Three and Twentieth Sunday after Trinity.

O GOD, our refuge and strength, Who art the author of all godliness; Be ready, we beseech thee, to hear the devout prayers of Thy Church; and grant that those things which we ask faithfully we may obtain effectually; through Jesus Christ our Lord. Amen.

Four and Twentieth Sunday after Trinity.

O LORD, we beseech Thee, absolve Thy people from their offences; that through Thy bountiful goodness we may all be delivered from the bands of those sins, which by our frailty we have committed: Grant this, O heavenly Father, for Jesus Christ's sake, our blessed Lord and Saviour. Amen.

Five and Twentieth Sunday after Trinity.

STIR up, we beseech Thee, O Lord, the wills of Thy faithful people; that they, plenteously bringing forth the fruit of good works, may of Thee be plenteously rewarded; through Jesus Christ our Lord. Amen.

FEAST OF THE DEDICATION OF THE CHURCH.
PRINCIPAL DOUBLE.

At Compline.

Daily throughout the Octaves Compl. a viii., as on Trinity Sunday, is said, when this Feast is observed between Trinity and the First Sunday in Advent, or between the Octave of the Epiphany and Ash Wednesday.
At other times the Compline of the season is not changed.

At Prime.

Antiphon.—Holiness, O Lord, becometh Thine house for ever. *In Eastertide.* Alleluia.
Antiphon.—Thanks be to Thee.

If this Feast fall within the Octaves of the Holy Trinity, then the Antiphon O holy, blessed is said over the Athanasian Creed.
The Responsory is said with Alleluia as on Trinity Sunday, unless the Feast fall between Septuagesima and Easter.

At Terce.

Antiphon.—My house shall be called the house of prayer. *In Eastertide.* Alleluia.
Chapter. 1 Cor. iii. 10.
Now let every man take heed how he buildeth thereupon. For other foundation can no man lay than that is laid, which is Jesus Christ.
R. Holiness, O Lord, becometh Thine house. Alleluia, Alleluia. *V.* Unto length of days. *R.* Alleluia, Alleluia.
V. Glory be. *R.* Holiness.
V. My house. *R.* Shall be called the house of prayer.

If this Feast fall between Septuagesima and Easter, all Alleluias are omitted.

FEAST OF THE DEDICATION OF THE CHURCH.

Collect.

O GOD, Who hast vouchsafed to call the Church Thy Bride, and to her who obtained grace by faith and devotion to grant a name of dignity; Grant unto all this Thy people, who serve Thy holy Name, that they may be found worthy to share the title of Thy Church; Who livest and reignest with the Father.

At Sext.

Antiphon.—This is the house of the Lord, which is firmly built; it is securely founded on a sure rock. *In Eastertide.* Alleluia.

Chapter. Rev. xxi. 3.

Behold, the tabernacle of God is with men, and He will dwell with them, and they shall be His people, and God Himself shall be with them, and be their God.

R. My house. Alleluia, Alleluia. *V.* Shall be called the house of prayer. *R.* Alleluia, Alleluia. *V.* Glory be. *R.* My house.

V. Blessed are they that dwell in Thy house, O Lord. *R.* They will be always praising Thee.

At None.

Antiphon.—Precious stones are all thy walls, and the towers of Jerusalem shall be built with gems.

Chapter. 1 Cor. iii. 8.

Every man shall receive his own reward according to his own labour. For we are labourers together with God; ye are God's husbandry, ye are God's building.

R. Blessed are they that dwell in Thy house, O Lord. Alleluia, Alleluia. *V.* They will be always praising Thee. *R.* Alleluia, Alleluia. *V.* Glory be. *R.* Blessed are they.

V. This is the house of the Lord which is firmly built. *R.* It is securely founded on a sure rock.

Full Service of the Dedication is continued for eight days with rulers of the Choir, including Sunday, unless a Feast of nine Lessons, or of Three Lessons with rulers, intervene.

If this Feast fall in Advent or Septuagesima, the Octaves have no rulers, and if a Feast of Three Lessons or an Octave day of a Saint fall within these Octaves, the whole service is of the Feast or Octave day, with memorial only of the Dedication. Also on the Sunday within the Octaves or on the Octave day, the whole service shall be of the Sunday with memorial only of the Dedication.

If it fall between the Circumcision and the Octave of Epiphany, or between Ash Wednesday and Wednesday in Holy Week, or between the Eve of the Ascension and the Eve of Whitsun, only a memorial of the Dedication is made within the Octaves and even on the Octave day. But if it fall within the Octaves of Epiphany, then the whole service of the Octave day of the Dedication shall be performed after the Octaves of Epiphany.

If it fall between Christmas Eve and the Circumcision, or between Wednesday in Holy Week and Low Sunday, or between Whitsun Eve and Trinity Sunday, then it is always transferred, viz. until after the Octaves of Epiphany, or after Low Sunday, or after the First Sunday after Trinity; and the Octaves are observed with rulers.

If it fall on Advent Sunday, or Ash Wednesday, or Passion Sunday, or

Palm Sunday, or Low Sunday, or Trinity Sunday, it is always transferred to the following day, if it be not occupied by a Feast with rulers, and Evensong shall be of the Dedication, and a solemn memorial of the Feast. The same is done if it fall on Ascension Day, but then there is no service of the Dedication within the Octaves until the Octave Day, except only a memorial.

The above rules hold good with respect to the Feast of the place when it has Octaves; e.g., the Nativity of St. John the Baptist, the Martyrdom of St. Peter and St. Paul, the Holy Trinity, St. Martin, and the like.

WITHIN THE OCTAVES.

At Prime and the other Hours, all as within Octaves.

None of the common memorials are made during the Octaves, unless a Feast without rulers occur. However, between Christmas and the Purification a solemn memorial of St. Mary is made, and between Low Sunday and the Ascension a solemn memorial of the Resurrection is made.

OCTAVE OF THE DEDICATION.

At Prime and the other Hours, all is as usual within Octaves.

At First and Second Evensong and at Mattins, as on the Festival.

END OF SUNDAY OFFICES.

Great Rubric concerning Sundays and Feasts.

On Saturdays throughout this season full service of holy Mary is customarily performed; unless some Feast of nine Lessons intervene, or Octaves with rulers, or a Feast without rulers but with proper Antiphons at Lauds, or Embertide, or Eves of Saints prevent it. If for such reasons the service of holy Mary be not performed on Saturday, then it shall be done on some Feria of the same week, when it can have its own first Evensong if possible. When full service of holy Mary be performed on a Monday, or on the morrow of any Feast of nine Lessons, or of three Lessons with rulers, then Evensong shall be of holy Mary with solemn memorial of the Feast or of the Sunday; unless the Sunday or Feast be for any reason deprived of its first Evensong, for then Evensong shall be of the Feast or Sunday with solemn memorial of holy Mary. Nevertheless within the Octaves of Epiphany, the Ascension, and the like, second Evensong of the Octaves is said, as is noted above after second Evensong of the Octave of the Epiphany. And when a Feast of any Saint or Octaves without rulers, and full service of St. Mary must be said on the same day, then a memorial only of the Feast or the Octaves is made.

Throughout Trinity-tide, if a Feast of nine Lessons is observed on a Saturday or on any Feria in the week, then neither at Evensong nor at Mattins is any memorial made, unless some Feast of three Lessons fall on the same day. When Feasts of nine Lessons fall within Octaves of Saints, a memorial of the Octaves is made, except on a double Feast; in that case no memorial is made of the Octaves, unless the Octaves have rulers. But after the Evensong of the day at Evensong of holy Mary, and after Mattins of the day at Mattins of holy Mary, are made memorials of the Holy Spirit, of the Feast of the place, of Relics, of All Saints, and of Peace.

If during Trinity-tide a double Feast fall on a Sunday, the whole service of the Feast, and nothing of the Sunday, unless it happen that the Sunday Mass has of necessity to be sung on the Sunday itself or in the same week; for then at both Evensongs and at Mattins are made silently memorials of the Sunday and of the Holy Trinity, viz. at first Evensong and at Mattins alike privately. Nevertheless the Procession to the Cross, whether the aforesaid memorials be made or no, is altogether omitted on Double Feasts.

If however the Feast of the Exaltation of the Holy Cross fall on a Sunday, then at first Evensong is made silently memorial of the Sunday and of the Holy Trinity, and then follows the Procession before the Cross, as on the Feast of the Invention of the Holy Cross, with the Sunday Mass in Chapter, at which is made memorial of the Trinity and of All Saints only. At second Evensong is made silently a memorial of the Sunday, with a solemn memorial of the Octaves. But if the Feast of the Exaltation fall on Monday, a memorial of the Sunday is made silently at the service, and afterwards Procession before the Cross.

On the Feast of St. Augustine, Doctor, a solemn memorial of St. John Baptist is made at second Evensong. If the Feast of St. Augustine fall on a Saturday, then at second Evensong is made a memorial of the Sunday and of the Trinity privately, with solemn memorial of St. John Baptist. The same is done when the Feast of St. Augustine falls on a Sunday.

And always throughout this season, when a memorial of Sunday is made at Evensong on Saturday, or at Mattins on Sunday, shall be said the Memorial of the Trinity.

At second Evensong of the Feasts of the Purification and Nativity of blessed Mary, and of Low Sunday, and of Trinity Sunday, Corpus Christi, and the Dedication of the church, no memorial is made of any Feast without rulers falling on the morrow, unless a Feast of nine Lessons be conjoined with it; in that case memorials of both Feasts are made silently. So on the Feast of St. Peter and St. Paul no memorial is made of the Octaves of St. John Baptist, unless the Octaves have rulers; nor is it customary to make a memorial of the Holy Trinity on the Feast of Corpus Christi, unless the Octaves of the Holy Trinity have rulers, for then solemn memorial is made of the Octaves, although the Feast of the place be on that day; nor on the Nativity of St. John Baptist is made memorial of the Octaves of Corpus Christi, unless the Octaves have rulers.

Memorials of double Feasts, and of Octaves with rulers, and of Commemoration of blessed Mary, and of the Feast of the place, shall be made solemnly even on double Feasts.

When any simple Feast of Nine Lessons is celebrated on Sunday, and there fall on the same day a Feast of three Lessons or Octaves without rulers, then first of all is made a memorial of the Feast or of the Octaves at First Evensong and at Mattins, and afterwards of the Sunday and of the Holy Trinity, and the Procession before the Cross is observed, except in that week the Sunday Mass be omitted; and except on double Feasts, for then there is no Procession on Saturday except on the Feast of the Exaltation of the Holy Cross. If some double Feast fall on Saturday, memorials of the Sunday and the Trinity are made silently, and there is no Procession before the Cross.

But if a simple Feast of nine Lessons be celebrated on Saturday, then at first Evensong of Sunday, first of all is made memorial of the Feast of nine Lessons, then of any Feast of three Lessons that may fall on the morrow, then of any Octave without rulers, then of the Holy Trinity.

If a simple Feast of nine Lessons be celebrated on a Monday, and on the same day another Feast of three Lessons or an Octave, then at Evensong on Sunday first of all is made memorial of the Feast of three Lessons, then of any Octave without rulers, and afterwards of the Sunday only. This is observed on all Sundays in this season except upon the occurrence of double Feasts, when a memorial of the Sunday is made at both Evensongs and at Mattins; then is said the memorial of the Holy Trinity at first Evensong and at Mattins, and there is Procession before the Cross at first Evensong, except when double Feasts fall on Saturdays or Sundays; for then there is no Procession before the Cross, and the Sunday Mass is said on any vacant Feria of that week. But if it happen that no notice be taken of the Sunday Mass through the week, and the season be prolix, i.e. if it be not said in Chapter on Sunday owing to double Feasts, nor on any Feria because of Feasts of nine or three Lessons or Octaves of Saints with rulers, and the season be prolix, then on the preceding Sunday the aforesaid memorials, viz. of the Sunday and of the Trinity, and the Procession before the Cross at first Evensong, are omitted. But if the season be short, then on Sunday is said the Sunday Mass in Chapter, or during the week on any Feria when Octaves with rulers are observed, and a memorial shall be made at Evensong and Mattins, of the Sunday and of the Holy Trinity, with Procession before the Cross. Yet if any simple Feast of nine Lessons, or Octaves with rulers, fall on a Sunday, and during the following week there be no vacant day, and the season be short, then on Sunday is said the Sunday Mass in Chapter, and memorial is made of the Sunday and of the Trinity at Evensong and at Mattins, with Procession before the Cross. Similarly is done on the Exaltation of the Holy Cross whenever it falls on Sunday, although it is a double Feast. If a double Feast during this season fall on Saturday, then there shall be no Procession before the Cross at second Evensong, which shall be of the Feast, nor is any memorial made audibly of the Sunday or of the Trinity, but in silence, except on the Exaltation of the Holy Cross; for then is made solemn memorial of the Octaves of the Nativity of blessed Mary; and the memorials of the Sunday and of the Trinity are said silently, and there is no Procession before the Cross.

When a simple Feast of nine Lessons within this season be celebrated on a Saturday, and on the preceding Friday the first Evensong of such Feast cannot be said owing to some Feast of nine Lessons, then Evensong of Saturday is of the Feast with memorial of Sunday and of the Trinity, and a Procession. However there shall be other Evensong of the Sunday with a memorial of the Feast.

This should be generally observed throughout the year, that all Feasts of nine Lessons, or of three Lessons with rulers, and all Sundays should have one Evensong at least; unless some double Feast prevent it, as in the case of the Sixth Day after the Nativity of our Lord, or when the Eve of Epiphany falls on a Sunday, or if the Feast of SS. Philip and James fall on a Saturday, then on the Saturday shall be Evensong of the Apostles, and on the Sunday Evensong of the Invention of the Holy Cross, and then the Sunday has no Evensong. Similarly when the Octave of the Assumption of blessed Mary falls on Saturday, then on the Saturday following shall be Evensong of the Octave, and on the Sunday Evensong of St. Bartholomew; and similarly in like cases.

When a double Feast falls on Saturday, and a simple Feast of nine Lessons on the Monday, and another double Feast on the Tuesday, then on Sunday Evensong shall be of the Feast of nine Lessons, and so the Sunday shall be deprived of both Evensongs. And a simple Feast of nine Lessons, falling between two double Feasts, loses both its Evensongs. On all double Feasts throughout the year there shall be first and second Evensong of the Feast, unless another double Feast prevent it, as in the week of the Nativity of our Lord, and the like. The Feast of St. Andrew, when it falls on Saturday is an exception; as also are double Feasts falling on the Saturdays before Passion Sunday and Palm Sunday, and on Wednesday in Holy Week, which have only first Evensong, although it be the Feast of the place or of the Dedication of the church. If the Feast of the place fall on Trinity Sunday, it is transferred to the morrow, if it be not occupied with a Feast of nine Lessons, and Evensong shall be of the Feast of the place, with solemn memorial of the Holy Trinity, and similarly is done in like cases, as is noted in the case of the Dedication of the Church.

And it should be noted that on Octaves with rulers, such as the Octaves of the Epiphany, the Ascension, Corpus Christi when its Octaves have rulers, the Visitation, Assumption, and Nativity of blessed Mary, there shall always be second Evensong of the Octaves, and only a memorial of a Feast or of a Sunday following on the morrow; except when a double Feast fall on the morrow or on the Octaves, or a Feast of nine Lessons, which cannot have a second Evensong. Similarly is done in the case of the Octaves of the Dedication of the church when they have rulers. And when Commemoration of blessed Mary or of the Feast of the place, is celebrated on the morrow of any Feast of nine Lessons, or of three Lessons with rulers, of which no first Evensong was said, then only a solemn memorial is made of the Commemoration. When Commemoration of blessed Mary or of the Feast of the place is celebrated on a Monday, then is said Evensong of the Commemoration and a memorial of the Sunday; except when First Evensong of the Sunday was not said, for then there is only a memorial of the Commemoration. If the Feast of St. Mary Magdalene, or of St. Margaret, or of St. Laurence, or of St. Martin the Bishop, or of St. Catherine fall on a Sunday, the customary memorials having been said, first of all a Procession is made to the Altar of the Saints, and then to the Cross.

THE DAVIDIC PSALTER ACCORDING TO THE USE OF SARUM.

Before the Day Hours.

IN THE NAME OF OUR LORD JESUS CHRIST. AMEN.

Before the beginning of each Hour is said always the Lord's Prayer; and at the end likewise, especially after Mattins and Evensong. Also Hail Mary. I believe in God. As Saint Hierome saith : "When thou beginnest any work, send on before thee the Lord's Prayer, sign thy brow with the holy Cross, according to that which is written: Before thou prayest, prepare thyself, and be not as one that tempteth the Lord."

A Short Prayer to be said before the Hours.

OPEN my mouth, O Lord, that I may bless Thy holy Name; and cleanse my heart from all vain and idle thoughts, that I may be worthy to be heard in the presence of Thy Divine Majesty; through Jesus Christ Thy Son, our Lord, Who liveth and reigneth with Thee and the Holy Ghost, one God, world without end. Amen.

At Prime.

V. O God, make speed to save ~~me.~~ *us*
R. O Lord, make haste to help ~~me.~~ *us*
V. Glory be to the Father, and to the Son: and to the Holy Ghost.
R. As it was in the beginning, is now, and ever shall be: world without end. Amen.
Alleluia.

[*From Septuagesima to Wednesday in Holy Week, instead of* Alleluia *is said:*

Praise to Thee, O Lord, King of eternal glory.]

Hymn.

Now that the lights of morn appear,
Seek we of God, with humble fear,
Grace to direct our steps to-day
To walk more nearly as we pray.

Upon our lips set Thou Thy guard,
Lest peace by angry tongues be marred;
From evil sights defend our eyes,
And shield our life from vanities.

Now pure be all our hearts within,
And undefiled by touch of sin,
And pride of flesh, O Christ, subdued
Through frugal use of daily food.

So may we, when the daylight dies,
And shades of night steal through the skies,
Pure from the world's pollution, raise
To Thee our evening hymns of praise.

To God Almighty praise be done;
Praise to the Father's only Son;
Praise now and ever, as is meet,
To God the Holy Paraclete.
Amen.

[*Instead of the afore-written doxology, is sung at the end of all hymns of this metre:*

From Christmas Day to the morrow of the Purification, except on the Feast and through the Octaves of Epiphany, and on all Feasts and through the Octaves of the blessed Virgin Mary, and on her Commemorations, throughout the year, and on the Feast of Corpus Christi, and through its Octaves, when the Service is of the Octaves:

All glory, Virgin-born, to Thee,
Jesu, Incarnate Deity,
Whom with the Father we adore,
And Holy Spirit evermore.

AT PRIME. 61

On the Feast and during the Octaves of Epiphany:

Jesu, all glory be to Thee
In this Thy glad Epiphany,
Whom with the Father we adore,
And Holy Spirit evermore.

From Low Sunday to the Ascension:

O Lord of life, to Thee we pray,
Triumphant o'er the grave to-day,
In this our Easter joy protect
From death and hell Thine own elect.

To Thee be sung Thy people's praise,
O risen Lord, through endless days,
Whom with the Father we adore,
And Holy Spirit evermore.

From the Ascension to Whitsun Day:

In Thee be all our joy, O Lord,
As Thou wilt be our high reward;
Be all our glory now in Thee
To ages of eternity.

To Thee be sung Thy people's praise,
Ascended Lord, through endless days,
Whom with the Father we adore,
And Holy Spirit evermore.

From Whitsun Day to Trinity:

In ages gone, like tongues of flame
On saintly souls Thy Spirit came;
O grant us peace, we humbly pray,
And cleanse Thy people's sins away.

To God the Father, God the Son,
And God the Spirit, praise be done;
And God's own Son upon us pour
The Spirit's gifts for evermore.]

(a) *Sunday Antiphon, except when otherwise appointed in the Proper:*

The Lord is my Shepherd.

(b) *On ordinary Ferias.*

Antiphon. — Hear my prayer, O God.

(c) *On Ferias in Advent.*

Antiphon. — Come and deliver us.

Psalm xxii.

MY God, my God, look upon me; why hast Thou forsaken me: and art so far from my health, and from the words of my complaint?

2 O my God, I cry in the day-time, but Thou hearest not: and in the night season also I take no rest.

3 And Thou continuest holy: O Thou worship of Israel.

4 Our fathers hoped in Thee: they trusted in Thee, and Thou didst deliver them.

5 They called upon Thee, and were holpen: they put their trust in Thee, and were not confounded.

6 But as for me, I am a worm, and no man: a very scorn of men, and the outcast of the people.

7 All they that see me laugh me to scorn: they shoot out their lips, and shake their heads, saying,

8 He trusted in God, that He would deliver him: let Him deliver him, if He will have him.

9 But Thou art He that took me out of my mother's womb: Thou wast my hope, when I hanged yet upon my mother's breasts.

10 I have been left unto Thee ever since I was born: Thou art my God even from my mother's womb.

11 O go not from me, for trouble is hard at hand: and there is none to help me.

12 Many oxen are come about me: fat bulls of Basan close me in on every side.

13 They gape upon me with their mouths: as it were a ramping and a roaring lion.

14 I am poured out like water, and all my bones are out of joint: my heart also in the midst of my body is even like melting wax.

15 My strength is dried up like a potsherd, and my tongue cleaveth to my gums: and Thou shalt bring me into the dust of death.

16 For many dogs are come about me: and the council of the wicked layeth siege against me.

17 They pierced my hands and my feet; I may tell all my bones: they stand staring and looking upon me.

18 They part my garments among them: and cast lots upon my vesture.

19 But be not Thou far from me, O Lord: Thou art my succour, haste Thee to help me.

20 Deliver my soul from the sword: my darling from the power of the dog.

21 Save me from the lion's mouth: Thou hast heard me also from among the horns of the unicorns.

22 I will declare Thy Name unto my brethren: in the midst of the congregation will I praise Thee.

23 O praise the Lord, ye that fear Him: magnify Him, all ye of the seed of Jacob, and fear Him, all ye seed of Israel;

24 For He hath not despised, nor abhorred, the low estate of the poor: He hath not hid His face from him, but when he called unto him He heard him.

25 My praise is of Thee

in the great congregation: my vows will I perform in the sight of them that fear Him.

26 The poor shall eat, and be satisfied: they that seek after the Lord shall praise Him; your heart shall live for ever.

27 All the ends of the world shall remember themselves, and be turned unto the Lord: and all the kindreds of the nations shall worship before Him.

28 For the kingdom is the Lord's: and He is the Governor among the people.

29 All such as be fat upon earth: have eaten, and worshipped.

30 All they that go down into the dust shall kneel before Him: and no man hath quickened his own soul.

31 My seed shall serve Him: they shall be counted unto the Lord for a generation.

32 They shall come, and the heavens shall declare His righteousness: unto a people that shall be born, whom the Lord hath made.

Psalm xxiii.

THE Lord is my Shepherd: therefore can I lack nothing.

2 He shall feed me in a green pasture: and lead me forth beside the waters of comfort.

3 He shall convert my soul: and bring me forth in the paths of righteousness, for His Name's sake.

4 Yea, though I walk through the valley of the shadow of death, I will fear no evil: for Thou art with me; Thy rod and Thy staff comfort me.

5 Thou shalt prepare a table before me against them that trouble me: Thou hast anointed my head with oil, and my cup shall be full.

6 But Thy lovingkindness and mercy shall follow me all the days of my life: and I will dwell in the house of the Lord for ever.

Glory be to the Father.

Psalm xxiv.

THE earth is the Lord's, and all that therein is: the compass of the world, and they that dwell therein.

2 For He hath founded it upon the seas: and prepared it upon the floods.

3 Who shall ascend into the hill of the Lord: or who shall rise up in His holy place?

4 Even he that hath clean hands, and a pure heart: and that hath not lift up his mind unto vanity, nor sworn to deceive his neighbour.

5 He shall receive the blessing from the Lord: and righteousness from the God of his salvation.

6 This is the generation of them that seek him: even of them that seek thy face, O Jacob.

7 Lift up your heads, O ye gates, and be ye lift up, ye everlasting doors: and the King of glory shall come in.

8 Who is the King of glory: it is the Lord strong and mighty, even the Lord mighty in battle.

9 Lift up your heads, O ye gates, and be ye lift up, ye everlasting doors: and the King of glory shall come in.

10 Who is the King of glory: even the Lord of hosts, He is the King of glory.

Psalm xxv.

UNTO Thee, O Lord, will I lift up my soul; my God, I have put my trust in Thee: O let me not be confounded, neither let mine enemies triumph over me.

2 For all they that hope in Thee shall not be ashamed: but such as transgress without a cause shall be put to confusion.

3 Show me Thy ways, O Lord: and teach me Thy paths.

4 Lead me forth in Thy truth, and learn me: for Thou art the God of my salvation; in Thee hath been my hope all the day long.

5 Call to remembrance, O Lord, Thy tender mercies: and Thy lovingkindnesses, which have been ever of old.

6 O remember not the sins and offences of my youth: but according to Thy mercy think Thou upon me, O Lord, for Thy goodness.

7 Gracious and righteous is the Lord: therefore will He teach sinners in the way.

8 Them that are meek shall He guide in judgment: and such as are gentle, them shall He learn His way.

9 All the paths of the Lord are mercy and truth: unto such as keep His covenant, and His testimonies.

10 For Thy Name's sake, O Lord: be merciful unto my sin, for it is great.

11 What man is he, that feareth the Lord: him shall He teach in the way that He shall choose.

12 His soul shall dwell at ease: and his seed shall inherit the land.

13 The secret of the Lord is among them that fear Him: and He will show them His covenant.

14 Mine eyes are ever looking unto the Lord: for He shall pluck my feet out of the net.

15 Turn Thee unto me, and have mercy upon me: for I am desolate, and in misery.

16 The sorrows of my heart are enlarged: O bring Thou me out of my troubles.

17 Look upon my adversity and misery: and forgive me all my sin.

18 Consider mine enemies, how many they are: and they bear a tyrannous hate against me.

19 O keep my soul, and deliver me: let me not be confounded, for I have put my trust in Thee.

20 Let perfectness and righteous dealing wait upon me: for my hope hath been in Thee.

21 Deliver Israel, O God: out of all his troubles.

Glory be to the Father.

Psalm xxvi.

BE Thou my Judge, O Lord, for I have walked innocently: my trust hath been also in the Lord, therefore shall I not fall.

2 Examine me, O Lord, and prove me: try out my reins and my heart.

3 For Thy lovingkindness is ever before mine eyes: and I will walk in Thy truth.

4 I have not dwelt with vain persons: neither will I have fellowship with the deceitful.

5 I have hated the congregation of the wicked: and will not sit among the ungodly.

6 I will wash my hands in innocency, O Lord: and so will I go to Thine altar;

7 That I may show the voice of thanksgiving: and tell of all Thy wondrous works.

8 Lord, I have loved the habitation of Thy house: and the place where Thine honour dwelleth.

9 O shut not up my soul with the sinners: nor my life with the bloodthirsty;

10 In whose hands is wickedness: and their right hand is full of gifts.

11 But as for me, I will

walk innocently: O deliver me, and be merciful unto me.

12 My foot standeth right: I will praise the Lord in the congregations.

Psalm liv.

SAVE me, O God, for Thy Name's sake: and avenge me in Thy strength.

2 Hear my prayer, O God: and hearken unto the words of my mouth.

3 For strangers are risen up against me: and tyrants, which have not God before their eyes, seek after my soul.

4 Behold, God is my helper: the Lord is with them that uphold my soul.

5 He shall reward evil unto mine enemies: destroy Thou them in Thy truth.

6 An offering of a free heart will I give Thee, and praise Thy name, O Lord: because it is so comfortable.

7 For He hath delivered me out of all my trouble: and mine eye hath seen his desire upon mine enemies.

Glory be to the Father.

Psalm cxviii.

O GIVE thanks unto the Lord, for He is gracious: because His mercy endureth for ever.

2 Let Israel now confess, that He is gracious: and that His mercy endureth for ever.

3 Let the house of Aaron now confess: that His mercy endureth for ever.

4 Yea, let them now that fear the Lord confess: that His mercy endureth for ever.

5 I called upon the Lord in trouble: and the Lord heard me at large.

6 The Lord is on my side: I will not fear what man doeth unto me.

7 The Lord taketh my part with them that help me: therefore shall I see my desire upon mine enemies.

8 It is better to trust in the Lord: than to put any confidence in man.

9 It is better to trust in the Lord: than to put any confidence in princes.

10 All nations compassed me round about: but in the Name of the Lord will I destroy them.

11 They kept me in on every side, they kept me in, I say, on every side: but in the Name of the Lord will I destroy them.

12 They came about me like bees, and are extinct even as the fire among the

thorns: for in the Name of the Lord I will destroy them.

13 Thou hast thrust sore at me, that I might fall: but the Lord was my help.

14 The Lord is my strength, and my song: and is become my salvation.

15 The voice of joy and health is in the dwellings of the righteous: the right hand of the Lord bringeth mighty things to pass.

16 The right hand of the Lord hath the pre-eminence: the right hand of the Lord bringeth mighty things to pass.

17 I shall not die, but live: and declare the works of the Lord.

18 The Lord hath chastened and corrected me: but He hath not given me over unto death.

19 Open me the gates of righteousness: that I may go into them, and give thanks unto the Lord.

20 This is the gate of the Lord: the righteous shall enter into it.

21 I will thank Thee, for Thou hast heard me: and art become my salvation.

22 The same stone which the builders refused: is become the head-stone in the corner.

23 This is the Lord's doing: and it is marvellous in our eyes.

24 This is the day which the Lord hath made: we will rejoice and be glad in it.

25 Help me now, O Lord: O Lord, send us now prosperity.

26 Blessed be he that cometh in the Name of the Lord: we have wished you good luck, ye that are of the house of the Lord.

27 God is the Lord Who hath showed us light: bind the sacrifice with cords, yea, even unto the horns of the altar.

28 Thou art my God, and I will thank Thee: Thou art my God, and I will praise Thee.

29 O give thanks unto the Lord, for He is gracious: and His mercy endureth for ever.

From Septuagesima to Easter, instead of Psalm cxviii., O give thanks, is said Psalm xciii., as follows:

Psalm xciii.

THE Lord is King, and hath put on glorious apparel: the Lord hath put on His apparel, and girded Himself with strength.

2 He hath made the round world so sure: that it cannot be moved.

3 Ever since the world began hath Thy seat been prepared: Thou art from everlasting.

4 The floods are risen, O Lord, the floods have lift up their voice: the floods lift up their waves.

5 The waves of the sea are mighty, and rage horribly: but yet the Lord, Who dwelleth on high, is mightier.

6 Thy testimonies, O Lord, are very sure: holiness becometh Thine house for ever.

Psalm cxix.

BLESSED are those that are undefiled in the way: and walk in the law of the Lord.

2 Blessed are they that keep His testimonies: and seek Him with their whole heart.

3 For they who do no wickedness: walk in His ways.

4 Thou hast charged: that we shall diligently keep Thy commandments.

5 Oh that my ways were made so direct: that I might keep Thy statutes!

6 So shall I not be confounded: while I have respect unto all Thy commandments.

7 I will thank Thee with an unfeigned heart: when I shall have learned the judgments of Thy righteousness.

8 I will keep Thy ceremonies: O forsake me not utterly.

9 Wherewithal shall a young man cleanse his way: even by ruling himself after Thy word.

10 With my whole heart have I sought Thee: O let me not go wrong out of Thy commandments.

11 Thy words have I hid within my heart: that I should not sin against Thee.

12 Blessed art Thou, O Lord: O teach me Thy statutes.

13 With my lips have I been telling: of all the judgments of Thy mouth.

14 I have had as great delight in the way of Thy testimonies: as in all manner of riches.

15 I will talk of Thy commandments: and have respect unto Thy ways.

16 My delight shall be in Thy statutes: and I will not forget Thy word.

Glory be to the Father.

Psalm cxix.

O DO well unto Thy servant: that I may live, and keep Thy word.

18 Open Thou mine eyes: that I may see the wondrous things of Thy law.

19 I am a stranger upon earth: O hide not Thy commandments from me.

20 My soul breaketh out for the very fervent desire: that it hath alway unto Thy judgments.

21 Thou hast rebuked the proud: and cursed are they that do err from Thy commandments.

22 O turn from me shame and rebuke: for I have kept Thy testimonies.

23 Princes also did sit and speak against me: but Thy servant is occupied in Thy statutes.

24 For Thy testimonies are my delight: and my counsellors.

25 My soul cleaveth to the dust: O quicken Thou me, according to Thy word.

26 I have acknowledged my ways, and Thou heardest me: O teach me Thy statutes.

27 Make me to understand the way of Thy commandments: and so shall I talk of Thy wondrous works.

28 My soul melteth away for very heaviness: comfort Thou me according unto Thy word.

29 Take from me the way of lying: and cause Thou me to make much of Thy law.

30 I have chosen the way of truth: and Thy judgments have I laid before me.

31 I have stuck unto Thy testimonies: O Lord, confound me not.

32 I will run the way of Thy commandments: when Thou hast set my heart at liberty.

Glory be to the Father.

(a) *On ordinary Sundays:*

Antiphon.—The Lord is my Shepherd, therefore can I lack nothing: He shall feed me in a green pasture.

(b) *On ordinary Ferias:*

Antiphon.—Hear my prayer, O God: and hearken unto the words of my mouth.

(c) *On Ferias in Advent:*

Antiphon.—Come and deliver us: O our God.

Creed of Athanasius.

Said daily, except from Thursday in Holy Week to the Saturday after Easter inclusive.

a\Sunday Antiphon, except between Christmas and the Octave of Epiphany, and between Easter and the Octave of Trinity—

Thee, God the Father Unbegotten, Thee, Only begotten Son, Thee, Holy Spirit, Paraclete: Holy and Undivided Trinity, Thee with our whole heart and mouth do we confess, praise, and bless: to Thee be glory for ever.

On all Double Feasts outside Easter Week and Trinity Week is said this Antiphon:

Thanks be to Thee, O God : thanks be to Thee, One very Trinity, One Most High Deity, One Holy Unity. *In Eastertide.* Alleluia.

Throughout Trinity Week, whatever be the Service, is said this Antiphon:

O holy, blessed, and glorious Trinity : Father, Son, and Holy Ghost.

On all other Sundays, and on all Simple Feasts of three or nine Lessons with rulers of the Choir; throughout Octaves with rulers; on Commemorations of blessed Mary and of the Feast of the place; except such as fall within Trinity Week, is said:

Thee all Thy creatures meetly praise : Thee they worship : Thee they glorify, O blessed Trinity.

On all Ferias, and Feasts of three Lessons without rulers; throughout Octaves without rulers; on Vigils and in Ember Seasons; outside Whitsun Week and Trinity Week, is said:

Glory to Thee, Co-equal Trinity, Unity Divine : as it was in the beginning, is now, and ever shall be. *In Eastertide*, Alleluia.

WHOSOEVER will be saved : before all things it is necessary that he hold the Catholick Faith. Which Faith except every one do keep whole and undefiled : without doubt he shall perish everlastingly.

And the Catholick Faith is this : That we worship one God in Trinity, and Trinity in Unity ;

Neither confounding the Persons : nor dividing the Substance.

For there is one Person of the Father, another of the Son : and another of the Holy Ghost.

But the Godhead of the Father, of the Son, and of the Holy Ghost, is all one : the Glory equal, the Majesty co-eternal.

Such as the Father is, such is the Son : and such is the Holy Ghost.

The Father uncreate, the Son uncreate : and the Holy Ghost uncreate.

The Father incomprehensible, the Son incomprehensible : and the Holy Ghost incomprehensible.

The Father eternal, the Son eternal : and the Holy Ghost eternal.

And yet they are not three eternals : but one eternal.

As also there are not three incomprehensibles, nor three uncreated : but one uncreated, and one incomprehensible.

So likewise the Father is Almighty, the Son Almighty: and the Holy Ghost Almighty.

And yet they are not three Almighties: but one Almighty.

So the Father is God, the Son is God: and the Holy Ghost is God.

And yet they are not three Gods: but one God.

So likewise the Father is Lord, the Son Lord: and the Holy Ghost Lord.

And yet not three Lords: but one Lord.

For like as we are compelled by the Christian verity: to acknowledge every Person by Himself to be God and Lord;

So are we forbidden by the Catholick Religion: to say, There be three Gods, or three Lords.

The Father is made of none: neither created, nor begotten.

The Son is of the Father alone: not made, nor created, but begotten.

The Holy Ghost is of the Father and of the Son: neither made, nor created, nor begotten, but proceeding.

So there is one Father, not three Fathers; one Son, not three Sons: one Holy Ghost, not three Holy Ghosts.

And in this Trinity none is afore, or after other: none is greater, or less than another;

But the whole three Persons are co-eternal together: and co-equal.

So that in all things, as is aforesaid: the Unity in Trinity, and the Trinity in Unity is to be worshipped.

He therefore that will be saved: must thus think of the Trinity.

Furthermore, it is necèssary to everlasting salvation: that he also believe rightly the Incarnation of our Lord Jesus Christ.

For the right Faith is, that we believe and confess: that our Lord Jesus Christ, the Son of God, is God and Man;

God, of the Substance of the Father, begotten before the worlds: and Man, of the Substance of His Mother, born in the world;

Perfect God, and perfect Man: of a reasonable soul and human flesh subsisting;

Equal to the Father, as touching His Godhead: and inferior to the Father, as touching His Manhood.

Who although He be God and Man: yet He is not two, but one Christ;

One; not by conversion

of the Godhead into flesh: but by taking of the Manhood into God;

One altogether; not by confusion of Substance: but by unity of Person.

For as the reasonable soul and flesh is one man: so God and Man is one Christ;

Who suffered for our salvation: descended into hell, rose again the third day from the dead.

He ascended into heaven, He sitteth on the right hand of the Father, God Almighty: from whence He shall come to judge the quick and the dead.

At Whose coming all men shall rise again with their bodies: and shall give account for their own works.

And they that have done good shall go into life everlasting: and they that have done evil into everlasting fire.

This is the Catholick Faith: which except a man believe faithfully, he cannot be saved.

Glory be to the Father.

Repeat the whole Antiphon.

Chapter.

a) On all Sundays, and on Festivals, and on Octave days and within Octaves with rulers; and on commemorations of blessed Mary and of the Feast of the place throughout the year, except in Easter Week:

1 *Timothy* i. 17.

Now unto the King eternal, immortal, invisible, the only wise God, be honour and glory for ever and ever. Amen.

Thanks be to God.

b) On all other Festivals, and on all Ferias from Low Sunday to Whitsuntide; and on Octave days and throughout Octaves without rulers, and on the Eves of Ascension, Whitsun, Christmas, and Epiphany, unless they fall on a Sunday:

Isaiah xxxiii. 2.

O Lord, be gracious unto us; we have waited for Thee: be Thou our arm every morning, our salvation also in the time of trouble.

c) On all other Ferias:

Zachariah viii. 19.

Love the truth and peace, saith the Lord of hosts.

And whenever this latter Chapter is said at Prime, the Petitions are said kneeling at all the Hours:

R. Jesus Christ, Son of the living God, have mercy upon us. V. Thou that sittest at the right hand of God. R. Have mercy upon us. V. Glory be. R. Jesus Christ.

The V. Thou that sittest varies at certain seasons, as is marked in the Proper.

AT PRIME.

V. O Lord, arise, help us. *R.* And deliver us for Thy Name's sake.

The Petitions.

Kyrie eleyson (thrice).
Christe eleyson (thrice).
Kyrie eleyson (thrice).

Our Father.

V. And lead us not into temptation. *R.* But deliver us from evil.
V. O let my soul live, and it shall praise Thee. *R.* And Thy judgments shall help me.
V. I have gone astray like a sheep that is lost. *R.* O seek Thy servant, for I do not forget Thy commandments.

I believe.

V. The Resurrection of the body. *R.* And the Life everlasting.
V. O let my mouth be filled with Thy praise. *R.* That I may sing of Thy glory and honour all the day long.
V. O Lord, turn Thy Face away from my sins. *R.* And blot out all mine offences.
V. Make me a clean heart, O God. *R.* And renew a right spirit within me.
V. Cast me not away from Thy Presence. *R.* And take not Thy Holy Spirit from me.
V. O give me the comfort of Thy help again. *R.* And stablish me with Thy free Spirit.
V. Deliver me, O Lord, from the evil man. *R.* And preserve me from the wicked man.
V. Deliver me from mine enemies, O God. *R.* Defend me from them that rise up against me.
V. O deliver me from the wicked doers. *R.* And save me from the bloodthirsty men.
V. So will I alway sing praise unto Thy Name. *R.* That I may daily perform my vows.
V. Hear us, O God of our salvation. *R.* Thou that art the Hope of all the ends of the earth, and of them that remain in the broad sea.
V. O God, make speed to save us. *R.* O Lord, make haste to help us.
V. Holy God; holy and mighty; holy and immortal. *R.* O Lamb of God, that takest away the sins of the world, have mercy upon us.
V. Praise the Lord, O my soul. *R.* And all that is within me praise His holy Name.

V. Praise the Lord, O my soul. *R.* And forget not all His benefits.

V. Who forgiveth all thy sin. *R.* And healeth all thine infirmities.

V. Who saveth thy life from destruction. *R.* And crowneth thee with mercy and lovingkindness.

V. Who filleth thy mouth with good things. *R.* Making thee young and lusty as the eagle.

Then is said in a low voice the Confession.

The Priest, turning to the Altar:

I confess to God, to blessed Mary, all Saints [*turning to the Choir*], and you, that I have sinned exceedingly in thought, word, and deed, by my own fault. [*Turning again to the Altar.*] I pray holy Mary, and all the Saints of God [*turning to the Choir*], and you, to pray for me.

The Choir reply, turning to the Priest:

Almighty God have mercy upon you, and forgive you all your sins; deliver you from every evil; confirm and strengthen you in all good, and bring you to everlasting life. Amen.

Then the Choir say I confess *in the same manner as the Priest. The Priest replies,* Almighty God, have mercy, etc., *as above. Then let the Priest add:*

The almighty and merciful Lord grant you absolution and remission of all your sins, time for true repentance, amendment of life, the grace and comfort of His Holy Spirit. Amen.

V. Wilt Thou not turn again and quicken us? *R.* That Thy people may rejoice in Thee.

V. Show us Thy mercy, O Lord. *R.* And grant us Thy salvation.

V. Vouchsafe, O Lord, this day. *R.* To keep us without sin.

V. O Lord, have mercy upon us. *R.* Have mercy upon us.

V. O Lord, let Thy mercy lighten upon us. *R.* As our trust is in Thee.

[*On Sundays and Festivals:*

V. Turn us again, Thou God of hosts. *R.* Show us the light of Thy countenance, and we shall be whole.

V. Hear my prayer, O Lord. *R.* And let my crying come unto Thee.

V. The Lord be with you. *R.* And with Thy spirit.

AT PRIME.

Let us pray.

On all Sundays not Doubles, and all Simple Feasts:

O LORD, our heavenly Father, almighty and everlasting God, Who hast safely brought us to the beginning of this day; Defend us in the same with Thy mighty power; and grant that this day we fall into no sin, neither run into any kind of danger; but that all our doings may be ordered by Thy governance, to do always that is righteous in Thy sight; through Jesus Christ our Lord, Who liveth and reigneth with Thee in the unity of the Holy Ghost, God for ever and ever. Amen.

On all Double Feasts except within the Octave of Easter is said:

SHOW us Thy mercy, O Lord, at the beginning of this day, that, going forth with gladness, we may rejoice in Thy praises all the day long; through Jesus Christ Thy Son, our Lord, Who liveth and reigneth with Thee in the unity of the Holy Ghost, ever one God, world without end. Amen.

V. The Lord be with you.
R. And with thy spirit.
V. Bless we the Lord.
R. Thanks be to God.]

On Ferias

B throughout the year, except from Christmas to the Octave of Epiphany, and from Maundy Thursday to the first Sunday after Trinity, is here said Psalm li. with this VR.

V. Hearken unto my voice, O Lord, when I cry unto Thee. R. Have mercy upon me, and hear me.

Psalm li.

HAVE mercy upon me, O God, after Thy great goodness: according to the multitude of Thy mercies do away mine offences.

2 Wash me throughly from my wickedness: and cleanse me from my sin.

3 For I acknowledge my faults: and my sin is ever before me.

4 Against Thee only have I sinned, and done this evil in Thy sight: that Thou mightest be justified in Thy saying, and clear when Thou art judged.

5 Behold, I was shapen in wickedness: and in sin hath my mother conceived me.

6 But lo, Thou requirest truth in the inward parts: and shalt make me to understand wisdom secretly.

7 Thou shalt purge me with hyssop, and I shall be clean: Thou shalt wash me, and I shall be whiter than snow.

8 Thou shalt make me hear of joy and gladness: that the bones which Thou hast broken may rejoice.

9 Turn Thy face from my sins: and put out all my misdeeds.

10 Make me a clean heart, O

God: and renew a right spirit within me.

11 Cast me not away from Thy presence: and take not Thy Holy Spirit from me.

12 O give me the comfort of Thy help again: and stablish me with Thy free Spirit.

13 Then shall I teach Thy ways unto the wicked: and sinners shall be converted unto Thee.

14 Deliver me from blood-guiltiness, O God, Thou that art the God of my health: and my tongue shall sing of Thy righteousness.

15 Thou shalt open my lips, O Lord: and my mouth shall show Thy praise.

16 For Thou desirest no sacrifice, else would I give it Thee: but Thou delightest not in burnt-offerings.

17 The sacrifice of God is a troubled spirit: a broken and contrite heart, O God, shalt Thou not despise.

18 O be favourable and gracious unto Sion: build Thou the walls of Jerusalem.

19 Then shalt Thou be pleased with the sacrifice of righteousness, with the burnt-offerings and oblations: then shall they offer young bullocks upon Thine altar.

Glory be to the Father.

[*Here follows in Lent:*

Psalm xxxii.

BLESSED is he whose unrighteousness is forgiven: and whose sin is covered.

2 Blessed is the man unto whom the Lord imputeth no sin: and in whose spirit there is no guile.

3 For while I held my tongue: my bones consumed away through my daily complaining.

4 For Thy hand is heavy upon me day and night: and my moisture is like the drought in summer.

5 I will acknowledge my sin unto Thee: and mine unrighteousness have I not hid.

6 I said, I will confess my sins unto the Lord: and so Thou forgavest the wickedness of my sin.

7 For this shall every one that is godly make his prayer unto Thee, in a time when Thou mayest be found: but in the great water-floods they shall not come nigh him.

8 Thou art a place to hide me in, Thou shalt preserve me from trouble: Thou shalt compass me about with songs of deliverance.

9 I will inform thee, and teach thee in the way wherein thou shalt go: and I will guide thee with mine eye.

10 Be ye not like to horse and mule, which have no understanding: whose mouths must be held with bit and bridle, lest they fall upon thee.

11 Great plagues remain for the ungodly: but whoso putteth his trust in the Lord, mercy embraceth him on every side.

12 Be glad, O ye righteous, and rejoice in the Lord: and be joyful, all ye that are true of heart.

Glory be to the Father.

Then is said on all Ferias, the Priest alone standing up:

V. O Lord, arise, help us.
R. And deliver us for Thy Name's sake.

V. Turn us again, O Lord

God of hosts. *R.* Show the light of Thy countenance, and we shall be whole.

V. Hear my prayer, O Lord. *R.* And let my crying come unto Thee.

V. The Lord be with you. *R.* And with thy spirit.

Let us pray.

Collect.

O LORD, our heavenly Father, almighty and everlasting God, Who hast safely brought us to the beginning of this day; Defend us in the same with Thy mighty power; and grant that this day we fall into no sin, neither run into any kind of danger; but that all our doings may be ordered by Thy governance, to do always that is righteous in Thy sight; through Jesus Christ our Lord, Who liveth and reigneth with Thee in the unity of the Holy Ghost, God for ever and ever. Amen.

V. The Lord be with you.
R. And with thy spirit.
V. Bless we the Lord.
R. Thanks be to God.

Then let the Priest say:

V. Right dear in the sight of the Lord. *R.* Is the death of His saints.

Then let the Priest say without The Lord be with you, *and without* Let us pray:

MAY holy Mary, mother of our Lord and God Jesus Christ, and all holy saints and elect of God, intercede and pray for us sinners to the Lord our God: that we may be worthy to be aided and saved by Him, Who in the perfect Trinity liveth and reigneth God, through endless ages. Amen.

V. O God, make speed to save us. *R.* O Lord, make haste to help us.

This V. and R. are said three times.

V. Glory be to the Father.
R. As it was.

Kyrie eleyson.
Christe eleyson.
Kyrie eleyson.

Our Father.

V. And lead us not into temptation. *R.* But deliver us from evil.

V. And let Thy loving mercy come unto us, O Lord. *R.* Even Thy salvation, according to Thy word.

V. And show Thy servants Thy work. *R.* And their children Thy glory.

V. And the glorious majesty of the Lord our God be upon us. *R.* And prosper Thou the works of our hands upon us: O prosper Thou our handiwork.

The following Collect is said on Double Feasts and whenever the Choir is ruled, except in Easter week, without The Lord be with you.

Let us pray.

ALMIGHTY and everlasting God, direct our actions, we beseech Thee, according to Thy good pleasure: that through the Name and merits of Thy well-beloved Son we may alway abound in good works, Who liveth and reigneth with Thee in the unity of the Holy Ghost, God, world without end. Amen.

V. The Lord be with you.
R. And with thy spirit.
V. Bless we the Lord.
R. Thanks be to God.

On all other Feasts and Ferias is said:

Let us pray.

O ALMIGHTY Lord, and everlasting God, vouchsafe, we beseech Thee, to direct, sanctify, and govern, both our hearts and bodies, in the ways of Thy laws, and in the works of Thy commandments; that through Thy most mighty protection, both here and ever, we may be preserved in body and soul; through Jesus Christ our Lord, Who liveth and reigneth.

V. The Lord be with you.
R. And with thy spirit.
V. Bless we the Lord.
R. Thanks be to God.

Then, after reading the list of persons to be prayed for, is said daily (except from Christmas Eve till the first Sunday after the Octave of Epiphany; from Maundy Thursday to the first Sunday after Trinity; on all Double Feasts, on All Souls' Day; and through the Octaves of Corpus Christi, the Assumption, the holy Name, and Dedication of the church):

Psalm cxxi.

I WILL lift up mine eyes unto the hills: from whence cometh my help.

2 My help cometh even from the Lord: Who hath made heaven and earth.

3 He will not suffer thy foot to be moved: and He that keepeth thee will not sleep.

4 Behold, He that keepeth Israel: shall neither slumber nor sleep.

5 The Lord Himself is thy keeper: the Lord is thy defence upon thy right hand;

6 So that the sun shall not burn thee by day: neither the moon by night.

7 The Lord shall preserve thee from all evil: yea, it is even He that shall keep thy soul.

8 The Lord shall preserve

AT PRIME.

thy going out, and thy coming in: from this time forth for evermore.
Glory be to the Father.
Kyrie eleyson.
Christe eleyson.
Kyrie eleyson.
Our Father.

V. And lead us not into temptation. *R.* But deliver us from evil.
V. O Lord, show Thy mercy upon us. *R.* And grant us Thy salvation.
V. O God, save Thy servants and handmaidens. *R.* Which put their trust in Thee.
V. Send them help, O Lord, from the sanctuary. *R.* And strengthen them out of Syon.
V. Be unto them a strong tower, O Lord. *R.* From the face of the enemy.
V. Let no enemy have advantage over them. *R.* Neither the son of wickedness approach to hurt them.
V. Lord, hear my prayer. *R.* And let my crying come unto Thee.
V. The Lord be with you. *R.* And with thy spirit.

Let us pray.

ASSIST us mercifully, O Lord, in these our supplications and prayers, and dispose the way of Thy servants towards the attainment of everlasting salvation; that, among all the changes and chances of this mortal life, they may ever be defended by Thy most gracious and ready help.

Collect.

ALMIGHTY and everlasting God, the eternal salvation of all believers; Receive our supplications and prayers, which we offer before Thee for Thy servants and handmaidens, imploring that, by the aid of Thy mercy, they may be recovered of their sickness, and evermore give thanks unto Thee in Thy holy Church; through.
R. Amen.

Let a priest say,

Bid a blessing. The Lord bless us. In the Name of the Father and of the Son and of the Holy Ghost. Amen.

At Terce.

V. O God, make speed to save me.
R. O Lord, make haste to help me.
V. Glory be to the Father, and to the Son, and to the Holy Ghost.
R. As it was in the beginning, is now, and ever shall be: world without end. Amen.
Alleluia.

[*From Septuagesima to Wednesday in Holy Week:*

Praise to Thee, O Lord, King of eternal glory.]

Hymn.

Come, Holy Ghost, with God the Son
And God the Father ever One;
Come, dwell within these hearts of Thine,
And shed abroad Thy grace Divine.

May'st Thou by every tongue be blest,
With heart and mouth Thy Name confessed;
Our spirits kindle from above,
Till others catch the fire of love.

All-loving Father, hear our cry,
Hear us, O Christ, our Lord most high,
Who in the Spirit's Unity
Dost reign to all eternity.

Sunday Antiphon.—Praise and eternal glory.

Ferial Antiphon.—O let Thy loving mercies.

On Ferias in Advent:

Antiphon.—O Lord, raise up Thy power.

Psalm cxix.

TEACH me, O Lord, the way of Thy statutes: and I shall keep it unto the end.

34 Give me understanding, and I shall keep Thy law: yea, I shall keep it with my whole heart.

35 Make me to go in the path of Thy commandments: for therein is my desire.

36 Incline my heart unto Thy testimonies: and not to covetousness.

37 O turn away mine eyes,

lest they behold vanity: and quicken Thou me in Thy way.

38 O stablish Thy word in Thy servant: that I may fear Thee.

39 Take away the rebuke that I am afraid of: for Thy judgments are good.

40 Behold, my delight is in Thy commandments: O quicken me in Thy righteousness.

41 Let Thy loving mercy come also unto me, O Lord: even Thy salvation, according unto Thy word.

42 So shall I make answer unto my blasphemers: for my trust is in Thy word.

43 O take not the word of Thy truth utterly out of my mouth: for my hope is in Thy judgments.

44 So shall I alway keep Thy law: yea, for ever and ever.

45 And I will walk at liberty: for I seek Thy commandments.

46 I will speak of Thy testimonies also, even before kings: and will not be ashamed.

47 And my delight shall be in Thy commandments: which I have loved.

48 My hands also will I lift up unto Thy commandments, which I have loved: and my study shall be in Thy statutes.

Glory be to the Father.

Psalm.

O THINK upon Thy servant, as concerning Thy word: wherein Thou hast caused me to put my trust.

50 The same is my comfort in my trouble: for Thy word hath quickened me.

51 The proud have had me exceedingly in derision: yet have I not shrinked from Thy law.

52 For I remembered Thine everlasting judgments, O Lord: and received comfort.

53 I am horribly afraid: for the ungodly that forsake Thy law.

54 Thy statutes have been my songs: in the house of my pilgrimage.

55 I have thought upon Thy Name, O Lord, in the night-season: and have kept Thy law.

56 This I had: because I kept Thy commandments.

57 Thou art my portion, O Lord: I have promised to keep Thy law.

58 I made my humble petition in Thy presence with my whole heart: O be

merciful unto me, according to Thy word.

59 I called mine own ways to remembrance: and turned my feet unto Thy testimonies.

60 I made haste, and prolonged not the time: to keep Thy commandments.

61 The congregations of the ungodly have robbed me: but I have not forgotten Thy law.

62 At midnight I will rise to give thanks unto Thee: because of Thy righteous judgments.

63 I am a companion of all them that fear Thee: and keep Thy commandments.

64 The earth, O Lord, is full of Thy mercy: O teach me Thy statutes.

Glory be to the Father.

Psalm.

O LORD, Thou hast dealt graciously with Thy servant: according unto Thy word.

66 O learn me true understanding and knowledge: for I have believed Thy commandments.

67 Before I was troubled, I went wrong: but now I have kept Thy word.

68 Thou art good and gracious: O teach me Thy statutes.

69 The proud have imagined a lie against me: but I will keep Thy commandments with my whole heart.

70 Their heart is as fat as brawn: but my delight hath been in Thy law.

71 It is good for me that I have been in trouble: that I may learn Thy statutes.

72 The law of Thy mouth is dearer unto me: than thousands of gold and silver.

73 Thy hands have made me and fashioned me: O give me understanding, that I may learn Thy commandments.

74 They that fear Thee will be glad when they see me: because I have put my trust in Thy word.

75 I know, O Lord, that Thy judgments are right: and that Thou of very faithfulness hast caused me to be troubled.

76 O let Thy merciful kindness be my comfort: according to Thy word unto Thy servant.

77 O let Thy loving mercies come unto me, that I may live: for Thy law is my delight.

78 Let the proud be confounded, for they go wickedly about to destroy me: but I will be occupied in Thy commandments.

AT TERCE.

79 Let such as fear Thee, and have known Thy testimonies: be turned unto me.

80 O let my heart be sound in Thy statutes: that I be not ashamed.

Glory be to the Father.

On Sundays.

Antiphon. — Praise and eternal glory to God, Father, Son, and blessed Paraclete, unto endless ages.

Chapter. 2 Cor. xiii. 14.

The grace of our Lord Jesus Christ, and the love of God, and the fellowship of the Holy Ghost, be with us all evermore.

R. Incline mine heart, O God, unto Thy testimonies. *V.* Turn away mine eyes, lest they behold vanity: and quicken Thou me in Thy way. *R.* Unto Thy testimonies. *V.* Glory be to the Father, and to the Son, and to the Holy Ghost. *R.* Incline mine heart, O God, unto Thy testimonies.

V. I said, Lord, be merciful unto me. *R.* Heal my soul, for I have sinned against Thee.

On Ferias.

Antiphon. — O let Thy loving mercies come unto me: that I may live.

Chapter. Jer. xvii. 14.

Heal me, O Lord, and I shall be healed; save me, and I shall be saved: for Thou art my praise.

R. Heal my soul; for I have sinned against Thee. *V.* I said, Lord, be merciful unto me. *R.* For I have sinned against Thee. *V.* Glory be to the Father, and to the Son, and to the Holy Ghost. *R.* Heal my soul, for I have sinned against Thee.

V. Lord, be Thou my Helper. *R.* Leave me not, neither forsake me, O God of my salvation.

On Ferias in Advent.

Antiphon.—O Lord, raise up Thy power: and come and save us.

Chapter. Heb. x. 37.

For yet a little while, and He that shall come will come, and will not tarry: there shall be no fear in our end, for He Himself is our Saviour.

R. Come and deliver us, O Lord God of hosts. *V.* Show the light of Thy countenance, and we shall be whole. *R.* O Lord God of hosts. *V.* Glory be to the Father, and to the Son, and to the Holy Ghost. *R.* Come and deliver us, O Lord God of hosts.

V. The heathen shall fear Thy Name, O Lord. *R.* And all the kings of the earth Thy majesty.

On all Ferias, except from Christmas Day to Epiphany, and Maundy Thursday to Trinity Sunday, here follow

The Petitions.

Kyrie, eleyson (*thrice*).
Christe, eleyson (*thrice*).
Kyrie, eleyson (*thrice*).

Our Father.

V. And lead us not into temptation. *R.* But deliver us from evil.

V. I said, Lord, be merciful unto me. *R.* Heal my soul, for I have sinned against Thee.

V. Turn Thee again, O Lord, at the last. *R.* And be gracious unto Thy servants.

V. Let Thy merciful kindness, O Lord, be upon us. *R.* As we do put our trust in Thee.

V. Let Thy priests be clothed with righteousness. *R.* And Thy saints sing with joyfulness.

V. O Lord, save the Queen. *R.* And mercifully hear us when we call upon Thee.

V. O Lord, save Thy servants and handmaidens. *R.* Which put their trust in Thee.

V. O Lord, save Thy people, and bless Thine inheritance. *R.* Govern them, and lift them up for ever.

V. Peace be within Thy walls. *R.* And plenteousness within Thy palaces.

V. Let us pray for the dead in Christ. *R.* Grant them, O Lord, eternal rest, and let light perpetual shine upon them.

V. Hearken unto my voice, O Lord, when I cry unto Thee. *R.* Have mercy upon me, and hear me.

Psalm li.

Have mercy upon me, O God (p. 75).

The whole Psalm is said without note, and with Glory be to the Father.

[*In Lent here follows (i.e. from the first Monday to Wednesday in Holy Week*).

Psalm xxxviii.

PUT me not to rebuke, O Lord, in Thine anger: neither chasten me in Thy heavy displeasure.

2 For Thine arrows stick fast in me: and Thy hand presseth me sore.

3 There is no health in my flesh, because of Thy displeasure: neither is there any rest in my bones, by reason of my sin.

4 For my wickednesses are

gone over my head : and are like a sore burden, too heavy for me to bear.

5 My wounds stink, and are corrupt : through my foolishness.

6 I am brought into so great trouble and misery : that I go mourning all the day long.

7 For my loins are filled with a sore disease : and there is no whole part in my body.

8 I am feeble, and sore smitten : I have roared for the very disquietness of my heart.

9 Lord, Thou knowest all my desire : and my groaning is not hid from Thee.

10 My heart panteth, my strength hath failed me : and the sight of mine eyes is gone from me.

11 My lovers and my neighbours did stand looking upon my trouble : and my kinsmen stood afar off.

12 They also that sought after my life laid snares for me : and they that went about to do me evil talked of wickedness, and imagined deceit all the day long.

13 As for me, I was like a deaf man, and heard not : and as one that is dumb, who doth not open his mouth.

14 I became even as a man that heareth not : and in whose mouth are no reproofs.

15 For in Thee, O Lord, have I put my trust : Thou shalt answer for me, O Lord my God.

16 I have required that they, even mine enemies, should not triumph over me : for when my foot slipped, they rejoiced greatly against me.

17 And I, truly, am set in the plague : and my heaviness is ever in my sight.

18 For I will confess my wickedness : and be sorry for my sin.

19 But mine enemies live, and are mighty : and they that hate me wrongfully are many in number.

20 They also that reward evil for good are against me : because I follow the thing that good is.

21 Forsake me not, O Lord my God : be not Thou far from me.

22 Haste Thee to help me : O Lord God of my salvation.

Glory be to the Father.]

The Priest alone standing up shall say:

V. O Lord, arise, help us. R. And deliver us for Thy Name's sake.

V. Turn us again, O Lord God of hosts. R. Show the light of Thy countenance, and we shall be whole.

V. Hear my prayer, O Lord. R. And let my crying come unto Thee.

V. The Lord be with you. R. And with thy spirit.

Let us pray.

Collect.

V. The Lord be with you. R. And with thy spirit. V. Bless we the Lord. R. Thanks be to God.

At Sext.

V. O God, make speed to save me.
R. O Lord, make haste to help me.
V. Glory be to the Father, and to the Son: and to the Holy Ghost.
R. As it was in the beginning, is now, and ever shall be: world without end. Amen.
Alleluia.

[*From Septuagesima to Wednesday in Holy Week:*

Praise to Thee, O Lord, King of eternal glory.]

Hymn.

Eternal Lord of truth and power,
Who rulest all from hour to hour,
Decking the morning skies with light,
Kindling the beams of noonday bright.

Quench thou in us the flames of strife,
From passion's riot shield our life;
And keep us, soul and body, free
From aught of ill, at peace with Thee.

All-loving Father, hear our cry,
O hear us, Saviour, from on high,
Who in the Spirit's unity
Dost reign to all eternity.
Amen.

Sunday Antiphon.—Let every mouth render praise and glory.
Ferial Antiphon.—Let me not.
On Ferias in Advent.—When Thou comest.

Psalm cxix.

MY soul hath longed for Thy salvation: and I have a good hope because of Thy word.

82 Mine eyes long sore for Thy word: saying, Oh when wilt Thou comfort me?

83 For I am become like a bottle in the smoke: yet do I not forget Thy statutes.

84 How many are the days of Thy servant: when wilt Thou be avenged of them that persecute me?

AT SEXT.

85 The proud have digged pits for me: which are not after Thy law.

86 All Thy commandments are true: they persecute me falsely; O be Thou my help.

87 They had almost made an end of me upon earth: but I forsook not Thy commandments.

88 O quicken me after Thy lovingkindness: and so shall I keep the testimonies of Thy mouth.

89 O Lord, Thy word: endureth for ever in heaven.

90 Thy truth also remaineth from one generation to another: Thou hast laid the foundation of the earth, and it abideth.

91 They continue this day according to Thine ordinance: for all things serve Thee.

92 If my delight had not been in Thy law: I should have perished in my trouble.

93 I will never forget Thy commandments: for with them Thou hast quickened me.

94 I am Thine, O save me: for I have sought Thy commandments.

95 The ungodly laid wait for me to destroy me: but I will consider Thy testimonies.

96 I see that all things come to an end: but Thy commandment is exceeding broad.

Glory be to the Father.

Psalm.

LORD, what love have I unto Thy law: all the day long is my study in it.

98 Thou through Thy commandments hast made me wiser than mine enemies: for they are ever with me.

99 I have more understanding than my teachers: for Thy testimonies are my study.

100 I am wiser than the aged: because I keep Thy commandments.

101 I have refrained my feet from every evil way: that I may keep Thy word.

102 I have not shrunk from Thy judgments: for Thou teachest me.

103 Oh how sweet are Thy words unto my throat: yea, sweeter than honey unto my mouth.

104 Through Thy commandments I get understanding: therefore I hate all evil ways.

105 Thy word is a lantern unto my feet: and a light unto my paths.

106 I have sworn, and am stedfastly purposed: to keep Thy righteous judgments.

107 I am troubled above measure: quicken me, O Lord, according to Thy word.

108 Let the free-will offerings of my mouth please Thee, O Lord: and teach me Thy judgments.

109 My soul is alway in my hand: yet do I not forget Thy law.

110 The ungodly have laid a snare for me: but yet I swerved not from Thy commandments.

111 Thy testimonies have I claimed as mine heritage for ever: and why? they are the very joy of my heart.

112 I have applied my heart to fulfil Thy statutes alway: even unto the end.

Glory be to the Father.

Psalm.

I HATE them that imagine evil things: but Thy law do I love.

114 Thou art my defence and shield: and my trust is in Thy word.

115 Away from me, ye wicked: I will keep the commandments of my God.

116 O stablish me according to Thy word, that I may live: and let me not be disappointed of my hope.

117 Hold Thou me up, and I shall be safe: yea, my delight shall be ever in Thy statutes.

118 Thou hast trodden down all them that depart from Thy statutes: for they imagine but deceit.

119 Thou puttest away all the ungodly of the earth like dross: therefore I love Thy testimonies.

120 My flesh trembleth for fear of Thee: and I am afraid of Thy judgments.

121 I deal with the thing that is lawful and right: O give me not over unto mine oppressors.

122 Make Thou Thy servant to delight in that which is good: that the proud do me no wrong.

123 Mine eyes are wasted away with looking for Thy health: and for the word of Thy righteousness.

124 O deal with Thy servant according unto Thy loving mercy: and teach me Thy statutes.

125 I am Thy servant, O grant me understanding: that I may know Thy testimonies.

126 It is time for Thee

AT SEXT.

Lord, to lay to Thine hand: for they have destroyed Thy law.

127 For I love Thy commandments: above gold and precious stone.

128 Therefore hold I straight all Thy commandments: and all false ways I utterly abhor.

Glory be to the Father.

(a) *On Sundays.*

Antiphon.—Let every mouth render praise and glory to the Father and the only begotten Son: and let everlasting praise be paid to the Holy Spirit with Them co-equal.

Chapter. 1 *John* v. 7.

There are Three that bear record in heaven, the Father, the Word, and the Holy Ghost: and these Three are One.

R. O Lord, Thy word endureth for ever in heaven. *V.* Thy truth also remaineth from one generation to another. *R.* For ever in heaven. *V.* Glory be to the Father, and to the Son, and to the Holy Ghost. *R.* O Lord, Thy word endureth for ever in heaven.

V. The Lord is my Shepherd, therefore can I lack nothing. *R.* He shall feed me in a green pasture.

(b) *On Ferias.*

Antiphon.—Let me not: be disappointed of my hope.

Chapter. 1 *Thess.* v. 21.

Prove all things; hold fast that which is good. Abstain from all appearance of evil.

R. I will alway give thanks unto the Lord. *V.* His praise shall ever be in my mouth. *R.* I will alway give thanks. *V.* Glory be to the Father, and to the Son, and to the Holy Ghost. *R.* I will alway give thanks unto the Lord.

V. The Lord is my Shepherd, therefore can I lack nothing. *R.* He shall feed me in a green pasture. *Petition*

(c) *On Ferias in Advent.*

Antiphon.—When Thou comest: deliver us, O Lord.

Chapter. Isa. xiii. 22.

Her time is near to come, and her days shall not be prolonged. For the Lord will have mercy on Jacob, and will yet choose Israel.

R. O Lord, show Thy mercy upon us. *V.* And grant us Thy salvation. *R.*

Thy mercy upon us. *V.* Glory be. *R.* O Lord.

V. Remember me, O Lord, according to the favour that Thou bearest unto Thy people. *R.* O visit us with Thy salvation.

Here follow the Petitions as at Terce, p. 84.

[*Then is said during Lent, in place of Psalm li.:*

Psalm lxvii.

GOD be merciful unto us, and bless us: and show us the light of His countenance, and be merciful unto us;

2 That Thy way may be known upon earth: Thy saving health among all nations.

3 Let the people praise Thee, O God: yea, let all the people praise Thee.

4 O let the nations rejoice and be glad: for Thou shalt judge the folk righteously, and govern the nations upon earth.

5 Let the people praise Thee, O God: let all the people praise Thee.

6 Then shall the earth bring forth her increase: and God, even our own God, shall give us His blessing.

7 God shall bless us: and all the ends of the world shall fear Him.

Glory be to the Father.]

All the rest as at Terce, p. 85.

At None.

V. O God, make speed to save me.
R. O Lord, make haste to help me.
V. Glory be to the Father, and to the Son: and to the Holy Ghost.
R. As it was in the beginning, is now, and ever shall be: world without end. Amen.
Alleluia.

[*From Septuagesima to Wednesday in Holy Week:*

Praise to Thee, O Lord, King of eternal glory.]

Hymn.

O God, creation's Strength and
    Stay,
Ruling the fleeting hours of day,
While all things change at Thy
    decree,
Thyself unchanged eternally;

Lord, grant us light at eventide,
Through death's dark shadows
    be our Guide:
Lover of souls, when all is past,
In mercy bring us home at last.

All-loving Father, hear our cry,
O hear us, Saviour, from on high,
Who in the Spirit's unity
Dost reign to all eternity.
    Amen.

Sunday Antiphon. — Of Whom are all things.
Ferial Antiphon. — Give me understanding.
On Ferias in Advent.— Come, O Lord, and tarry not.

Psalm cxix.

THY testimonies are wonderful: therefore doth my soul keep them.

130 When Thy word goeth forth: it giveth light and understanding unto the simple.

131 I opened my mouth, and drew in my breath: for my delight was in Thy commandments.

132 O look Thou upon me, and be merciful unto me: as Thou usest to do unto those that love Thy Name.

133 Order my steps in Thy word: and so shall no wickedness have dominion over me.

134 O deliver me from the wrongful dealings of men: and so shall I keep Thy commandments.

135 Show the light of Thy countenance upon Thy servant: and teach me Thy statutes.

136 Mine eyes gush out with water: because men keep not Thy law.

137 Righteous art Thou, O Lord: and true is Thy judgment.

138 The testimonies that Thou hast commanded: are exceeding righteous and true.

139 My zeal hath even consumed me: because mine enemies have forgotten Thy words.

140 Thy word is tried to the uttermost: and Thy servant loveth it.

141 I am small, and of no reputation: yet do I not forget Thy commandments.

142 Thy righteousness is an everlasting righteousness: and Thy law is the truth.

143 Trouble and heaviness have taken hold upon me: yet is my delight in Thy commandments.

144 The righteousness of Thy testimonies is everlasting: O grant me understanding, and I shall live.

Glory be to the Father.

Psalm.

I CALL with my whole heart: hear me, O Lord, I will keep Thy statutes.

146 Yea, even unto Thee do I call: help me, and I shall keep Thy testimonies.

147 Early in the morning do I cry unto Thee: for in Thy word is my trust.

148 Mine eyes prevent the night-watches: that I might be occupied in Thy words.

149 Hear my voice, O Lord, according unto Thy lovingkindness: quicken me, according as Thou art wont.

150 They draw nigh that of malice persecute me: and are far from Thy law.

151 Be Thou nigh at hand, O Lord: for all Thy commandments are true.

152 As concerning Thy testimonies, I have known long since: that Thou hast grounded them for ever.

153 O consider mine adversity, and deliver me: for I do not forget Thy law.

154 Avenge Thou my cause, and deliver me:

quicken me, according to Thy word.

155 Health is far from the ungodly: for they regard not Thy statutes.

156 Great is Thy mercy, O Lord: quicken me, as Thou art wont.

157 Many there are that trouble me, and persecute me: yet do I not swerve from Thy testimonies.

158 It grieveth me when I see the transgressors: because they keep not Thy law.

159 Consider, O Lord, how I love Thy commandments: O quicken me, according to Thy lovingkindness.

160 Thy word is true from everlasting: all the judgments of Thy righteousness endure for evermore.

Glory be to the Father.

Psalm.

PRINCES have persecuted me without a cause: but my heart standeth in awe of Thy word.

162 I am as glad of Thy word: as one that findeth great spoils.

163 As for lies, I hate and abhor them: but Thy law do I love.

164 Seven times a day do I praise Thee: because of Thy righteous judgments.

165 Great is the peace that they have who love Thy law: and they are not offended at it.

166 Lord, I have looked for Thy saving health: and done after Thy commandments.

167 My soul hath kept Thy testimonies: and loved them exceedingly.

168 I have kept Thy commandments and testimonies: for all my ways are before Thee.

169 Let my complaint come before Thee, O Lord: give me understanding, according to Thy word.

170 Let my supplication come before Thee: deliver me, according to Thy word.

171 My lips shall speak of Thy praise: when Thou hast taught me Thy statutes.

172 Yea, my tongue shall sing of Thy word: for all Thy commandments are righteous.

173 Let Thine hand help me: for I have chosen Thy commandments.

174 I have longed for Thy saving health, O Lord: and in Thy law is my delight.

175 O let my soul live, and it shall praise Thee: and Thy judgments shall help me.

176 I have gone astray

like a sheep that is lost: O seek Thy servant, for I do not forget Thy commandments.

Glory be to the Father.

On Sundays.

Antiphon. — Of Whom and through Whom and in Whom are all things; to Him be glory for ever.

Chapter. *Eph.* iv. 5.

One Lord, one faith, one baptism, one God and Father of all, Who is above all, and through all, and in us all, Who is blessed for ever.

R. I call with my whole heart; hear me, O Lord. *V.* I will keep Thy statutes. *R.* Hear me, O Lord. *V.* Glory be to the Father, and to the Son, and to the Holy Ghost. *R.* I call with my whole heart; hear me, O Lord.

V. O cleanse Thou me from my secret faults. *R.* Keep Thy servant also from presumptuous sins.

On Ferias.

Antiphon. — Give me understanding, according to Thy word.

Chapter. *Gal.* vi. 2.

Bear ye one another's burdens, and so fulfil the law of Christ.

R. O deliver me, and be merciful unto me. *V.* My foot standeth right; I will praise the Lord in the congregations. *R.* And be merciful unto me. *V.* Glory be to the Father, and to the Son, and to the Holy Ghost. *R.* O deliver me, and be merciful unto me.

V. O cleanse Thou me from my secret faults. *R.* Keep Thy servant also from presumptuous sins.

On Ferias in Advent.

Antiphon.—Come, O Lord, and tarry not: do away the offences of Thy people Israel.

Chapter. *Micah* iv. 2.

Come, and let us go up to the mountain of the Lord, and to the house of the God of Jacob; and He will teach us of His ways, and we will walk in His paths: for the law shall go forth of Sion, and the word of the Lord from Jerusalem.

R. The Lord shall arise upon thee, O Jerusalem. *V.* And His glory shall be seen upon thee. *R.* The Lord shall arise. *V.* Glory be to the Father, and to the Son, and to the Holy Ghost. *R.*

The Lord shall arise upon thee, O Jerusalem.

V. Turn us again, O Lord God of hosts. *R.* Show the light of Thy countenance, and we shall be whole.

Here follow the Petitions as at Terce, p. 84.

[*Here in Lent (i.e. from the first Monday to Wednesday in Holy Week) is said:*

Psalm cii.

HEAR my prayer, O Lord: and let my crying come unto Thee.

2 Hide not Thy face from me in the time of my trouble: incline Thine ear unto me when I call; O hear me, and that right soon.

3 For my days are consumed away like smoke: and my bones are burnt up as it were a firebrand.

4 My heart is smitten down, and withered like grass: so that I forget to eat my bread.

5 For the voice of my groaning: my bones will scarce cleave to my flesh.

6 I am become like a pelican in the wilderness: and like an owl that is in the desert.

7 I have watched, and am even as it were a sparrow: that sitteth alone upon the house-top.

8 Mine enemies revile me all the day long: and they that are mad upon me are sworn together against me.

9 For I have eaten ashes as it were bread: and mingled my drink with weeping;

10 And that because of Thine indignation and wrath: for Thou hast taken me up, and cast me down.

11 My days are gone like a shadow: and I am withered like grass.

12 But, Thou, O Lord, shalt endure for ever: and Thy remembrance throughout all generations.

13 Thou shalt arise, and have mercy upon Sion: for it is time that Thou have mercy upon her, yea, the time is come.

14 And why? Thy servants think upon her stones: and it pitieth them to see her in the dust.

15 The heathen shall fear Thy Name, O Lord: and all the kings of the earth Thy Majesty;

16 When the Lord shall build up Sion: and when His glory shall appear;

17 When He turneth Him unto the prayer of the poor destitute: and despiseth not their desire.

18 This shall be written for those that come after: and the people which shall be born shall praise the Lord.

19 For He hath looked down from His sanctuary: out of the heaven did the Lord behold the earth;

20 That He might hear the mournings of such as are in captivity: and deliver the children appointed unto death;

21 That they may declare the Name of the Lord in Sion: and His worship at Jerusalem;

22 When the people are gathered together: and the kingdoms also, to serve the Lord.

23 He brought down my strength in my journey: and shortened my days.

24 But I said, O my God, take me not away in the midst of mine age : as for Thy years, they endure throughout all generations.

25 Thou, Lord, in the beginning hast laid the foundation of the earth : and the heavens are the work of Thy hands.

26 They shall perish, but Thou shalt endure : they all shall wax old as doth a garment ;

27 And as a vesture shalt Thou change them, and they shall be changed : but Thou art the same, and Thy years shall not fail.

28 The children of Thy servants shall continue : and their seed shall stand fast in Thy sight.

Glory be to the Father.]

All the rest as at Terce, p. 85.

At Compline.

V. Turn us, O God, our Saviour. *R.* And let Thine anger cease from us.
V. O God, make speed to save me. *R.* O Lord, make haste to help me.
V. Glory be to the Father, and to the Son: and to the Holy Ghost.
R. As it was in the beginning, is now, and ever shall be: world without end. Amen.
Alleluia.

[*From Septuagesima to Wednesday in Holy Week:*

Praise to Thee, O Lord, King of eternal glory.]

¶ Compline I.

Antiphon.—Have mercy upon me, O Lord.

Psalm iv.

HEAR me when I call, O God of my righteousness: Thou hast set me at liberty when I was in trouble; have mercy upon me, and hearken unto my prayer.

2 O ye sons of men, how long will ye blaspheme mine honour: and have such pleasure in vanity, and seek after leasing?

3 Know this also, that the Lord hath chosen to Himself the man that is godly: when I call upon the Lord, He will hear me.

4 Stand in awe, and sin not: commune with your own heart, and in your chamber, and be still.

5 Offer the sacrifice of righteousness: and put your trust in the Lord.

6 There be many that say: Who will show us any good?

7 Lord, lift Thou up: the light of Thy countenance upon us.

8 Thou hast put gladness in my heart: since the time that their corn, and wine, and oil, increased.

9 I will lay me down in peace, and take my rest: for it is Thou, Lord, only, that makest me dwell in safety.

Glory be to the Father.

Psalm xxxi.

IN Thee, O Lord, have I put my trust: let me never be put to confusion, deliver me in Thy righteousness.

2 Bow down Thine ear to me: make haste to deliver me.

3 And be Thou my strong rock, and house of defence: that Thou mayest save me.

4 For Thou art my strong rock, and my castle: be Thou also my guide, and lead me for Thy Name's sake.

5 Draw me out of the net, that they have laid privily for me: for Thou art my strength.

6 Into Thy hands I commend my spirit: for Thou hast redeemed me, O Lord, Thou God of truth.

Glory be to the Father.

Psalm xci.

WHOSO dwelleth under the defence of the most High: shall abide under the shadow of the Almighty.

2 I will say unto the Lord, Thou art my hope, and my strong hold: my God, in Him will I trust.

3 For He shall deliver thee from the snare of the hunter: and from the noisome pestilence.

4 He shall defend thee under His wings, and Thou shalt be safe under His feathers: His faithfulness and truth shall be thy shield and buckler.

5 Thou shalt not be afraid for any terror by night: nor for the arrow that flieth by day;

6 For the pestilence that walketh in darkness: nor for the sickness that destroyeth in the noon-day.

7 A thousand shall fall beside thee, and ten thousand at thy right hand: but it shall not come nigh thee.

8 Yea, with thine eyes shalt thou behold: and see the reward of the ungodly.

9 For Thou, Lord, art my hope: Thou hast set Thine house of defence very high.

10 There shall no evil happen unto thee: neither shall any plague come nigh thy dwelling.

11 For He shall give His angels charge over thee: to keep thee in all thy ways.

12 They shall bear thee in their hands: that thou hurt not thy foot against a stone.

13 Thou shalt go upon the lion and adder: the young lion and the dragon

AT COMPLINE.

shalt thou tread under thy feet.

14 · Because he hath set his love upon Me, therefore will I deliver him: I will set him up, because he hath known My Name.

15 He shall call upon Me, and I will hear him: yea, I am with him in trouble; I will deliver him, and bring him to honour.

16 With long life will I satisfy him: and show him My salvation.

Glory be to the Father.

Psalm cxxxiv.

BEHOLD now, praise the Lord: all ye servants of the Lord;

2 Ye that by night stand in the house of the Lord: even in the courts of the house of our God.

3 Lift up your hands in the sanctuary: and praise the Lord.

4 The Lord that made heaven and earth: give thee blessing out of Sion.

Glory be to the Father.

Antiphon.— Have mercy upon me, O Lord: and hearken unto my prayer.

Chapter. Jer. xiv. 9.

Thou, O Lord, art in the midst of us, and we are called by Thy Name; leave us not, O Lord our God.

R. Thanks be to God.

This chapter is said throughout the year, except from Maundy Thursday to Low Sunday.

Hymn.

To Thee, Creator Lord, we pray,
Ere now the daylight dies away;
God of our life, Thy vigil keep
Around us while Thy children sleep.

Cheer, Lord, our darkness with Thy light;
Chase far the hideous shapes of night;
O let no spot of sin defile,
Nor ghostly foe our souls beguile.

Almighty Father, hear our cry,
Through Jesus Christ our Lord most high,
Who in the Spirit's unity
Reigneth with Thee eternally.

V. Keep us, O God. *R.* As the apple of an eye; hide us under the shadow of Thy wings.

Antiphon.—Come, O Lord.

The Song of Simeon. *Luke* ii. 29.

LORD, now lettest Thou Thy servant depart in peace: according to Thy word.

For mine eyes have seen: Thy salvation,

Which Thou hast pre-

pared: before the face of all people;
To be a light to lighten the Gentiles: and to be the glory of Thy people Israel.
Glory be to the Father.

Antiphon.—Come, O Lord, and visit us in peace: that we may rejoice before Thee with a perfect heart.

[*The ordinary Antiphon, i.e. during Epiphany and Trinity seasons:*

Save us, O Lord, while waking, and guard us while sleeping: that when we are awake we may watch with Christ, and when we sleep we may rest in peace.]

Here follow the Petitions, p. 108.

This Compline is said throughout Advent, except on Double Feasts when the Hymn is changed, and Saviour, Who didst the ransom pay, *is said. On Commemorations of blessed Mary, when celebrated in Advent, the Hymn ends:*

All glory, Virgin-born, to Thee,
Jesu, Incarnate Deity,
Whom with the Father we adore,
And Holy Spirit evermore.

¶ COMPLINE II.
On Christmas Eve.

Antiphon to the Psalms.—Be ye ready: like unto men that wait for their Lord, when He shall return from the wedding.

Hymn.

Saviour, Who didst the ransom pay,
Refuge of souls from day to day,
This night protect us by Thy power,
And shield us in the evil hour.

Be near us, and in pity spare,
Lord Jesus, at Thy servants' prayer;
From sin's pollution wash us white;
Turn Thou our darkness into light.

Grant that our hearts may wake to Thee,
Watchful against the enemy;
Our souls keep pure from touch of sin,
Thy temple undefiled within.

O great Restorer, from on high
Bend down and hear our humble cry;
May we, when morning breaks again,
Rise pure in heart and free from stain.

To God Almighty praise be done,
Praise to the Father's only Son;
Praise now and ever, as is meet,
To God the holy Paraclete. Amen.

V. Keep us, O Lord. *R.* As the apple of an eye; hide us under the shadow of Thy wings.

Antiphon to Nunc Dimittis.—Watch ye all and pray, for ye know not when the time is: watch ye therefore, for ye know not when the Master of the house will come: at even, or at midnight, or at cock-crowing, or in the morning: lest coming suddenly He find you sleeping.

Here follow the Petitions, and Compline ends as usual.

¶ COMPLINE III.
On Christmas Day.

Antiphon to the Psalms.—Unto us is born this day in the city of David: a Saviour, which is Christ the Lord.

Hymn. Saviour, Who didst the ransom pay.

With Doxology, All glory, Virgin-born, to Thee.

V. Keep us.

Antiphon to Nunc Dimittis.—Alleluia. The Word was made flesh, Alleluia : and dwelt among us. Alleluia, Alleluia.

Petitions, etc., as usual.

This Compline is said until the Circumcision.

¶ COMPLINE IV.

On the Feast of the Circumcision.

Antiphon to the Psalms.—When the Lord was born, the choirs of angels sang, saying : Salvation to our God, Which sitteth upon the throne, and to the Lamb.

Hymn. Saviour, Who didst the ransom pay.

With Doxology, All glory, Virgin-born, to Thee.

V. Keep us.

Antiphon to Nunc Dimittis.—Alleluia. The Word was made flesh, Alleluia : and dwelt among us. Alleluia, Alleluia.

Petitions, etc., as usual.

This Compline is said until the Eve of Epiphany.

¶ COMPLINE V.

On the Eve of Epiphany.

Antiphon to the Psalms.—Light of light, O Christ, Thou hast appeared : to Whom the wise men offer gifts. Alleluia, Alleluia, Alleluia.

Hymn. Saviour, Who didst the ransom pay.

With Doxology, Jesu, all glory be to Thee (p. 61).

V. Keep us.

Antiphon to Nunc Dimittis.—Alleluia. All they from Sheba shall come, Alleluia : they shall bring gold and incense. Alleluia, Alleluia.

Petitions, etc., as usual.

This Compline is said throughout the Octaves of Epiphany.

¶ COMPLINE VI.

On the morrow of the Octave of Epiphany.

Antiphon to the Psalms.—Have mercy upon me, O Lord : and hearken unto my prayer.

Hymn. To Thee, Creator, Lord, we pray.

With Doxology, All glory, Virgin-born, to Thee, *until the morrow of the Purification.*

V. Keep us.

Antiphon to Nunc Dimittis.—Save us, O Lord, while waking, and guard us while sleeping : that when we are awake we may watch with Christ, and when we sleep we may rest in peace.

Petitions, etc., as usual.

This Compline is said from the morrow of the Octave of Epiphany until the beginning of Lent; and from the morrow of the Feast of the Holy Trinity until the beginning of Advent: except on Doubles and during the Octaves of Feasts of Our Lady, of the Dedication of a church, and of the Holy Name, and in Commemorations of blessed Mary.

¶ COMPLINE VII.

On the First Sunday in Lent.

Antiphon to the Psalms.—Lord, lift Thou up the light of

Thy countenance upon us : Thou hast put gladness in my heart.

Chapter. Thou, O Lord, art in the midst of us, and we are called by Thy name : leave us not, O Lord our God.

R. I will lay me down in peace, and take my rest. *V.* I will not suffer mine eyes to sleep, nor mine eyelids to slumber. *R.* I will take my rest. *V.* Glory be to the Father, and to the Son, and to the Holy Ghost. *R.* I will lay me down in peace, and take my rest.

Hymn.

O Christ. Who art this dark world's Light,
And dost dispel the shades of night,
Thyself our Dayspring we confess,
Thou blessed Sun of righteousness.

We humbly pray Thee, Lord of light,
Protect us through the hours of night;
Grant us to taste how sweet the rest
Of those who sleep on Jesus' breast.

Bright be our dreams, our slumbers pure,
Nor Satan with his wiles allure;
No evil in our flesh find place,
To rob us of Thy saving grace.

What time our eyes are closed in sleep,
Grant that our hearts their vigil keep;
Stretch out Thine arm, and shield from shame
Thy servants who adore Thy Name.

Behold, O God our Strength, and see
The malice of our enemy;
Be Thou our Guardian and our Guide,
Who to redeem our souls hast died.

Remember us, O Jesu blest,
While in this sinful flesh opprest;
Our souls' Defender, Master, Friend,
O Lord, be with us to the end.

To God Almighty praise be done,
Praise to the Father's only Son,
Praise now and ever, as is meet,
To God the Holy Paraclete. Amen.

V. Keep us.

Antiphon to Nunc Dimittis.—
When thou seest the naked, cover thou him : and despise not thine own flesh : then shall thy light break forth, and the glory of the Lord shall be thy rereward.

Petitions, etc., as usual. On Ferias during Lent Ps. cxliii. is said after Ps. li.

This Compline is said until the Third Sunday in Lent.

¶ Compline VIII.

On the Third Sunday in Lent.

Antiphon to the Psalms.— Lord, lift Thou up the light of Thy countenance upon us : Thou hast put gladness in my heart.

Chapter. Thou, O Lord, art in the midst of us, and we are called by Thy Name : leave us not, O Lord our God.

R. I will lay me down in peace, and take my rest. *V.* I will not suffer mine eyes to sleep, nor mine eyelids to slumber. *R.* I will take my rest. *V.* Glory be to the Father, and to the Son, and to the Holy Ghost. *R.* I will lay me down in peace, and take my rest.

Hymn. O Christ, who art this dark world's Light.

V. Keep us.

AT COMPLINE.

Antiphon to Nunc Dimittis.—In the midst of life we are in death: of whom may we seek for succour but of Thee, O Lord, Who for our sins art justly displeased? Yet, O Lord God most holy, O Lord most mighty, O holy and most merciful Saviour, deliver us not into the bitter pains of eternal death.

On Saturdays and Sundays, and at both Complines of Feasts of nine Lessons, here follows:

V. Cast me not away in the time of age: forsake me not when my strength faileth me.

R. O Lord God most holy, O Lord most mighty, O holy and most merciful Saviour, deliver us not into the bitter pains of eternal death.

V. Shut not Thy merciful ears to our prayer.

R. O Lord most mighty, O holy and most merciful Saviour, deliver us not into the bitter pains of eternal death.

V. Thou that knowest the secrets of our hearts: be merciful unto our sins.

R. O holy and most merciful Saviour, deliver us not into the bitter pains of eternal death.

Petitions, etc., as usual.

This Compline is said until Passion Sunday.

¶ COMPLINE IX.
On Passion Sunday.

Antiphon to the Psalms. — Have mercy upon me, O Lord: and hearken unto my prayer.

Chapter. Thou, O Lord, art in the midst of us, and we are called by Thy Name: leave us not, O Lord our God.

Clerk.—R. Into Thy hands. *The choir proceed:* O Lord, I commend my spirit. *Clerk.*— V. For thou hast redeemed me, O Lord, Thou God of truth. *Choir:* I commend my spirit. *Then the Clerk recommences:* Into Thy hands, etc.

Hymn.

Thou child of God, remember
  The Font of thy salvation,
The sacred Seal forget not
  Of holy confirmation.

What time the soft night-voices
  To dewy sleep entice thee,
Then, signed o'er brow and bosom,
  Let Christ's dear Cross suffice thee.

From fear and power of darkness
  The holy Cross shall save thee;
For ghostly aid thy Master
  This blessed symbol gave thee.

Its gentle benediction
  Night's wandering shapes shall banish,
Before it in confusion
  All fiends of hell shall vanish.

Depart, thou subtil serpent,
  Depart, thou arch-deceiver,
Dare not with thy delusions
  To vex Christ's true believer.

Away! for Christ is with us,
  The holy Name thou hearest;
Away! with all thy legions
  Before the Sign thou fearest.

What, though the flesh be weary,
  And rest a moment taketh;
Yet ever 'mid its slumbers
  The soul to Christ awaketh.

All praise to Thee, O Father,
  To Son and Holy Spirit;
All praise and endless glory
  To Thine eternal merit. Amen.

V. Keep us.

Antiphon to Nunc Dimittis.—O King, glorious amid Thy saints,

Who art ever to be adored, yet of majesty ineffable; Thou, Lord, art in the midst of us, and we are called by Thy Name; leave us not, O our God: and in the day of judgment vouchsafe to number us among Thy saints, O King most blessed.

V. O King most blessed, govern Thy servants in the right way.
R. Among Thy saints, O King most blessed.
V. By holy fasts to mend our sinful lives.
R. O King most blessed.
V. To keep aright the solemn Paschal mysteries.
R. Among Thy saints, O King most blessed.

This Compline is said daily until Maundy Thursday, whatever be the service; except that the VV. and RR. are only said on Saturdays and Sundays, Double Feasts which fall in Passiontide, and on Wednesday in Holy Week.

¶ COMPLINE X.
On Maundy Thursday.

The office begins immediately with the Antiphon, without note, the VV. and RR. being omitted.

Antiphon. — Christ became obedient.

Psalms.—Hear me when I call.
In Thee, O Lord, have I put.
Behold now, praise the Lord.
Lord, now lettest Thou.

All said under the same Antiphon, without Glory be to the Father.

Antiphon. — Christ became obedient unto death for us: even the death of the cross.

V. The Lord be with you.
R. And with Thy spirit.
Let us pray.

Collect.

ALMIGHTY God, we beseech Thee graciously to behold this Thy family, for which our Lord Jesus Christ was contented to be betrayed, and given up into the hands of wicked men, and to suffer death upon the cross, Who now liveth and reigneth with Thee and the Holy Ghost, ever one God, world without end. Amen.

V. The Lord be with you.
R. And with thy spirit.
V. Bless we the Lord.
R. Thanks be to God.

The office is said throughout without note, and in a low voice.

¶ COMPLINE XI.
On Good Friday.

The office begins as on Maundy Thursday, except that the choir genuflect at the first words of the Antiphon.

Antiphon. — Christ became obedient.

Psalms.—Hear me when I call.
In Thee, O Lord.
Behold now, praise.
Lord, now lettest Thou.

Without Glory be to the Father.

Antiphon. — Christ became obedient unto death for us: even the death of the cross.

AT COMPLINE.   105

Here is said, all kneeling:

Our Father *and* Hail, Mary.

Psalm li.—Have mercy upon me.

Without Glory be to the Father; *all kneeling. Then immediately shall be said the Collect, without* The Lord be with you, *and without* Let us pray. *And Compline shall thus end, without* Bless we the Lord.

Collect.

ALMIGHTY God, we beseech Thee graciously to behold this Thy family, for which our Lord Jesus Christ was contented to be betrayed, and given up into the hands of wicked men, and to suffer death upon the cross. Amen.

¶ COMPLINE XII.
On Easter Eve.

The office begins as usual, but without Turn us, O God.

V. O God, make speed to save me.
R. O Lord, make haste to help me.
V. Glory be to the Father. *R.* As it was. Alleluia.

Antiphon.—Alleluia.

Psalms.—Hear me when I call.
In Thee, O Lord.
Behold now, praise the Lord.
Lord, now lettest Thou.

Antiphon.—Alleluia, Alleluia, Alleluia, Alleluia.

The Psalms are said under one Antiphon with Glory be to the Father. *Then follows immediately—*

V. The Lord be with you.
R. And with thy spirit.

Let us pray.

Collect.

O LORD, we beseech Thee, pour upon us the fulness of Thy loving Spirit: that like as Thou dost gladden our hearts with Thy Paschal mysteries, so by Thy grace we may be ever united in love to Thee: through Jesus Christ Thy Son our Lord, who liveth and reigneth with Thee in the unity of the same Spirit, ever one God, world without end. Amen.

V. The Lord be with you.
R. And with thy spirit.
V. Bless we the Lord.
R. Thanks be to God.

And here it is to be noted that this Collect shall be said daily at Compline until the first Compline of Low Sunday.

¶ COMPLINE XIII.
On Easter Day.

All as on Easter Eve, except that after the Antiphon has been repeated is sung the Graile:

This is the day: which the Lord hath made; we will rejoice and be glad in it.

Then the Priest shall say:

V. In Thy resurrection, O Christ.
R. Let heaven and earth rejoice. Alleluia.
V. The Lord be with you.
R. And with thy spirit.

Let us pray.

THE PSALTER.

Collect

(as on Easter Eve).

V. The Lord be with you.
R. And with thy spirit.
V. Bless we the Lord.
R. Thanks be to God.

Compline shall be said thus until Saturday in the Octaves.

¶ COMPLINE XIV.
On Low Sunday.

The office begins as usual.

V. Turn us, O God our Saviour.
R. And let Thine anger cease from us.
V. O God, make speed, etc.

Antiphon to the Psalms.—Alleluia, Alleluia, Alleluia, Alleluia.

Psalms as usual.

Chapter. Thou, O Lord, art in the midst of us, etc.
R. Thanks be to God.

Hymn.

O Jesu, Saviour of our race,
Word of the Father, King of grace;
Thou secret Source of life and light,
Our Guardian here by day and night.

Thou madest all things by Thy power,
Thou rulest all from hour to hour:
Now wearied with the toils of day,
A quiet night we humbly pray.

A little season here below
Abide we in this vale of woe;
Grant while the flesh is wrapped in sleep
The heart with Thee may vigil keep.

Thy servants, Lord, beseech of Thee,
Protection from the enemy;
Deliver from eternal loss
Souls purchased by Thy holy cross.

O Lord of life, to Thee we pray,
Triumphant o'er the grave to-day,
In this our Easter joy protect
From death and hell Thine own elect.

To Thee be sung Thy people's praise,
O risen Lord, through endless days:
Whom with the Father we adore
And Holy Spirit evermore. Amen.

V. Keep us.

Antiphon over Nunc Dimittis.
—Alleluia: The Lord is risen,
Alleluia: as He said unto you.
Alleluia, Alleluia.

Then the Petitions follow as usual. It is here to be noted that all is said standing throughout Eastertide.

This Compline is said until the Ascension of our Lord on Festivals and Ferias alike, except that in Commemorations of St. Mary the Doxology to the hymn, instead of To Thee be sung, *etc., is—*

All glory, Virgin-born, to Thee,
Jesu, Incarnate Deity,
Whom with the Father we adore
And Holy Spirit evermore. Amen.

¶ COMPLINE XV.
On the Eve of the Ascension.

Antiphon over the Psalms.
—Alleluia, Alleluia, Alleluia, Alleluia.

Hymn.

O Jesu, our Salvation's tower,
Creator of almighty power,
Strong Son of God, for us made Man,
To finish all the Father's plan.

What pity led Thee, Lord, to spare
Our sinful souls, their guilt to bear;
That cruel death to undergo
To save us from eternal woe?

The bars of hell Thy love did break;
Hell's prisoners Thou didst captive take,

AT COMPLINE. 107

And in high triumph lead Thine own
Victorious to the Father's throne.

Now, Lord, for very love's delight,
Deliver us from evil plight;
Hear Thou, and grant Thy servants grace
To see the glory of Thy face.

In Thee be all our joy, O Lord,
As Thou wilt be our high reward;
Be all our glory now in Thee,
And unto all eternity.

To Thee be sung Thy people's praise,
Ascended Lord, through endless days,
Whom with the Father we adore,
And Holy Spirit evermore. Amen.

V. Keep us.

Antiphon over Nunc Dimittis.
—Alleluia. Christ ascending up on high, Alleluia, hath led captivity captive. Alleluia, Alleluia.

This Compline is said daily until Whitsun, on Festivals and Ferias alike, except that in Commemorations of blessed Mary, after the verse of the hymn, In Thee be all our joy, *is said,* All glory, Virgin-born, *etc.*

¶ COMPLINE XVI.

On Whitsun Eve.

Antiphon over the Psalms.—
Alleluia, Alleluia, Alleluia, Alleluia.

Hymn. Saviour, Who didst the ransom pay.

With this doxology:

In ages gone, like tongues of flame
On saintly souls Thy Spirit came;
O grant us peace, we humbly pray,
And cleanse Thy people's sins away.

To God the Father, God the Son,
And God the Spirit, praise be done;
And God's own Son upon us pour
The Spirit's gifts for evermore.

Antiphon over Nunc Dimittis.
—Alleluia. The Holy Ghost the Comforter, Alleluia : shall teach you all things. Alleluia, Alleluia.

Petitions, etc., as usual, standing.

¶ COMPLINE XVII.

On Whitsun Day.

All as on Whitsun Eve, except that on this day and the three days following, instead of the Hymn, is said this Sequence.

Now let the choir of the Lord sing sweetly the Names of the Highest.
Messiah, Saviour, Emmanuel, Lord of Sabaoth;
He is the Only begotten, Way, Life, Arm of God, ὁμοούσιον.
Beginning, and First-born, God's Wisdom, and Power,
Alpha, the Head and the End, Omega,
Fountain and Source of all good, our Paraclete and Mediator,
Lamb and Sheep, Calf, Serpent, Ram, Lion, and Worm,
Mouth, Word, and Radiance, Sun, Glory, God's Image, and Light,
Bread, Blossom, Vine, Mountain, Door, Rock, Corner-stone,
Angel, and Spouse, Shepherd, Prophet, and Priest,
Immortal, the Lord, God, Almighty, and Jesus;

Save us, we pray Thee:
Whose is the glory
Through ages eternal.
Amen.

On the remaining days of the Festival is said, Saviour, Who didst the ransom pay, *with Whitsuntide doxology.*

¶ Compline XVIII.

On the Festival of the Holy Trinity.

Antiphon over the Psalms.—Have mercy upon me, O God: and hearken unto my prayer.

Hymn. Saviour, Who didst the ransom pay.

Antiphon over Nunc Dimittis.—Lord, grant us Thy Light: that, being freed from the darkness of our hearts, we may come to the true Light, which is Christ.

This Compline is said on all Double Festivals between Trinity and Advent, and between the Octave of Epiphany and the First Sunday in Lent; except on the Festivals and through the Octaves of the Holy Name and of blessed Mary, and on the Feasts of Relics, and of All Saints. It is said also on the Festival and through the Octaves of the Dedication of a church, whatever be the Service, except it fall in Advent, Lent, or Eastertide; and if it fall in the Summer, or at any time when it can have an Octave day with rulers.

¶ Compline XIX.

On the Feast of Relics and of All Saints.

Antiphon over the Psalms.—At the prayers of all saints, grant health of body and soul to Thy servants, O Christ.

Hymn. Saviour, Who didst the ransom pay.

Antiphon over Nunc Dimittis.—Lord, grant us Thy Light, etc.

As on Trinity Sunday.

¶ Compline XX.

On the Purification of B. Mary.

Antiphon over the Psalms.—A Virgin, she conceived the Word: a Virgin remained she: a Virgin, brought she forth the King of kings.

Hymn. Saviour, Who didst.
With Christmas doxology.

Antiphon over Nunc Dimittis.—We glorify thee, O mother of God: for of thee the Christ was born: help all those that glorify thee.

This Antiphon is said on all Feasts and throughout the Octaves of blessed Mary, and in Commemorations of the same, throughout the whole year, except in Advent, and on the Annunciation, and during Eastertide.

¶ Compline XXI.

On the Feasts of the Visitation and Assumption.

Antiphon over the Psalms.—Holy Mary the Virgin, intercede for the whole world, since thou hast brought forth the King of the earth.

The rest as on the Purification.

¶ Compline XXII.

On the Nativity of Blessed Mary.

Antiphon over the Psalms.—Blessed and unwedded Virgin, glorious Queen of the world, intercede for us with the Lord.

The rest as on the Purification.

The Petitions.

~~Kyrie, eleyson~~ (*thrice*).
~~Christe, eleyson~~ (*thrice*).
~~Kyrie, eleyson~~ (*thrice*).

AT COMPLINE.

[handwritten: Lord Christ have mercy upon us / Lord]

Our Father. Hail, Mary.

V. And lead us not into temptation. *R.* But deliver us from evil.

V. I will lay me down in peace. *R.* And take my rest.

I believe.

V. The resurrection of the body. *R.* And the life everlasting.

V. Let us bless the Father, the Son, and the Holy Spirit. *R.* Let us praise and highly exalt Him for ever.

V. Blessed be Thou, O Lord, in the firmament of heaven. *R.* Glorious in praise, and highly to be exalted for ever.

V. May the Almighty and merciful Lord bless us and keep us. *R.* Amen.

Then is said the Confession in a low voice, so as to be heard by the Choir, in this manner:

The Priest, turning toward the Altar:

I confess to God, to blessed Mary, all Saints, [*turning to the Choir*] and you, that I have sinned exceedingly, in thought, word, and deed, by my fault. [*Turning to the Altar.*] I pray holy Mary, and all the Saints of God, [*turning to the Choir*] and you, to pray for me.

The Choir reply, turning to him:

Almighty God have mercy upon you, and forgive you all your sins; deliver you from all evil; confirm and strengthen you in all good, and bring you to everlasting life. Amen.

Then the Choir say the Confession, turning first to the Altar, and then to the Priest, in the same manner as the Priest. Then the Priest, having said, Almighty God, have mercy, shall add:

The almighty and merciful Lord grant you absolution and remission of your sins, time for true repentance, amendment of life, the grace and comfort of His Holy Spirit. Amen.

V. Wilt Thou not turn again and quicken us, O Lord? *R.* That Thy people may rejoice in Thee.

V. Show us Thy mercy, O Lord. *R.* And grant us Thy salvation.

V. Vouchsafe, O Lord. *R.* To keep us this night without sin.

V. Have mercy upon us, O Lord. *R.* Have mercy upon us.

V. Let Thy mercy lighten upon us, O Lord. *R.* As we do put our trust in Thee.

On Sundays and all Festivals.

V. Turn us again, O Lord God of hosts. *R.* Show the

light of Thy countenance, and we shall be whole.
V. Lord, hear my prayer.
R. And let my crying come unto Thee.
V. The Lord be with you.
R. And with thy spirit.

Let us pray.

LIGHTEN our darkness, we beseech Thee, O Lord; and by Thy great mercy defend us from all perils and dangers of this night; for the love of Thy only Son, our Saviour, Jesus Christ, Who liveth and reigneth with Thee in the unity of the Holy Ghost, ever one God, world without end. Amen.

V. The Lord be with you.
R. And with thy spirit.
V. Bless we the Lord.
R. Thanks be to God.

On Ferias throughout the year, except from Christmas to the first Sunday after the Octave of Epiphany, and in Eastertide until the first Sunday after Trinity:

V. Hearken unto my voice, O Lord, when I cry unto Thee. *R.* Have mercy upon me, and hear me.

Psalm li.

The Psalm is said throughout without note, with Glory be to the Father; and when this Psalm is ap- *pointed to be said, everything is said kneeling, from Kyrie, eleyson, till after the Collect.*

Here in Lent shall follow:

Psalm cxliii.

HEAR my prayer, O Lord, and consider my desire: hearken unto me for Thy truth and righteousness' sake.

2 And enter not into judgment with Thy servant: for in Thy sight shall no man living be justified.

3 For the enemy hath persecuted my soul; he hath smitten my life down to the ground: he hath laid me in the darkness, as the men that have been long dead.

4 Therefore is my spirit vexed within me: and my heart within me is desolate.

5 Yet do I remember the time past; I muse upon all Thy works: yea, I exercise myself in the works of Thy hands.

6 I stretch forth my hands unto Thee: my soul gaspeth unto Thee as a thirsty land.

7 Hear me, O Lord, and that soon, for my spirit waxeth faint: hide not Thy face from me, lest I be like unto them that go down into the pit.

8 O let me hear Thy lovingkindness betimes in the morning, for in Thee is my trust: show Thou me the way that I should walk in, for I lift up my soul unto Thee.

9 Deliver me, O Lord, from mine enemies: for I flee unto Thee to hide me.

10 Teach me to do the thing that pleaseth Thee, for Thou art my God: let Thy loving Spirit

AT COMPLINE.

lead me forth into the land of righteousness.

11 Quicken me, O Lord, for Thy Name's sake: and for Thy righteousness' sake bring my soul out of trouble.

12 And of Thy goodness slay mine enemies: and destroy all them that vex my soul; for I am Thy servant.

Glory be to the Father.

Here let the Priest alone stand up and say:

V. O Lord, arise, help us.
R. And deliver us for Thy Name's sake.
V. Turn us again, Thou God of hosts. R. Show the light of Thy countenance, and we shall be whole.
V. Hear my prayer, O Lord. R. And let my crying come unto Thee.
V. The Lord be with you.
R. And with thy spirit.

Let us pray.

LIGHTEN our darkness, we beseech Thee, O Lord; and by Thy great mercy defend us from all perils and dangers of this night; for the love of Thy only Son, our Saviour Jesus Christ, Who liveth and reigneth with Thee in the unity of the Holy Ghost, ever one God, world without end. Amen.

V. The Lord be with you.
R. And with thy spirit.
V. Bless we the Lord.
R. Thanks be to God.

Every day throughout the year, after Compline of the day, and after Mattins of the day, except on Double Feasts, and through the Octaves of Corpus Christi, the Visitation, Assumption, and Nativity of blessed Mary, and of the Dedication of the church, and of the Name of Jesus, and on All Souls' Day, and upon Christmas Eve to the first Sunday after the Octave of Epiphany, and from Wednesday in Holy Week to the first Sunday after Trinity, is said the prayer For the Peace of the Church, kneeling, without note.

Psalm cxxiii.

UNTO Thee lift I up mine eyes: O Thou that dwellest in the heavens.

2 Behold, even as the eyes of servants look unto the hand of their masters, and as the eyes of a maiden unto the hand of her mistress: even so our eyes wait upon the Lord our God, until He have mercy upon us.

3 Have mercy upon us, O Lord, have mercy upon us: for we are utterly despised.

4 Our soul is filled with the scornful reproof of the wealthy: and with the despitefulness of the proud.

Glory be to the Father.

Then follows:

Kyrie, eleyson.
Christe, eleyson.
Kyrie, eleyson.

Our Father.

Then aloud without note:

V. And lead us not into temptation. R. But deliver us from evil.

V. O Lord, arise, help us. R. And deliver us for Thy Name's sake.

V. Turn us again, O Lord God of hosts. R. Show the light of Thy countenance, and we shall be whole.

V. Lord, hear my prayer. R. And let my cry come unto Thee.

V. The Lord be with you. R. And with thy spirit.

Collect.

MERCIFULLY hear the prayers of Thy Church, O Lord, that she, being delivered from all error and adversity, may serve Thee in rest and freedom; and grant us Thy peace all the days of our life; through Christ our Lord. Amen.

COMMON OF SAINTS.

COMMON OF APOSTLES.
EXCEPT IN EASTERTIDE.

At First Evensong the Collect of the Eve is said, if it have a proper one; if not, the Collect of the day.

At Prime.

Antiphon.—This is My commandment: that ye love one another, as I have loved you.

At Terce.

Antiphon.—Greater love hath no man than this: that a man lay down his life for his friends.

Chapter. Ephesians ii. 19.

Now therefore ye are no more strangers and foreigners, but fellow citizens with the saints, and of the household of God; and are built upon the foundation of the apostles and prophets.

R. Their sound is gone out into all lands. *V.* And their words into the ends of the world. *R.* Into all lands. *V.* Glory be. *R.* Their sound.

V. Thou shalt make them princes in all lands. *R.* They shall remember Thy Name, O Lord.

The Collect of the day is said, if it have one; but if not, then is said this Collect of the Common:

Collect.

HEAR Thy people, O Lord, who pray in union with the intercession of Thy holy Apostle N.; that they may be defended evermore by Thy ready help, and serve Thee with a quiet mind; through.

At Sext.

Antiphon.—Ye are My friends: if ye do whatsoever I command you, saith the Lord.

Chapter. Acts v. 12.

By the hands of the apostles were many signs and wonders wrought among the people: and the people magnified them.

R. Thou shalt make them princes in all lands. *V.* They shall remember Thy Name, O Lord. *R.* In all lands. *V.* Glory be. *R.* Thou shalt make.

V. Great is the honour of Thy friends, O God. *R.* Great is the might of their dominion.

At None.

Antiphon.—In your patience: possess ye your souls.

Chapter. Acts v. 41.

The apostles departed from the presence of the council, rejoicing that they were counted worthy to suffer shame for the Name of Jesus.

℟. Great is the honour of Thy friends, O Lord. ℣. Great is the might of their dominion. ℟. Of Thy friends, O Lord. ℣. Glory be. ℟. Great is the honour.

℣. They have declared the marvellous acts of God. ℟. They have also told of His greatness.

OF ONE MARTYR.
EXCEPT IN EASTERTIDE.

At Prime.

Antiphon.—Whosoever therefore shall confess Me before men: him will I confess also before My Father.

At Terce.

Antiphon.—He that followeth Me shall not walk in darkness: but shall have the light of life, saith the Lord.

Chapter. James i. 12.

Blessed is the man that endureth temptation: for when he is tried, he shall receive the crown of life, which the Lord hath promised to them that love Him.

If a Bishop.
Heb. v. 1.

Every high priest taken from among men is ordained for men in things pertaining to God, that he may offer both gifts and sacrifices for sins.

℟. With glory and worship: Thou hast crowned him, O Lord. ℣. Thou makest him to have dominion of the works of Thy hands. ℟. Thou hast crowned him, O Lord. ℣. Glory be. ℟. With glory.

℣. Thou hast set upon his head, O Lord. ℟. A crown of pure gold.

Collect.

INCLINE Thy merciful ears, O Lord, to us Thy servants, who make now our supplication before Thee; and, at the intercession of blessed N., Thy martyr, protect us evermore with Thy perpetual lovingkindness; through our Lord.

Another Collect.

GRANT, we beseech Thee, Almighty Lord, that as we keep the Feast of blessed N., Thy martyr, so by his intercession we may evermore increase in love of Thy Name; through.

If a Bishop.

O GOD, by whose grace we celebrate the holy Feast of blessed N., Thy Martyr and Bishop; Mercifully hear the prayers of Thy servants, and grant that as we keep his festival here on earth, so by his merits and prayers we may receive Thy heavenly succour; through.

At Sext.

Antiphon.—If any man serve Me, let him follow Me: and where I am, there shall My servant be.

Chapter. Ecclus. xlv.

He learned righteousness, and beheld very marvellous things: and he prevailed with the Most High, and was found among the number of the saints.

OF MANY MARTYRS OR CONFESSORS.

If a Bishop.
Heb. v. 4.

No man taketh this honour unto himself, but he that is called of God, as was Aaron. As He saith also in another place, Thou art a priest for ever after the order of Melchisedec.

R. Thou hast set : upon his head, O Lord. *V.* A crown of pure gold. *R.* Upon his head, O Lord. *V.* Glory be. *R.* Thou hast set.

V. The righteous shall flourish like a palm tree, in the house of the Lord.

R. And shall spread abroad like a cedar in Libanus.

At None.

Antiphon.—Father, I will that where I am : there shall also My servant be.

Chapter. Ecclus. xlv.

The Lord clothed him with a robe of glory, and a crown of beauty hath He placed on his head.

If a Bishop.
Ecclus. xxiv. 2.

In the congregation of the Most High shall Wisdom open her mouth, and triumph before His power; she shall be exalted in the midst of the people, and wonderful in her sanctity.

R. The righteous shall flourish like a palm tree : in the house of the Lord. *V.* He shall spread abroad like a cedar in Libanus. *R.* In the house of the Lord. *V.* Glory be. *R.* The righteous.

V. The righteous shall blossom as a lily. *R.* He shall flourish for ever before the Lord.

The following Chapters are said alternately with the above during the week.

At TERCE. *Chapter. Ecclus.* xiv. 22. Blessed is the man that doth meditate good things in wisdom, and that reasoneth of holy things by his understanding, and in his conduct payeth heed unto the providence of God.

At SEXT. *Chapter. Ecclus.* xv. 3. With the bread of life and understanding shall she feed him, and give him the water of saving wisdom to drink.

At NONE. *Chapter. Ecclus.* xv. 4. He shall be stayed on her, and shall not be moved : and shall rely upon her, and shall not be confounded. She shall exalt him above his neighbours, and the Lord our God shall cause him to inherit an everlasting name.

OF MANY MARTYRS OR CONFESSORS.
EXCEPT IN EASTERTIDE.

At Prime.

Antiphon.—But the souls of the righteous are in the hand of God : and there shall no torment touch them.

At Terce.

Antiphon.—With the palm the saints did attain to the kingdom : crowns of glory have they merited from the hand of the Lord.

Chapter. Wisdom x. 17.
God will render to His saints a

reward of their labours, and will guide them in a marvellous way.

If Confessors.
Heb. vii. 23.

Under the law were made many priests, because they were not suffered to continue by reason of death: but Jesus, because He continueth ever, hath an unchangeable priesthood.

R. Be glad, O ye righteous: and rejoice in the Lord. V. And be joyful, all ye that are true of heart. R. And rejoice in the Lord. V. Glory be. R. Be glad.

V. Let the righteous be glad, and rejoice before God. R. Let them also be merry and joyful.

Collect.

O ALMIGHTY and everlasting God, grant us to hold in continual veneration the glorious deeds of Thy Martyrs N. and N.: that being freed from all worldly perils, we may be found worthy of heavenly joys; through Jesus Christ Thy Son our Lord, Who liveth and reigneth with Thee in the unity of the Holy Ghost, ever one God, world without end. Amen.

If Bishops.

ALMIGHTY and everlasting God, Who in the hearts of Thy holy Martyrs and Bishops N. and N., didst kindle the fire of Thy love; Inflame our souls, we pray Thee, with the like fervour of faith and charity, that as we rejoice in their triumphs, so we may profit by their examples; through.

At Sext.

Antiphon.—The bodies of the saints are buried in peace, but their name liveth for evermore.

Chapter. Wisdom x. 18.

Wisdom brought them through the Red Sea, and led them through much water; but she drowned their enemies, and cast them up out of the bottom of the deep.

If Confessors.
Wisdom v.

Ye saints and righteous, rejoice in the Lord; God hath chosen you for an heritage for Himself.

R. Let the righteous be glad, and rejoice before God. V. Let them also be merry and joyful. R. And rejoice before God. V. Glory be. R. Let the righteous.

V. The souls of the righteous are in the hand of God. R. And there shall no torment touch them.

At None.

Antiphon.—Let the saints be joyful with glory; let them rejoice in their beds.

Chapter. Wisdom x. 20.

The righteous spoiled the ungodly, and praised Thy holy Name, O Lord, and magnified with one accord Thy hand, that fought for them, O Lord our God.

If Confessors.
Wisdom v. 15.

But the righteous live for evermore; their reward also is with the Lord, and the care of them is with the Most High.

OF A CONFESSOR AND BISHOP.

R. The souls of the righteous are: in the hand of God. V. And there shall no torment touch them. R. In the hand of God. V. Glory be. R. The souls.

V. Wonderful art Thou in Thy saints, O God. R. And glorious in Thy majesty.

The following Chapters are said alternately with the above during the week.

AT TERCE. *Chapter.* Heb. xi. 33. The saints through faith subdued kingdoms, wrought righteousness, obtained promises in Christ.

AT SEXT. *Chapter.* Heb. xi. 36. The saints had trial of cruel mockings and scourgings, yea, moreover of bonds and imprisonment: they were stoned, they were sawn asunder, were tempted, were slain with the sword.

AT NONE. *Chapter.* Heb. xi. 37. They wandered about in sheepskins and goatskins; being destitute, afflicted, tormented; of whom the world was not worthy.

OF A CONFESSOR AND BISHOP.

EXCEPT IN EASTERTIDE.

At Prime.

Antiphon. — Behold a great priest, who in his days pleased God: and was found righteous.

If an Abbat or Doctor.

The Lord guided the righteous man: in right paths, and showed him the kingdom of God.

At Terce.

Antiphon.—In glory was there none like unto him: who kept the law of the Most High.

Chapter. Ecclus. xliv. 22.

With him did the Lord establish the blessing of all men: and the covenant, and made it rest upon his head.

If an Abbat or Doctor.

Ecclus. xxxix. 5.

The righteous will give his heart to resort early unto the Lord that made him, and will pray before the Most High.

R. The Lord loved him, and beautified him with comely ornaments. V. He clothed him with a robe of glory. R. And beautified him with comely ornaments. V. Glory be. R. The Lord.

V. The Lord guided the righteous man in right paths. R. And showed him the kingdom of God.

Collect.

ALMIGHTY and everlasting God, who makest us glad by this day's Festival in honour of blessed N., Thy Confessor and Bishop; We humbly beseech Thee that as we devoutly observe his Festival, so by his loving intercessions we may attain to everlasting life; through Jesus Christ Thy Son our Lord, Who liveth and reigneth with Thee in the unity of the Holy Ghost, one God, world without end. Amen.

Or this.

GRANT, we beseech Thee, Almighty God, that as we celebrate this holy solemnity of blessed N., Thy Confessor and Bishop, so we may evermore increase in true religion, and finally be made partakers of Thy heavenly treasure; through.

But if an Abbat, substitute the word Abbat *for* Bishop, *in the Collect.*

At Sext.

Antiphon.—A faithful and wise steward: whom his Lord made ruler over His household.

Chapter. Ecclus. xliv. 23.

The Lord acknowledged him in His blessing, He kept His mercy for him, and he found favour in the sight of the Lord.

If an Abbat or Doctor.
Ecclus. xxxix. 6.

When the great Lord will, he shall be filled with the spirit of understanding; he shall pour out wise sentences, and give thanks unto the Lord in his prayer.

R. The Lord guided the righteous man in right paths. V. And showed him the kingdom of God. R. In right paths. V. Glory be. R. The Lord guided.

V. The righteous shall flourish like a palm tree in the house of the Lord. R. And spread abroad like a cedar in Libanus.

At None.

Antiphon.—Good and faithful servant: enter Thou into the joy of thy Lord.

Chapter.—*Ecclus.* xlv. 3.

He made Him glorious in the sight of kings, and gave Him a crown of glory.

If an Abbat or Doctor.

Ecclus. xxxix. 7.

The Lord shall direct his counsel and knowledge, and he shall glory in the law of the covenant of the Lord.

R. The righteous shall flourish like a palm tree in the house of the Lord. V. He shall spread abroad like a cedar in Libanus. R. In the house of the Lord. V. Glory be. R. The righteous.

V. The righteous shall blossom as a lily. R. He shall flourish for ever before the Lord.

The following Chapters are said on the Feast of a Confessor who is neither Bishop nor Abbat.

AT TERCE. *Wisdom* x. 10. The Lord guided the righteous man in right paths, showed him the kingdom of God, and gave him knowledge of holy things, made him rich in his travails, and multiplied the fruit of his labours.

AT SEXT. *Wisdom* x. 12. The Lord defended him from his enemies, and kept him safe from those that lay in wait, and in a sore conflict gave him the victory, that he might know that godliness is stronger than all.

AT NONE. *Wisdom* x. 13. When the righteous was sold, Wisdom forsook him not, but delivered him from sin.

———

OF A VIRGIN AND MARTYR.

At Prime.

Antiphon. — This is a wise virgin: whom the Lord found watching.

At Terce.

Antiphon.—This is a wise virgin: and one of the number of the prudent.

Chapter. *Ecclus.* li. 13.
O Lord my God, Thou hast exalted my dwelling-place above the earth, and I have prayed for deliverance from death.

Of a Virgin not a Martyr.
2 *Cor.* x. 17.
He that glorieth, let him glory in the Lord. For not he that commendeth himself is approved, but whom the Lord commendeth.

R. Full of grace are thy lips. V. Because God hath blessed thee for ever. R. Are thy lips. V. Glory be. R. Full of grace.
V. With thy glory and thy majesty. R. Go, ride prosperously and reign.

Collect.

HEAR our prayer, O God of our salvation: that as with joy and gladness we keep the feast of blessed N., Thy Virgin and Martyr, so we may learn of Thee the true devotion of spirit; through Jesus Christ Thy Son our Lord, Who liveth and reigneth with Thee in the unity of the Holy Ghost, one God world without end. Amen.

Of a Virgin not a Martyr.

ALMIGHTY and everlasting God, Lover of virginity and Author of all virtue; Grant, we beseech Thee, that as we celebrate the most chaste life of holy N., Thy Virgin, so by her merits and prayers we too may be made pleasing unto Thee in all manner of godly conversation; through Jesus Christ Thy Son our Lord, Who liveth.

At Sext.

Antiphon.—This is a virgin, holy and glorious: for the Lord of all things has chosen her.

Chapter. *Ecclus.* li. 11.
I will praise Thy Name continually, and will sing praise with thanksgiving; because my prayer was heard.

Of a Virgin not a Martyr.
2 *Cor.* xi. 2.
I am jealous over you with godly jealousy: for I have espoused you to one husband, that I may present you as a chaste virgin to Christ.

R. With thy glory and thy majesty. V. Go, ride prosperously and reign. R. With thy majesty. V. Glory be. R. With thy glory.
V. God hath given her the help of His countenance. R. God is in the midst of her, therefore shall she not be removed.

At None.

Antiphon.—Come, thou bride of Christ, receive the crown:

which the Lord hath laid up for thee for ever.

Chapter. Ecclus. li. 12.

Thou savedst me from destruction, and deliveredst me from the evil time: therefore will I give thanks, and praise Thee, and bless Thy Name, O Lord my God.

Of a Virgin not a Martyr.
Wisdom vii. 30.

Vice shall not prevail against wisdom: wisdom reacheth from one end to another mightily; and sweetly doth she order all things.

R. God hath given her the help of His countenance. *V.* God is in the midst of her, therefore shall she not be removed. *R.* The help of His countenance. *V.* Glory be. *R.* God hath given.

V. The virgins that be her fellows shall bear her company. *R.* And shall be brought unto Thee.

OF MANY VIRGINS.

At Prime.

Antiphon.— O ye holy Virgins of God, pray for us, that we may obtain pardon of our sins through your prayers.

At Terce.

Antiphon.—At midnight there was a cry made, Behold, the Bridegroom cometh; go ye out to meet him.

Chapter. Wisdom iv. 1.

How beautiful is chastity with virtue! for the memorial there-of is immortal: because it is known with God and with men.

R. The virgins that be her fellows shall bear her company. *V.* And shall be brought unto Thee. *R.* Shall bear her company. *V.* Glory be. *R.* The virgins.

V. At midnight there was a cry made. *R.* Behold, the Bridegroom cometh; go ye out to meet Him.

Collect as in the Proper.

At Sext.

Antiphon.—The wise virgins: took oil in their vessels with their lamps.

Chapter. 2 *Cor.* xi. 2.

I am jealous over you with godly jealousy: for I have espoused you to one husband, that I may present you as a chaste virgin to Christ.

R. At midnight there was a cry made. *V.* Behold, the Bridegroom cometh; go ye out to meet Him. *R.* There was a cry made. *V.* Glory be. *R.* At midnight.

V. The wise virgins took oil in their vessels with their lamps. *R.* And they went forth to meet the Bridegroom and the Bride.

Collect as in the Proper.

At None.

Antiphon.—Then all those virgins arose: and trimmed their lamps.

Chapter. Wisdom vii. 30.

Vice shall not prevail against wisdom: wisdom reacheth from one end to another mightily;

and sweetly doth she order all things.

R. The wise virgins took oil in their vessels with their lamps. V. And they went forth to meet the Bridegroom and the Bride.

R. With their lamps. V. Glory be. R. The wise virgins.

V. The virgins that be her fellows shall bear her company. R. And shall be brought unto Thee.

Collect as in the Proper.

HERE ENDETH THE COMMON OF SAINTS.

PROPER OF SAINTS.

ST. ANDREW, APOSTLE.

If this Feast fall within Advent, then at First Evensong is made a solemn memorial of Advent and afterwards of St. Mary.

Whenever the Feast falls, within Advent or not, there is always a Procession at First Evensong, after the memorials, to the altar of St. Andrew, if there be one, with candle-bearers and thurifers, and the boy bearing the book before the Priest, without Cross, the Choir following. While the Cantors sing the verse the Priest censes the altar. He then says the Collect, without The Lord be with you, but with Let us pray. Returning, the anthem of St. Mary is sung; but, if it be within Advent, the anthem of All Saints, with the Collect.

And so let the Procession be performed on all Feasts of Saints at First Evensong throughout the year, if there be altars dedicated to them in the church: and if a Collect of the Eve is said at Evensong, then at the Procession is said the Collect of the Feast. But when the Collect of the Feast is said at Evensong, then at the Procession is said the Collect of the Common, unless the Procession have a proper Collect, as on the Feast of St. Nicholas, St. Katherine, etc.; and always in returning is said the anthem of St. Mary except a memorial of her have been said at Evensong already; for then in returning is said the anthem of All Saints.

Nor should their service be celebrated at their altars, as Evensong, Mattins, or the other Hours, according to the use of Sarum, except only the Mass of the Saint in the morning.

At Compline.

If this Feast fall before Advent, all is said as on Trinity Sunday. If it fall within Advent, the Compline of the season is said with the Hymn, Saviour, Who didst the ransom pay.

At Mattins, if the Feast fall within Advent, Te Deum is not said; nor are the altar and Choir censed, as is customary on Double Feasts.

A memorial is made of Advent, and of St. Mary, at Mattins, Mass, and Evensong, if the Feast fall within Advent.

At Prime.

Antiphon.—Hail, Cross most precious; bear the disciple of Him who hung on thee, my Master Christ.

Antiphon.—Thanks be to Thee.

At Terce.

Antiphon. — Blessed Andrew kept praying, O Lord, King of eternal glory, support me, hanging here in torture.

Chapter. Romans x. 10.

With the heart man believeth unto righteousness; and with the mouth confession is made unto salvation. For the Scripture saith, Whosoever believeth on Him shall not be ashamed.

R. Their sound is gone out into

all lands. *V.* And their words into the end of the world. *R.* Into all lands. *V.* Glory be. *R.* Their sound.

V. Thou shalt make them princes in all lands. *R.* They shall remember Thy Name, O Lord.

Collect.

ALMIGHTY GOD, Who didst give such grace unto Thy holy Apostle Saint Andrew, that he readily obeyed the calling of Thy Son Jesus Christ, and followed Him without delay; Grant unto us all, that we, being called by Thy holy Word, may forthwith give up ourselves obediently to fulfil Thy holy commandments; through the same Jesus Christ our Lord, Who liveth and reigneth with Thee in the unity of the Holy Ghost, one God, world without end. Amen.

[1552]

Or this.

WE humbly beseech Thy majesty, O Lord, that as Thou didst give blessed Andrew the Apostle to be a teacher and ruler of Thy Church, so he may make perpetual intercession before Thee for us Thy servants; through.

At Sext.

Antiphon.—Suffer me not, O Lord, Thy servant, to be parted from Thee: time it is that Thou commit my body to the earth.

Chapter. Romans x. 12.

For there is no difference between the Jew and the Greek: for the same Lord over all is rich unto all that call upon Him.

R. Thou shalt make them princes in all lands. *V.* They shall remember Thy name, O Lord. *R.* In all lands. *V.* Glory be. *R.* Thou shalt make.

V. Great is the honour of Thy friends, O Lord. *R.* Great is the might of their dominion.

At None.

Antiphon.—Thou didst cast into hell, O Lord, him who persecuted the righteous: and upon the wood of the cross Thou wast the Captain of the righteous.

Chapter. Romans x. 13.

Whosoever shall call upon the name of the Lord shall be saved.

R. Great is the honour of Thy friends, O Lord. *V.* Great is the might of their dominion. *R.* Of Thy friends, O Lord. *V.* Glory be. *R.* Great is the honour.

V. All men that see it shall say, This hath God done. *R.* For they shall perceive that it is His work.

If this Feast fall on Advent Sunday, it shall always be transferred to the following day: even when the church is dedicated to St. Andrew. And when the Feast is thus transferred, then on the Sunday Evensong shall be of the Feast, with a solemn Memorial of the Sunday, and afterwards of St. Mary. If the Feast fall on the Saturday before Advent, then Evensong shall be of the Sunday, with a solemn memorial of the Feast, and of St. Mary.

On the Octave day all shall be said as on this Feast. On other days within the Octave falling within Advent, the Service is of Advent, with a memorial of St. Andrew before that of blessed Mary. If the Feast fall on the Thursday before Advent, then

the Service on Friday is all done as within Octaves. On Saturday there is full Service of St. Mary.
But if this Feast fall on any other Feria, then only a Memorial of St. Andrew is made within the Octaves, until the Octave day.

December 6.
ST. NICHOLAS, BISHOP.

At First Evensong memorials are made of St. Andrew, of Advent, and of St. Mary.
Then follows the Procession to the altar of St. Nicholas.

At Prime.

Antiphon.—Blessed Nicholas, while yet a boy, brought his body into subjection by much fasting.
Antiphon.—Thee, all Thy creatures.

At Terce.

Antiphon.—He was ever in the courts of holy Church, storing his soul with her precepts.

Chapter. Ecclus. xliv. 17.

Behold a great priest, who in his days pleased God and was found righteous, and in time of wrath was taken in exchange for the world.

R. The Lord loved him and beautified him with comely ornaments. V. He clothed him with a robe of glory. R. And beautified him with comely ornaments. V. Glory be. R. The Lord.

V. The Lord guided the righteous man in right paths. R. And showed him the kingdom of God.

Collect.

O GOD, Who hast honoured Thy Bishop, blessed Nicholas, with innumerable miracles; Grant unto us, we pray Thee, that by his merits and prayers we may escape the fires of hell; through.

At Sext.

Antiphon.—Through his godly and pious living he was thought worthy to obtain of God the honour of the priesthood.

Chapter. Ecclus. xliv. 22.

With him did the Lord establish the blessing of all men: and the covenant, and made it rest upon his head.

R. The Lord guided the righteous man in right paths. V. And showed him the kingdom of God. R. In right paths. V. Glory be. R. The Lord.

V. The righteous shall flourish like a palm tree in the house of the Lord. R. And spread abroad like a cedar in Libanus.

At None.

Antiphon.—O man ever to be honoured, by whose merits they are delivered from all mishap, who out of a perfect heart ask his prayers.

Chapter. Ecclus. xliv. 23.

The Lord acknowledged him in His blessing. He kept His mercy for him, and he found favour in the sight of the Lord.

R. The righteous shall flourish like a palm tree in the house of

THE CONCEPTION OF THE BLESSED VIRGIN MARY.

the Lord. *V.* He shall spread abroad like a cedar in Libanus. *R.* In the house of the Lord. *V.* Glory be. *R.* The righteous.
V. The righteous shall blossom as a lily. *R.* He shall flourish for ever before the Lord.

DECEMBER 7.
OCTAVE OF ST. ANDREW, APOSTLE.

It is to be noted that when the Octave of St. Andrew falls on the Saturday, then is done full Service of St. Mary, and only a memorial of the Octave, and Mass in Chapter.

At Mattins memorials are made of Advent and St. Mary, and afterwards of All Saints.
If the Octave fall on Sunday, or if the Feast of St. Nicholas be transferred from Sunday to this day, or the Octave fall on a Saturday, then only a memorial of the Octave at first Evensong and at Mattins shall be made, with Mass in Chapter.

At Prime and the other Hours all is done as within Octaves.

DECEMBER 8.
THE CONCEPTION OF THE BLESSED VIRGIN MARY.

At First Evensong only the High Altar is censed.

At Compline.

The Advent Compline is said, except that the Doxology to the Hymn is, All glory, Virgin-born, to Thee.

At Mattins a memorial of Advent is made.

At Prime.

Antiphon.—The conception of holy Mary the Virgin to-day we celebrate: whose glorious life doth lighten all the Churches.
Antiphon.—Thanks be to Thee, O God.

At Terce.

Antiphon.—The conception of the glorious Virgin Mary, born of the seed of Abraham, of the tribe of Judah: of the mighty stock of David.

Chapter. Ecclus. xxiv. 17.
As the vine brought I forth pleasant savour, and my flowers are the fruit of honour and riches.

R. Holy Mother of God, ever Virgin Mary. *V.* Pray for us to the Lord our God. *R.* Ever Virgin Mary. *V.* Glory be. *R.* Holy Mother.
V. After child-bearing thou remainedst a pure virgin. *R.* O Mother of God, pray for us.

Collect.

O GOD, who hast mercy upon all men, hear the supplication of us Thy servants, that we who celebrate the conception of the Virgin Mother of God may by her prayers be delivered from all dangers that beset us; through the same.

At Sext.

Antiphon.—Glorious is Mary risen from a royal race: and through her intercession we devoutly beg help for soul and spirit.

Chapter. Ecclus. xxiv. 19.
Come unto me, all ye that be desirous of me, and fill your-

selves with my fruits: for my memorial is sweeter than honey, and mine inheritance than the honeycomb.

R. After child-bearing thou remainedst a pure Virgin. *V.* O Mother of God, pray for us. *R.* Thou remainedst a pure Virgin. *V.* Glory be. *R.* After child-bearing.

V. Thou art become fair and pleasant. *R.* In thy delights, O holy Mother of God.

At None.

Antiphon. With joy we celebrate the conception of blessed Mary: that she may pray for us to Jesus Christ the Lord.

Chapter. Ecclus. xxiv. 22.

He that obeyeth me shall never be confounded, and they that work by me shall not do amiss; they that magnify me shall have eternal life.

R. Thou art become fair and pleasant. *V.* In thy delights, O holy Mother of God. *R.* And pleasant. *V.* Glory be. *R.* Thou art become.

V. God hath elected her and pre-elected her. *R.* And made her to dwell in His tabernacle.

If this Feast fall on a Sunday, it is transferred to the morrow, and always at both Evensongs, at Mattins, and at Mass is made a solemn memorial of Advent, on whatever Feria it fall; except when the Dedication of the church is the Conception of blessed Mary; for then it is not transferred, yet a solemn memorial of Advent is made, notwithstanding that such a Feast, in a church of that Dedication only, is a Greater Double according to the Use of Sarum, and one of the Principals.

DECEMBER 14.
ST. LUCY, VIRGIN AND MARTYR.

At both Evensongs and Mattins memorials are made of Advent and St. Mary.

At Prime.

Antiphon. — While blessed Lucy prayed, St. Agatha appeared to her: and consoled the handmaid of Christ.

At Terce.

Antiphon. — Lucy, maiden, why seekest thou of me what thou canst thyself bestow upon thy mother?

At Sext.

Antiphon. — For thy sake, Lucy maiden, the State of Syracuse shall be honoured by the Lord Jesus Christ.

At None.

Antiphon.—Lucy, my sister, virgin vowed to God, why seekest thou of me what thou canst thyself bestow upon thy mother?

All else is of the Common of a Virgin and Martyr (see p. 119).

DECEMBER 31.
ST. THOMAS, APOSTLE.

At both Evensongs and Mattins memorials are made of Advent and St. Mary.

If this Feast fall on a Sunday, it is transferred to the morrow, unless it be the Feast of the place.

But if it fall on Friday or Saturday in Ember-week, only a memorial of the Fast is made at Mattins; but *after the Mass of the Apostle is said the Mass of the Fast, both at the High Altar; then the proper Service of the Feria at Mattins is omitted that year, and the Collect said as a memorial.*

All the Service is of the Common of an Apostle, with the following Collect:

Collect.

ALMIGHTY and ever-living God, Who for the more confirmation of the faith didst suffer Thy holy Apostle Thomas to be doubtful in Thy Son's resurrection; Grant us so perfectly, and without all doubt, to believe in Thy Son Jesus Christ, that our faith in Thy sight may never be reproved. Hear us, O Lord, through the same Jesus Christ, to Whom, with Thee and the Holy Ghost, be all honour and glory, now and for evermore. Amen.

Or this.

GRANT to us, Lord, we beseech Thee, so to rejoice in the solemnities of Thy blessed Apostle St. Thomas, that we may ever be protected by his prayers, and with a true devotion follow his faith; through.

DECEMBER 31.
ST. SILVESTER, POPE AND CONFESSOR.

At First Evensong and at Mattins memorials are made (1) of the Nativity, (2) of St. Stephen, (3) of St. John, (4) of the Holy Innocents, (5) of St. Thomas.

All the Service is of the Common of a Confessor and Bishop (see p. 117), with this Collect:

Collect.

GRANT, we beseech Thee, Almighty God, that as we celebrate this holy solemnity of blessed Silvester, Thy Confessor and Bishop, so we may evermore increase in true religion, and finally be made partakers of Thy heavenly treasure; through.

JANUARY 8.
ST. LUCIAN, PRIEST AND MARTYR, AND HIS COMPANIONS.

All as within the Octaves of Epiphany, with memorial of St. Lucian, viz. the Collect of the Common of Many Martyrs.

JANUARY 13.
ST. HILARY, BISHOP AND CONFESSOR.

The Service at the Hours is all as within the Octaves of Epiphany.

Memorial of St. Hilary.

HEARKEN to our supplications, O Lord, and at the intercession of blessed Hilary, Thy Confessor and Bishop, whose Feast we celebrate, graciously pour upon us Thy perpetual mercy; through.

JANUARY 18.
ST. PRISCA, VIRGIN AND MARTYR.

All of the Common, p. 119, with this Collect:

GRANT, we beseech Thee, Almighty God, that as we

keep the Feast of blessed Prisca, Thy Virgin and Martyr, so we may both be made glad by this yearly solemnity, and may follow the example of her wonderful faith; through.

From the Octave of Epiphany to Quinquagesima, the Service of St. Mary is performed every Saturday; unless a Feast of nine Lessons prevent it, in which case it is performed on any other Feria in the week.

JANUARY 20.

SS. FABIAN AND SEBASTIAN, MARTYRS.

At Mattins and Evensong memorial of St. Mary.

At Prime.

Antiphon.—Sebastian, the servant of God, was a captain exceeding zealous; secretly in soldier's guise he would strengthen the hearts of the Christians, exhorting to hope, and to reach after eternal glory.

At Terce.

Antiphon.—If I be a true servant of Christ, and if all things which this woman has heard of my mouth and believed be true: then let Him who opened the mouth of Zacharias the prophet of the Lord open her mouth.

At Sext.

Antiphon.—At this word of Sebastian, Christ's martyr: immediately the mouth of Nicostratus' wife was opened.

At None.

Antiphon. — Holy Sebastian said to Nicostratus: Our Saviour on behalf of sinners vouchsafed to reveal His presence.

All else of the Common of Many Martyrs (see p. 115), except the Collect.

Collect.

O GOD, Who to Thy blessed martyrs Fabian and Sebastian didst grant constancy in suffering; Give us grace in such wise to follow their examples, that for love of Thee we may neither court the favour of the world nor fear its enmity; through.

JANUARY 21.

ST. AGNES, VIRGIN AND MARTYR.

At First Evensong memorial of SS. Fabian and Sebastian, and of St. Mary.
At Mattins memorial of St. Mary.

At Prime.

Antiphon.—Entering the place of shame, Agnes found the angel of the Lord ready to assist her.

At Terce.

Antiphon.—With me abideth the angel of the Lord, to keep me in all my ways.

At Sext.

Antiphon.—I am espoused to Him Whom angels serve: before Whose beauty sun and moon bow down.

At None.

Antiphon. — Rejoice and be glad with me, for with all this company I have attained unto thrones of light.

All else of the Common of a Virgin and Martyr, p. 119, except the Collect.

Collect.

ALMIGHTY and everlasting God, Who hast chosen the weak things of the world to confound the strong; Mercifully grant that we who keep the Feast of blessed Agnes Thy Martyr may enjoy the protection of her prayers before Thee; through.

JANUARY 22.
ST. VINCENT, MARTYR.
Feast of nine Lessons.

At First Evensong, *memorial of St. Agnes and of St. Mary.*

At Mattins and Second Evensong, *memorial of St. Mary.*

At Prime.

Antiphon.—The deacon Vincent was taken from the little horse and hurried to torture: chiding the delay of the executioners, he hastened eagerly to his martyrdom.

At Terce.

Antiphon. — So fearlessly mounting on to the instrument of glowing iron of his own accord, he remained motionless, and turning his eyes to heaven, prayed to the Lord.

At Sext.

Antiphon.—And thus God's athlete, inclosed in his dreadful prison-house: was comforted by the wondrous ministry of angels, and much solaced by their converse.

At None.

Antiphon.—Therefore did their praises go up to the most high God: and far and wide the voices of the angelic choir did fling the sweetness of their melody.

All else of the Common of a Martyr, p. 114, except the Collect.

Collect.

HEARKEN to our prayers, O Lord: that we who for our evil deeds do confess ourselves worthy to be punished, by the intercession of Thy blessed martyr Vincent may be mercifully relieved; through.

JANUARY 25.
CONVERSION OF ST. PAUL, APOSTLE.
Feast of nine Lessons.

At First Evensong and at Mattins, *memorial of St. Mary.*
If this Feast fall on any Sunday before Septuagesima the whole service is of the Apostle; and memorials are made first of the Sunday, and afterwards of St. Mary.

At Prime.

Antiphon.—Saul, which is also called Paul, increased the more in strength, and confounded the Jews.

Antiphon.—Thee all Thy creatures.

At Terce.

Antiphon.—Brother Saul, the Lord, even Jesus, that appeared unto thee in the way as thou camest, hath sent me, that thou mightest receive thy sight, and be filled with the Holy Ghost.

Chapter. Acts ix. 1.

Saul, yet breathing out threatenings and slaughter against the disciples of the Lord, came near Damascus. And suddenly there shined round about him a light from heaven.

R. Their sound is gone out into all lands. V. And their words into the ends of the world. R. Into all lands. V. Glory be. R. Their sound.

V. Thou shalt make them princes in all lands. R. They shall remember Thy Name, O Lord.

Collect.

O GOD, Who, through the preaching of the blessed Apostle Saint Paul, hast caused the light of the Gospel to shine throughout the world; Grant, we beseech Thee, that we, having his wonderful conversion in remembrance, may show forth our thankfulness unto Thee for the same, by following the holy doctrine which he taught; through Jesus Christ Thy Son our Lord, Who liveth and reigneth with Thee and the Holy Ghost, ever one God, world without end. Amen.

At Sext.

Antiphon.—And Ananias putting his hands on him, immediately there fell from his eyes as it had been scales: and he received sight forthwith, and arose, and was baptized: and when he had received meat, he was strengthened.

Chapter. Acts ix. 15.

Go thy way, Ananias, inquire for Saul: for he is a chosen vessel unto Me, to bear My Name before the Gentiles, and kings, and the children of Israel.

R. Thou shalt make them princes in all lands. V. They shall remember Thy Name, O Lord. R. In all lands. V. Glory be. R. Thou shalt make.

V. Great is the honour of Thy friends, O Lord. Great is the might of their dominion.

At None.

Antiphon.—Paul entering into the synagogues, preached Jesus to the Jews: affirming that this is very Christ.

Chapter. Acts ix. 7.

And Ananias went his way, and entered into the house; and putting his hands on him said, Brother Saul, the Lord, even Jesus, Who appeared unto thee in the way as thou camest, hath sent me, that thou mightest receive thy sight, and be filled with the Holy Ghost.

R. Great is the honour of Thy friends, O Lord. V. Great is the might of their dominion. R. Of Thy friends, O Lord. V. Glory be. R. Great is.

V. They have declared the marvellous acts of God. R. They have also told of His greatness.

PURIFICATION OF THE BLESSED VIRGIN MARY.

February 2.
THE PURIFICATION OF THE BLESSED VIRGIN MARY.
Greater Double.

At Prime.

Antiphon.—Symeon was just and devout, waiting for the consolation of Israel, and the Holy Ghost was upon him.
Antiphon.—Thanks be to Thee.

At Terce.

Antiphon. — It was revealed unto Symeon by the Holy Ghost: that he should not see death until he had seen the Lord.

Chapter. Malachi iii. 1.

Behold, I send My messenger, and he shall prepare the way before Me: and the Lord, whom ye seek, shall suddenly come to His temple, even the Messenger of the covenant, Whom ye delight in.

R. Holy Mother of God, ever Virgin Mary. *V.* Intercede for us with the Lord our God. *R.* Ever Virgin Mary. *V.* Glory be. *R.* Holy Mother.
V. After child-bearing thou remainedst a pure Virgin. *R.* O Mother of God, pray for us.

Collect.

ALMIGHTY and everliving God, we humbly beseech Thy Majesty; that as Thine only begotten Son was this day presented in the temple in substance of our flesh, so we may be presented unto Thee with pure and clean hearts; by the same Thy Son Jesus Christ our Lord, Who liveth.

At Sext.

Antiphon.—Symeon took the Child up in his arms, and gave thanks, blessing the Lord.

Chapter. Malachi iii. 2.

For He is like a refiner's fire, and like fullers' sope: and He shall sit as a refiner and purifier of silver: and He shall purify the sons of Levi.

R. After child-bearing thou remainedst a pure Virgin. *V.* O Mother of God, pray for us. *R.* Thou remainedst a pure Virgin. *V.* Glory be. *R.* After child-bearing.
V. Thou art become fair and pleasant. *R.* In thy delights, O holy Mother of God.

At None.

Antiphon. — Mine eyes have seen Thy salvation: which Thou hast prepared before the face of all people.

Chapter. Malachi iii. 3.

And He shall purge them as gold and silver, that they may offer unto the Lord an offering in righteousness.

R. Thou art become fair and pleasant. *V.* In thy delights, O holy Mother of God. *R.* Fair and pleasant. *V.* Glory be. *R.* Thou art become.
V. God hath elected her and pre-elected her. *R.* He hath made her to dwell in His tabernacle.

At Second Evensong no memorial is made of St. Blasius; but a solemn memorial of Septuagesima, Sexagesima, or Quinquagesima is made, if this Feast so fall.

If Septuagesima Sunday fall on this day, the whole service is of the Feast, but without Alleluia and Te Deum; and a solemn memorial of the Sunday is made at both Evensongs, at Mattins, and at Mass.

Similarly is done if Sexagesima or Quinquagesima Sunday fall on this day.

If this Feast fall on the Saturday next before Septuagesima, Second Evensong is of the Feast, and a solemn memorial of the Sunday is made, but without Alleluia.

The Feast of the Purification indeed never is altered, because of the mystery of the days of purification: in order that the number of the days of purification may be observed. Now the mystery of purification, according to the Mosaic precept, was, that when a woman bare a man-child, she should abstain for forty days from entering the temple and from marriage rights, and on the fortieth day should come with her neighbours, and with victims and gifts, and entering the temple, should accomplish her purification. Since this was the law of the Old Covenant, the Feast of the Purification never alters on account of Septuagesima, etc.

FEBRUARY 3.
ST. BLASIUS, BISHOP.

Feast of three Lessons. All of th Common of a Martyr and Bishop, p. 114, with this Collect.

Collect.

LORD, grant that Thy blessed Martyr Blasius may implore Thy mercy upon us; that as we celebrate his Feast, we may ever enjoy his patronage with Thee; through.

If this Feast fall on a Saturday, only a memorial is made of it. If it fall on a Sunday, a solemn memorial is made at First Evensong, Mattins, and Mass. *The same rule holds of all Feasts of three Lessons from this day till Ash Wednesday.*

FEBRUARY 5.
ST. AGATHA, VIRGIN AND MARTYR.

Feast of nine Lessons.

At Prime.

Antiphon.—Who art thou that comest to cure me of my wounds? I am the apostle of Christ: fear nothing in me, my daughter.

Antiphon.—Thee all Thy creatures.

At Terce.

Antiphon.—This world's medicine have I never used for my body: but I possess the Lord Jesus Christ, who with a single word restoreth all things.

At Sext.

Antiphon.—I give Thee thanks, O Lord, that Thou art mindful of me, and hast sent Thine apostle to me to cure my wounds.

At None.

Antiphon.—Upon the living God I call: since He hath vouchsafed to cure me of all my wounds and to heal my body.

All else of the Common of a Virgin and Martyr, p. 119, except this Collect.

Collect.

O GOD, Who, amidst the many marvels of Thy power, hast granted to weak women the martyr's crown; Mercifully assist us so to follow the example of Thy blessed Martyr Agatha, whose Festival we celebrate, that we come to Thine everlasting kingdom; through.

FEBRUARY 14.
ST. VALENTINE, MARTYR.

Feast of three Lessons. All of the Common of a Bishop and Martyr (see p. 114), except the Collect.

Collect.

GRANT, we beseech Thee, Almighty God, that we, who keep the Feast of Thy blessed Martyr Valentine, may be delivered through his intercession from all dangers that threaten us; through.

FEBRUARY 24.
ST. MATTHIAS, APOSTLE.
INFERIOR DOUBLE.

If this Feast fall before Lent, Compline is said as on Trinity Sunday; if within Lent, Compline does not change.
All of the Common of an Apostle (see p. 113), except the Collect.

Collect.

O ALMIGHTY GOD, Who into the place of the traitor Judas didst choose Thy faithful servant Matthias to be of the number of the twelve Apostles; Grant that Thy Church, being alway preserved from false Apostles, may be ordered and guided by faithful and true pastors; through Jesus Christ our Lord, Who liveth and reigneth with Thee in the unity of the Holy Ghost, ever one God, world without end. Amen. [1549]

Or this.

O GOD, Who didst choose blessed Matthias into the college of Thine Apostles; Grant, we pray Thee, that through his intercession we may ever perceive Thy love and pity towards us; through.

If this Feast fall on Ash Wednesday, it is transferred to the following day, even though it be the Feast of the place. In leap year the Feast of St. Matthias is kept on Feb. 25. If it fall on Saturday after Ash Wednesday, it has a Second Evensong, with solemn memorial of the Sunday. The Lenten Compline is not changed.

MARCH 1.
ST. DAVID, BISHOP AND CONFESSOR.

Feast of nine Lessons. All of the Common, p. 117, except the Collect.

Collect.

O ALMIGHTY and everlasting God, Who for blessed David, Thy Confessor and Bishop, didst even before his birth marvellously provide a place of habitation by the hand of Thy holy angel; Mercifully grant, that as we venerate him on earth, so by his merits and prayers we may share with him the joy of the beatific Vision in the heavens; through.

MARCH 2.
ST. CHAD, BISHOP AND CONFESSOR.

Feast of nine Lessons. All of the Common, p. 117, except the Collect.

Collect.

O GOD, Who hast decked the Church throughout the whole world with the merits of Thy saints; Grant, we beseech Thee, that by the prayers of blessed Chad, Thy Bishop, we may be counted worthy in Thy protecting love to attain to the company of Thy blessed ones; through.

March 7.
SS. PERPETUA AND FELICITAS, VIRGINS AND MARTYRS.

Feast of three Lessons. All of the Common of Many Virgins and Martyrs, p. 120, except the Collect.

Collect.

GRANT to us, O Lord our God, with ceaseless devotion to venerate Thy victorious Martyrs Perpetua and Felicitas; that we, who may not worthily do them honour, may yet with humble service celebrate their memory; through.

March 12.
ST. GREGORY, POPE AND DOCTOR.
DOUBLE FEAST.

All of the Common of a Confessor and Bishop, see p. 117, except the Collect.

Collect.

O GOD, Who hast bestowed the reward of eternal blessedness upon the soul of Thy servant Gregory; Mercifully grant that we who are oppressed with the weight of our sins, by his patronage with Thee may be aided and relieved; through.

Whenever this Feast may fall, it is kept under the same rule as the Feast of the Annunciation; yet if it fall on the Saturday before the first Sunday in Lent, it is then celebrated, and Second Evensong will be of this Feast, with a solemn memorial of the Sunday; the Lenten Compline does not change; but after First Evensong is said Compline as on Trinity Sunday.

March 18.
ST. EDWARD, KING AND MARTYR.

Feast of nine Lessons. All of the Common of a Martyr (see p. 114), with this Collect.

Collect.

O GOD, Who hast won for Thyself an eternal kingdom; Mercifully behold this Thy family now celebrating the martyrdom of King Edward, and grant, that as Thou hast vouchsafed unto him a crown of heavenly glory, so at his prayers we may be made worthy to attain everlasting joy; through.

If this Feast, or those of St. Cuthbert or St. Benedict, chance to fall in Passion-tide, they shall be kept upon the Feasts of their Translations.

March 21.
ST. BENEDICT, ABBOT.

Feast of nine Lessons. All of the Common of a Confessor and Abbot (see p. 117), with this Collect.

Collect.

ALMIGHTY and everlasting God, Who on this day didst deliver Thy most blessed Con-

ANNUNCIATION OF THE BLESSED VIRGIN MARY.

fessor Benedict from the prison-house of the flesh, exalting him unto Thy heavenly kingdom; Grant, we pray Thee, to Thy servants who celebrate his feast, pardon of all their sins, that they, who with glad hearts rejoice in his exaltation, may through his prayers be made partakers of his blessedness; through.

MARCH 25.
THE ANNUNCIATION OF THE BLESSED VIRGIN MARY.
LESSER DOUBLE.

If this Feast fall in Lent, then at both Evensongs and at Mattins is made a solemn memorial of the Fast. The Lenten Compline is not changed.

At Prime.

Antiphon.—The angel of the Lord announced unto Mary, and she conceived by the Holy Ghost.

Antiphon.—Thanks be to Thee.

At Terce.

Antiphon.—Fear not, Mary, thou hast found grace with the Lord: behold, thou shalt conceive and bring forth a Son.

Chapter. Isaiah vii. 14.

Behold, a Virgin shall conceive, and bear a Son, and shall call His name Immanuel. Butter and honey shall He eat, that He may know to refuse the evil, and choose the good.

R. Full of grace are thy lips. V. Because God hath blessed thee for ever. R. Are Thy lips. V. Glory be. R. Full of grace.

V. With thy glory and thy majesty. R. Go, ride prosperously, and reign.

Collect.

WE beseech Thee, O Lord, pour Thy grace into our hearts; that, as we have known the incarnation of Thy Son Jesus Christ by the message of an angel, so by His cross and passion we may be brought into the glory of His resurrection; through the same Jesus Christ our Lord. Amen. [*Post Communion.*]

Or this.

O GOD, Who didst grant Thy Word to take flesh from the womb of blessed Mary ever Virgin, at the message of an angel; Mercifully grant to us Thy servants, that we, who truly believe her to be the Mother of God, may ever be assisted by her prayers; through the same.

At Sext.

Antiphon.—How shall that be, thou angel of God, seeing that I know not a man? Hearken, O Mary, Virgin of Christ, the Holy Ghost shall come upon thee, and the power of the Highest shall overshadow thee.

Chapter. Isaiah xi. 1.

There shall come forth a rod out of the stem of Jesse, and a Branch shall grow out of his roots: and the Spirit of the Lord shall rest upon Him.

R. With thy glory and thy majesty. V. Go, ride prosperously, and reign. R. With thy majesty. V. Glory be. R. With thy glory.

V. God hath given her the help of His countenance. R. God is in the midst of her, therefore shall she not be removed.

At None.

Antiphon.—Behold the handmaid of the Lord: be it unto me according to thy word.

Chapter. Isaiah xxvi. 21.

Behold the Lord cometh out of His holy place: He shall come and save His people from their sins.

R. God hath given her the help of His countenance. V. God is in the midst of her, therefore shall she not be removed. R. The help of His countenance. V. Glory be. R. God hath given.

V. The virgins that be her fellows shall bear her company. R. And shall be brought unto Thee.

When this Feast happens to fall on any Sunday in Lent, it is always transferred to the morrow. If it fall on a Saturday in Lent, Second Evensong is of St. Mary with a solemn memorial of the Sunday following: except on the Saturday before Passion Sunday or Palm Sunday; for then Evensong of the Sunday is said, with a solemn memorial of the Feast.

But when the Feast of the Annunciation falls on a Monday: always on Sunday, Evensong is of the Feast, with a solemn memorial of the Sunday.

If it fall on the Wednesday in Holy Week, the service is of the Feast, but Evensong is of the Feria, with a solemn memorial of the Feast.

If it fall between Wednesday in Holy Week and the morrow of Low Sunday, it is transferred to the first Sunday on which it can have two Evensongs.

Similarly is done in the case of all Double Feasts thus falling.

If the Feast of the Annunciation fall in Eastertide, then at both Evensongs and at Mattins is made a solemn memorial of the Resurrection. The Hymns all end with the Christmas Doxology; and all the Antiphons and Responsories end with Alleluia.

APRIL 3.

ST. RICHARD, BISHOP AND CONFESSOR.

All of the Common of a Confessor and Bishop (see p. 117).

Collect.

O GOD, Who by the merits of blessed Richard, Thy Confessor and Bishop, hast made Thy Church to shine with wonderful miracles; Grant that we Thy servants may by his intercessions attain to the glory of eternal blessedness; through.

If this Feast fall in Passion-tide, it is altogether omitted. If it fall on Low Sunday, it is transferred to the Tuesday following, and at Second Evensong of St. Ambrose is made a solemn memorial of St. Richard.

APRIL 4.

ST. AMBROSE, BISHOP, CONFESSOR, AND DOCTOR.

DOUBLE FEAST.

Collect.

O GOD, Who didst give blessed Ambrose to Thy people to be a minister of everlasting salvation; Grant, we beseech Thee, that as we honour him as a teacher of the way of life on

ST. ALPHEGE, BISHOP AND MARTYR.

earth, so we may ever have him as our intercessor in the heavens; through.

This Feast is kept according to the same rule as the Feast of the Annunciation (see p. 136).

Antiphons, etc., at all the Hours of the Common of a Confessor and Bishop.

If the Feast fall after Easter, then all is as on the Feast of St. Alphege.

APRIL 19.
ST. ALPHEGE, BISHOP AND MARTYR.

Feast of three Lessons, without Rulers.

At Prime.

Antiphon. — Thy saints, O Lord, shall flourish as a lily, Alleluia: as the odour of balsam shall they be before Thee. Alleluia.

At Terce.

Antiphon.— Ye saints and righteous, rejoice in the Lord, Alleluia: God hath chosen you to be His heritage. Alleluia.

Chapter. Hebrews v. 1.

Every high priest taken from among men is ordained for men in things pertaining to God, that he may offer both gifts and sacrifices for sin.

R. Your sorrow: Alleluia! Alleluia! *V.* Shall be turned into joy. *R.* Alleluia! Alleluia! *V.* Glory be. *R.* Your sorrow. Alleluia! Alleluia!

V. Right dear in the sight of the Lord. *R.* Is the death of His saints. Alleluia!

Collect.

O GOD, Who didst honour Thy Confessor blessed Alphege with the dignity of the priesthood and the palm of martyrdom; Mercifully grant, that, assisted by his intercessions with Thee, we may with him attain to the bliss of everlasting life; through.

At Sext.

Antiphon.—Within the veil, O Lord, Thy Saints cry: Alleluia! Alleluia! Alleluia!

Chapter. Hebrews v. 4.

No man taketh this honour unto himself, but he that is called of God, as was Aaron. As He saith also in another place, Thou art a priest for ever after the order of Melchizedek.

R. Right dear in the sight of the Lord. Alleluia! Alleluia! *V.* Is the death of His Saints. *R.* Alleluia! Alleluia! *V.* Glory be. *R.* Right dear.

V. Rejoice in the Lord, ye righteous. *R.* For it becometh well the just to be thankful. Alleluia!

At None.

Antiphon.—In heavenly realms is the dwelling-place of the saints: Alleluia! and their rest is in eternity. Alleluia!

Chapter. Ecclus. xv.

In the congregations of the Most High shall Wisdom open her mouth, and triumph before His power; she shall be exalted in the midst of her people, and she shall be wonderful in her sanctity.

R. Rejoice in the Lord, ye righteous. Alleluia! Alleluia!
V. For it becometh well the just to be thankful. R. Alleluia! Alleluia! V. Glory be. R. Rejoice.
V. The voice of joy and health. R. Is in the dwellings of the righteous. Alleluia.

April 23.
ST. GEORGE, MARTYR.

Feast of three Lessons with rulers. All as upon the Feast of St. Alphege, except the Chapters and Collect.

AT TERCE. *Chapter. James* i. 12. Blessed is the man that endureth temptation: for when he is tried, he shall receive the crown of life, which the Lord hath promised to them that love Him.

AT SEXT. *Chapter. Ecclus.* xlv. He learned righteousness, and beheld very marvellous things: and he prevailed with the Most High, and was found among the number of the saints.

AT NONE. *Chapter. Ecclus.* xlv. The Lord clothed him with a robe of glory, and a crown of beauty hath He placed on his head.

Collect.

O GOD, Who makest us to exult in the merits of Thy blessed Martyr George; Mercifully grant that, by the gift of Thy grace, we may attain the benefits which we ask; through.

If this Feast fall on Low Sunday, it is transferred to the following day, and at Second Evensong of the Sunday a solemn memorial is made of the Feast.

April 25.
ST. MARK, EVANGELIST.
DOUBLE FEAST.

All as on the Feast of St. Alphege, except the Chapters and Collects.

AT TERCE. *Chapter. Eph.* iv. 7. Unto every one of us is given grace according to the measure of the gift of Christ. Wherefore He saith, When He ascended up on high, He led captivity captive, and gave gifts unto men.

AT SEXT. *Chapter. Eph.* iv. 10. He that descended is the same that ascended up far above all heavens, that He might fill all things.

AT NONE. *Chapter. Eph.* iv. 11. And He gave some, apostles; and some, prophets; and some, evangelists; and some, pastors and teachers; for the perfecting of the saints.

Collect.

O ALMIGHTY GOD, Who hast instructed Thy holy Church with the heavenly doctrine of Thy Evangelist Saint Mark; Give us grace, that, being not like children carried away with every blast of vain doctrine, we may be established in the truth of Thy holy Gospel; through Jesus Christ our Lord. Amen. [1549]

ST. PHILIP AND ST. JAMES, APOSTLES.

Or this.

O GOD, Who didst honour Thy blessed Evangelist Saint Mark with grace to preach the Gospel; Grant, we beseech Thee, that we may ever profit by his teaching, and be defended by his prayers; through.

If this Feast chance to fall in Easter week, it is transferred to the first convenient day after Low Sunday, on which both Evensongs can be celebrated. If it fall on any Sunday after Low Sunday, it is not transferred, and a solemn memorial only is made of the Sunday and afterwards of the Resurrection.

MAY 1.
ST. PHILIP AND ST. JAMES, APOSTLES.

DOUBLE FEAST.

At First Evensong and at Mattins a memorial of the Resurrection is made.

At Prime.

Antiphon.—Lord, show us the Father: and it sufficeth us. Alleluia.

Antiphon. — Thanks be to Thee.

At Terce.

Antiphon. — Philip, he that hath seen Me hath seen the Father.

Chapter. Wisdom v. 1.

Then shall the righteous man stand in great boldness before the face of such as have afflicted him, and made no account of his labours.

R. Then were the disciples glad. Alleluia! Alleluia! V. When they saw the Lord. R. Alleluia! Alleluia! V. Glory be. R. Then were the disciples.
V. Lord, show us the Father. R. And it sufficeth us. Alleluia!

Collect.

O ALMIGHTY GOD, Whom truly to know is everlasting life; Grant us perfectly to know Thy Son Jesus Christ to be the way, the truth, and the life; that, following the steps of Thy holy Apostles, Saint Philip and Saint James, we may steadfastly walk in the way that leadeth to eternal life; through the same Thy Son Jesus Christ our Lord, Who liveth and reigneth with Thee in the unity of the Holy Ghost, ever one God, world without end. Amen. [1549]

Or this.

O GOD, Who makest us glad with the yearly solemnity of Thy Apostles Philip and James; Grant, we pray Thee, that, as we rejoice in their merits, so we may follow their examples; through.

At Sext.

Antiphon.—I am the Way, the Truth, and the Life: no man cometh to the Father, but by Me. Alleluia!

Chapter. Acts iv. 33.

With great power gave the Apostles witness of the resurrection of the Lord Jesus: and great grace was upon them all.

R. Lord, show us the Father. Alleluia! Alleluia! V. And it sufficeth us. R. Alleluia! Alle-

PROPER OF SAINTS.

luia! *V.* Glory be. *R.* Lord, show us.

V. Let not your heart be troubled. *R.* Neither let it be afraid. Alleluia!

At None.

Antiphon.—If ye abide in Me, and My words abide in you: ye shall ask what ye will, and it shall be done unto you. Alleluia!

Chapter. Acts v. 41.

And the Apostles departed from the council, rejoicing that they were counted worthy to suffer shame for the name of Jesus. Alleluia!

R. Let not your heart be troubled. Alleluia! Alleluia! *V.* Neither let it be ashamed. *R.* Alleluia! Alleluia! *V.* Glory be. *R.* Let not your heart.

V. The Lord was known of them. *R.* In breaking of bread. Alleluia!

If this Feast chance to fall on Low Sunday, it is transferred to the following day, and on Sunday Evensong is of the Feast with solemn memorial of the Sunday. In that case, on Monday Evensong is of the Holy Cross, with solemn memorial of the Apostles.

If this Feast fall on the Eve of the Ascension, it is kept on that day; and at First Evensong of the Ascension solemn memorial of the Apostles is made.

If it fall on Ascension Day, it is transferred until the following day; at Second Evensong of the Ascension solemn memorial is made of the Apostles, and on the next day Evensong is of the Apostles, with solemn memorial of the Holy Cross.

Let the same rule be followed with respect to the Feast of the Holy Cross.

May 3.
THE INVENTION OF THE HOLY CROSS.
LESSER DOUBLE.

No memorial of the Resurrection is made, but if the Feast fall on Sunday, a memorial is made of the Sunday at both Evensongs and at Mattins.

At Prime.

Antiphon.—Helena, the mother of Constantine, went to Jerusalem. Alleluia!

Antiphon. — Thanks be to Thee.

At Terce.

Antiphon.—Then commanded she them all to be burnt with fire: but they, in terror, gave up Judas to her. Alleluia!

Chapter. Galatians vi. 14.

God forbid that I should glory save in the cross of our Lord Jesus Christ, by Whom the world is crucified unto me, and I unto the world.

R. This sign of the Cross shall be in heaven. Alleluia! *V.* When the Lord cometh to judgment. *R.* Alleluia! Alleluia! *V.* Glory be. *R.* This sign.

V. Tell it out among the nations. *R.* That the Lord hath reigned from the tree. Alleluia!

Collect.

O GOD, Who by the marvellous invention of the saving Cross didst renew the wonders of Thy Passion; Grant that by the ransom paid upon the tree of life, we may attain to the bliss of everlasting life; Who with the Father.

ST. JOHN BEFORE THE LATIN GATE.

At Sext.

Antiphon.— Quoth St. Helen unto Judas, Fulfil my behest and live; show me what place is called Calvary: where is hid the precious Cross of the Lord. Alleluia!

Chapter. 1 Cor. i. 18.

The preaching of the cross is to them that perish foolishness; but unto us which are saved it is the power of God.

R. Tell it out among the nations. Alleluia! Alleluia! *V.* That the Lord hath reigned from the tree. *R.* Alleluia! Alleluia! *V.* Glory be. *R.* Tell it out.

V. We adore Thee, O Christ, and we bless Thee. *R.* Because by Thy Cross Thou hast redeemed the world. Alleluia!

At None.

Antiphon.—When Judas had prayed: the place in which the holy Cross lay hid was rent. Alleluia!

Chapter. 1 Cor. i. 23.

But we preach Christ crucified, unto the Jews a stumbling-block, and unto the Greeks foolishness; but unto them which are called, both Jews and Greeks, Christ the power of God, and the wisdom of God.

R. We adore Thee, O Christ, and we bless Thee. Alleluia! Alleluia! *V.* Because by Thy Cross Thou hast redeemed the world. *R.* Alleluia! Alleluia! *V.* Glory be. *R.* We adore.

V. Let all the earth worship Thee, O God. *R.* And praise Thy Name. Alleluia!

If this Feast fall on Saturday, there is no procession at second Evensong, nor any memorial except of the following Sunday. If however it fall within Ascensiontide, a memorial of the Ascension is made.

If it fall on Ascension Eve it is celebrated on that day: and at first Evensong of the Ascension a solemn memorial of the Cross is made.

But if it fall on Ascension Day, it is transferred to the morrow, and a solemn memorial of the Cross is made at second Evensong of the Ascension.

The reason why no memorial of the Resurrection is made on the Invention of the Holy Cross is, that when two contraries concur, one must be omitted.

MAY 6.

ST. JOHN BEFORE THE LATIN GATE, APOSTLE AND EVANGELIST.

Feast of three Lessons with rulers. All as on the Feast of St. Alphege (see p. 137), except as follows:

AT TERCE. *Chapter. Ecclus.* xv. 1. He that feareth the Lord will do good: and he that hath knowledge of the law shall obtain wisdom. And as a mother shall she meet him.

AT SEXT. *Chapter. Ecclus.* xv. 3. With the bread of life and understanding shall she feed him, and give him to drink the water of wisdom and salvation. He shall be stayed upon her, and shall not be moved: and shall rely upon her, and shall not be confounded. She shall exalt him above his neighbours.

AT NONE. *Chapter. Ecclus.* xv. 5. In the midst of the church she opened his mouth, and the

Lord filled him with the spirit of wisdom and understanding: with a robe of glory He clothed him.

If this Feast, or that of St. Dunstan, fall on the Eve of the Ascension, it is kept on that day; but at first Evensong of the Ascension no memorial is made of these feasts audibly.

If either of these Feasts should fall on Ascension Day, it is transferred to the morrow, and at second Evensong of the Ascension memorial is made of the Feast secretly.

Collect.

O GOD, Who seest that we are beset with evils on every side: we pray Thee, grant to us the protection of the glorious intercession of Thy blessed apostle and evangelist Saint John; through.

MAY 19.
ST. DUNSTAN, BISHOP AND CONFESSOR.

Feast of nine Lessons. If this Feast fall in Eastertide, the service is all as on the Feast of St. Alphege, p. 137. Otherwise all is of the Common of a Bishop and Confessor, p. 117.

If this Feast or that of St. Augustine, or of St. Barnabas the apostle, fall before Whit-Sunday, they are reckoned Feasts of three Lessons with rulers. If they fall after Whit-Sunday, they have nine Lessons.

Collect.

O GOD, Who hast translated blessed Dunstan Thy Bishop unto Thy heavenly kingdom: grant to us by his merits and prayers to attain to everlasting joys; through.

MAY 26.
ST. AUGUSTINE, BISHOP AND CONFESSOR.
APOSTLE OF THE ENGLISH.

INFERIOR DOUBLE.

The service follows the same rule as on the Feast of St. Dunstan.

Collect.

O GOD, Who didst give blessed Augustine Thy Bishop to be the first teacher of the people of the English: grant, we beseech Thee, that as we celebrate his merits here on earth, so we may ever perceive the effect of his prayers with Thee in the heavens; through.

If this Feast fall on the Eve of Ascension, it is kept on that day; but Evensong is of the Ascension with solemn memorial of St. Augustine. If it fall on Ascension Day, it is transferred to the morrow; and at second Evensong of the Ascension is made solemn memorial of St. Augustine. If it fall within Whitsun week, it is transferred until after the Feast of the Holy Trinity.

MAY 27.
VENERABLE BEDE, PRIEST AND CONFESSOR.

All of the Common of a Confessor not a Bishop, p. 117, except it fall in Eastertide, when the service is all as on the Feast of St. Alphege, p. 137.

JUNE 1.
ST. NICOMEDE, MARTYR.

Feast of three Lessons. All of the Common of a Martyr, p. 114, except the Collect; unless the Feast fall in Eastertide, when the service is all as on the Feast of St. Alphege, p. 137.

Collect.

O GOD, Who makest us glad with the merits and prayers of Thy blessed martyr Nicomede. Grant, we pray Thee, that as we ask his help, so by the gift of Thy grace we may obtain the same; through.

JUNE 5.
ST. BONIFACE AND HIS COMPANIONS, MARTYRS.

Feast of three Lessons. All of the Common of Many Martyrs, p. 115, except the Collect; but if this Feast fall in Eastertide, then the service is all as on the Feast of St. Alphege, p. 137.

Collect.

ALMIGHTY and everlasting God, Who didst bestow upon blessed Boniface and his companions the palm of martyrdom; Grant, we pray Thee, that as Thou hast vouchsafed to them the crown, so by their merits and prayers we may obtain Thy pardon; through.

JUNE 11.
ST. BARNABAS, APOSTLE.

Feast of nine Lessons. If this Feast fall in Eastertide, then the service is all as on the Feast of St. Alphege, except the chapters and Collect, p. 137.

AT TERCE. *Chapter. Eph.* ii. 19. Now therefore ye are no more strangers and foreigners, but fellow citizens with the saints, and of the household of God; and are built upon the foundation of the apostles and prophets.

AT SEXT. *Chapter. Acts v.* 12. By the hands of the apostles were many signs and wonders wrought among the people: and the people magnified them.

AT NONE. *Chapter. Acts v.* 41. And the apostles departed from the presence of the council, rejoicing that they were counted worthy to suffer shame for the Name of Jesus.

Collect.

O LORD God Almighty, Who didst endue Thy holy Apostle Barnabas with singular gifts of the Holy Ghost; Leave us not, we beseech Thee, destitute of Thy manifold gifts, nor yet of grace to use them alway to Thy honour and glory; through Jesus Christ Thy Son our Lord, Who liveth and reigneth with Thee in the unity of the same Spirit, ever one God, world without end. Amen. [1549]

Or this.

GRANT to thy Church, O Lord, we beseech Thee, the help of Thy protection, at the prayers of Thy blessed apostle Saint Barnabas: and as Thou didst give him to adorn her by his doctrine and sufferings, so make him to be her continual intercessor with Thee; through.

If the Feast however do not fall in Eastertide, all is of the Common of Apostles, with Collect as above.

JUNE 20.

TRANSLATION OF ST. EDWARD, KING AND MARTYR.

Feast of nine Lessons. All of the Common of a Martyr, p. 114.

Collect.

O GOD, Who hast won for Thyself an eternal kingdom; Mercifully behold this Thy family now celebrating the translation of King Edward: and grant that as Thou hast vouchsafed unto him a crown of heavenly glory, so at his prayers we may be made worthy to attain everlasting joy; through.

JUNE 22.

ST. ALBAN, PROTOMARTYR OF ENGLAND.

Feast of nine Lessons. All of the Common of a Martyr, p. 114.

Collect.

O GOD, Who didst hallow this day by the martyrdom of blessed Alban; Grant, we pray Thee, that as year by year we celebrate his feast, so we may be preserved by his unceasing aid; through.

If the Feast of St. Alban fall on the First Sunday after Trinity, it is transferred to the following day.

JUNE 24.

ST. JOHN THE BAPTIST.

LESSER DOUBLE.

At First Evensong. *If this Feast fall within the Octaves of Corpus Christi or of Trinity, no memorial is made of the Octaves, unless they be kept with rulers, in which case a memorial is made, and then the procession shall go to the Altar of St. John with Candle-bearers and Thurifers, and the boy carrying the book, without cross, singing the Responsory. While the verse is sung, the priest shall cense the Altar. In returning, the anthem of St. Mary is sung.*

At Compline.

All as on Trinity Sunday, p. 108.

At Prime.

Antiphon.—Elizabeth, the wife of Zacharias, brought forth a son, great in the sight of the Lord, John the Baptist, Forerunner of the Lord.

Antiphon.—Thanks be to Thee.

If this Feast fall within the Octave of Trinity Sunday, then the Antiphon to the Creed of St. Athanasius shall be O holy, blessed.

At Terce.

Antiphon.—They made signs to his father, how he would have him called: and he wrote saying, His name is John.

Chapter. Isaiah xlix. 1.

Listen, O isles, unto me, and hearken, ye people from far: the Lord hath called me from the womb, from the bowels of my mother hath He made mention of my name.

R. With glory and worship Thou hast crowned him, O Lord. V. Thou makest him to have dominion of the works of Thy hands. R. Thou hast crowned him, O Lord. V. Glory be. R. With glory.

V. Thou hast set upon his head, O Lord. *R.* A crown of pure gold.

Collect.

ALMIGHTY God, by Whose providence Thy servant John Baptist was wonderfully born, and sent to prepare the way of Thy Son our Saviour, by preaching of repentance; Make us so to follow his doctrine and holy life, that we may truly repent according to his teaching; and after his example constantly speak the truth, boldly rebuke vice, and patiently suffer for the truth's sake; through.   [1549].

Or this.

O GOD, Who hast made this day glorious by the nativity of blessed John; Grant to Thy servants the grace of spiritual joys, and guide the hearts of all Thy faithful people in the way that leadeth unto eternal life; through.

At Sext.

Antiphon.—Thou shalt call his name John: and many shall rejoice at his birth.

Chapter. Isaiah xlix. 5.

Thus saith the Lord that formed me from the womb to be His servant, I will give thee for a light to the Gentiles, that thou mayest be My salvation unto the end of the earth.

R. Thou hast set upon his head, O Lord. *V.* A crown of pure gold. *R.* Upon his head, O Lord. *V.* Glory be. *R.* Thou hast set.

V. The righteous shall flourish like a palm-tree, in the house of the Lord. *R.* And shall spread abroad like a cedar in Libanus.

At None.

Antiphon.—The child shall be great in the sight of the Lord: for His hand also is with him.

Chapter. Isaiah xlix. 7.

Kings shall see and arise, princes also shall worship the Lord thy God, and the Holy One of Israel Who hath chosen thee.

R. The righteous shall flourish like a palm tree, in the house of the Lord. *V.* He shall spread abroad like a cedar in Libanus. *R.* In the house of the Lord. *V.* Glory be. *R.* The righteous.

V. The righteous shall blossom as a lily. *R.* He shall flourish for ever before the Lord.

Through the Octaves, i.e. on June 25, 26, 27, 28, and on the Octave-day, July 1, the Service is all as on the Festival, except on the Sunday, when the Service is of the Sunday, with memorial of St. John.

JUNE 29.

ST. PETER AND ST. PAUL, APOSTLES AND MARTYRS.

LESSER DOUBLE.

No memorial of St. John is made at either Evensong or at Mattins.

At Compline.

All as on Trinity Sunday (see p. 108).

At Prime.

Antiphon.—Peter and John went up together into the temple: at the hour of prayer, being the ninth hour.

Antiphon. — Thanks be to Thee.

At Terce.

Antiphon.—Silver and gold have I none: but such as I have give I thee.

Chapter. Acts xii. 5.

Peter therefore was kept in prison; but prayer was made without ceasing of the Church to God for him.

R. Their sound is gone out into all lands. *V.* And their words into the ends of the world. *R.* Into all lands. *V.* Glory be. *R.* Their sound.

V. Thou shalt make them princes in all lands. *R.* They shall remember Thy Name, O Lord.

Collect.

O ALMIGHTY God, Who by Thy Son Jesus Christ didst give to Thine Apostle, Saint Peter, many excellent gifts, and commandest him earnestly to feed Thy flock; Make, we beseech Thee, all Bishops and Pastors diligently to preach Thy holy word, and the people obediently to follow the same, that they may receive the crown of everlasting glory; through. [1549.]

Or this.

O GOD, Who hast hallowed this day by the martyrdom of Thine Apostles Peter and Paul; Grant unto Thy Church in all things to follow their holy precepts, through whom she received the beginning of her religion; through.

At Sext.

Antiphon. — The angel said unto Peter: cast thy garment about thee, and follow me.

Chapter. Acts xii. 7.

And behold the angel of the Lord came upon him, and a light shined in the prison; and he smote Peter on the side, and raised him up, saying, Arise up quickly. And his chains fell off from his hands.

R. Thou shalt make them princes in all lands. *V.* They shall remember Thy Name, O Lord. *R.* In all lands. *V.* Glory be. *R.* Thou shalt make.

V. Great is the honour of Thy friends, O Lord. *R.* Great is the might of their dominion.

At None.

Antiphon.—Thou art Peter: and upon this rock I will build My Church.

Chapter. Acts xii. 9.

Peter went out and followed the angel, and wist not that it was true which was done by him; but thought he saw a vision.

R. Great is the honour of Thy friends, O Lord. *V.* Great is the might of their dominion. *R.* Of Thy friends, O Lord. *V.* Glory be. *R.* Great is.

V. They have declared the marvellous acts of God. *R.* They have also told of His greatness.

During the Octaves, if precedence be given to the Feast of the Apostles, the Service is all of the Common of Apostles, with Collect of the Proper; except on the Octave Day of St. John

THE VISITATION OF BLESSED MARY. 147

the Baptist; on the Feast of the Visitation, and the Feast of St. Martin. On the Sunday within the Octaves, if no other Feast fall on that day, the Service is of the Sunday, with memorial of the Apostles.

JUNE 30.

For the Proper Service of this day, see p. 175; but if the Commemoration of St. Paul be not observed, all the Service is as on the Feast of St. Peter, with a memorial of St. John Baptist.

JULY 1.
OCTAVE OF ST. JOHN THE BAPTIST.

All as on the Festival; unless the Octave fall on a Sunday, in which case the Service is of the Sunday, with memorials of St. John Baptist and of St. Peter and St. Paul.

JULY 2.
THE VISITATION OF BLESSED MARY.

GREATER DOUBLE.

At Compline.
All as in Compl. xxi., p. 108.

At Prime.
Antiphon.

The morn of grace now climbs the mountain height,
Bringing with brightness of celestial light
To righteous souls the Sun of righteousness,
The dawn of man's new day of blessedness.

At Terce.
Antiphon.

Now where the mothers meet with holy joy,
Prophesies speechlessly the herald boy;
E'en from the womb the servant hails his King,
And to the Child the child doth praises bring.

Chapter. Ecclus. xxiv. 18.

I am the mother of fair love, and fear, and knowledge, and holy hope: in me is all the grace of the way and the truth, in me is all the hope of life and virtue.

R. Full of grace are thy lips. V. Because God hath blessed thee for ever. R. Are thy lips. V. Glory be. R. Full of grace.

V. With thy glory and thy majesty. R. Go, ride prosperously, and reign.

Collect.

O GOD, Who didst cause the most holy Virgin Mary, mother of Thine only begotten Son, to visit blessed Elizabeth with the grace of mutual comfort; Mercifully grant to us Thy servants, that we may be comforted by His continual visitations, and sheltered from all adversities by Thy protecting power; through the same.

At Sext.
Antiphon.

The aged mother, great with child God-given,
Beholds the fleece wet with the Dew of heaven;

PROPER OF SAINTS.

Sees the bush burn with unconsuming flames;
The Rod of Jesse buds, Elizabeth proclaims.

Chapter. Canticles ii. 10.

Rise up, my love, my dove, my fair one, and come away; for lo! the winter is past, the rain is over and gone, the flowers appear on the earth, the time of singing birds is come.

R. With thy glory and thy majesty. *V.* Go, ride prosperously, and reign. *R.* With thy majesty. *V.* Glory be. *R.* With thy glory.

V. God hath given her the help of His countenance. *R.* God is in the midst of her, therefore shall she not be removed.

At None.

Antiphon.

Now full of grace, Mary the mother holy
Doth in her Saviour fervently rejoice,
Who hath regard unto His handmaid lowly,
Singing Magnificat with joyful voice.

Chapter. Canticles ii. 14.

Come, my dove, that art in the clefts of the rocks, in the secret places of the stairs, let me see thy countenance, let me hear thy voice; for sweet is thy voice, and thy countenance is comely.

R. God hath given her the help of His countenance. *V.* God is in the midst of her, therefore shall she not be removed.

R. The help of His countenance. *V.* Glory be. *R.* God hath given.

V. God hath elected her and pre-elected her. *R.* He hath made her to dwell in His tabernacle.

At Second Evensong is made a memorial of Sunday if it so happen.

Compline is said as is noted above, and the same daily throughout the Octaves, except on the Feast of St. Martin, and on the Octave of the Apostles, on which days all is said at Compline as on Trinity Sunday.

Throughout the Octaves, whenever the service is of the Visitation, all is done as within Octaves.

On the Sunday within the Octaves, if it be not occupied with a Feast of nine Lessons, at First Evensong memorials are made of the Sunday and of the Holy Trinity, and Procession before the Cross. In returning is sung the anthem of All Saints.

JULY 4.
THE TRANSLATION OF ST. MARTIN, BISHOP.

Feast of nine Lessons. All of the Common of a Confessor and Bishop, p. 117.

Collect.

O GOD, Who hast given blessed Martin to be a minister of eternal salvation to Thy people; Mercifully grant that, as he performed Thy commandments upon earth, so he may ever intercede for us in the heavens; through.

A memorial is made of the Apostles and of the Visitation.

ST. MARY MAGDALENE.

July 6.
OCTAVE OF ST. PETER AND ST. PAUL.

All of the Common of Apostles (see p.113) except the Collect, which is of the Proper (see p. 146), and the Chapters, which are as follows:

At Terce. *Chapter. Ecclus.* xliv. 10. These were merciful men, whose righteousness hath not been forgotten. With their seed shall continually remain a good inheritance, and their children are within the covenant.

At Sext. *Chapter. Ecclus.* xliv. 14. The bodies of the saints are buried in peace: but their name liveth for evermore.

At None. *Chapter. Ecclus.* xliv. 15. The people will tell of the wisdom of the saints, and all the Church will show forth their praise.

Memorial of the Visitation at both Evensongs and at Mattins.

July 9.
OCTAVE OF THE VISITATION OF BLESSED MARY.
All as on the Festival.

July 15.
TRANSLATION OF ST. SWITHUN AND HIS COMPANIONS, BISHOPS AND CONFESSORS.

Feast of nine Lessons. All of the Common of many Confessors (see p. 115), with the following Collect:

Collect.

O ALMIGHTY and everlasting God, Who hast made this day glorious by the translation of blessed Swithun, Thy Confessor and Bishop, and his companions; Grant to Thy Church to rejoice in this feast; that as we venerate their solemnity on earth, so we may be aided by their intercessions in heaven; through.

July 20.
ST. MARGARET, VIRGIN AND MARTYR.

Feast of nine Lessons. All of the Common of a Virgin and Martyr (see p. 119).

Collect.

O GOD, Who on this day didst cause Thy blessed virgin Margaret to attain to heaven by the Martyr's palm; Grant us, we pray Thee, so to follow her example, that we may be worthy to be admitted into Thy presence; through.

July 22.
ST. MARY MAGDALENE.
Feast of nine Lessons.

At Prime.

Antiphon.—With high praises all the world exults on this solemnity of St. Mary Magdalene.
Antiphon. — Thee all Thy creatures.

At Terce.

Antiphon.—Mary anoints the Lord, receiving Him with sincere heart, and is by Him purified by the holy fount of baptism.

Chapter. Proverbs xxxi. 10. Who can find a virtuous woman? for her price is far above rubies.

The heart of her husband doth safely trust in her, so that he shall have no need of spoil.

R. Full of grace are thy lips. *V.* Because God hath blessed thee for ever. *R.* Are thy lips. *V.* Glory be. *R.* Full of grace.

V. With thy glory and thy majesty. *R.* Go, ride prosperously, and reign.

Collect.

GRANT, O most merciful Father, that as blessed Mary Magdalene, loving Thine only begotten Son above all things, did obtain pardon of her sins, so by her prayers she may procure from Thy mercy eternal blessedness for us; through the same.

At Sext.

Antiphon.—Pray for us sinners, Mary, who by thy tears didst obtain the washing away of thine own sins.

Chapter. Proverbs xxxi. 17.

She girdeth her loins with strength, and strengtheneth her arms. She perceiveth that her merchandise is good: her candle goeth not out by night.

R. With thy glory and thy majesty. *V.* Go, ride prosperously, and reign. *R.* With thy majesty. *V.* Glory be. *R.* With thy.

V. God hath given her the help of His countenance. *R.* God is in the midst of her, therefore shall she not be removed.

At None.

Antiphon.—Intercede earnestly for us with Jesus the Lord, Mary Magdalene.

Chapter. Proverbs xxxi. 30.

A woman that feareth the Lord, she shall be praised. Give her of the fruit of her hands, and let her own works praise her in the gates.

R. God hath given her the help of His countenance. *V.* God is in the midst of her, therefore shall she not be removed. *R.* The help of His countenance. *V.* Glory be. *R.* God hath given.

V. The virgins that be her fellows shall bear her company. *R.* And shall be brought unto Thee.

JULY 25.
ST. JAMES, APOSTLE.
DOUBLE FEAST.

All of the Common of Apostles, p. 113.

Collect.

GRANT, O merciful God, that as Thy holy apostle Saint James, leaving his father and all that he had, without delay, was obedient unto the calling of Thy Son Jesus Christ, and followed Him; so we, forsaking all carnal and worldly affections, may be evermore ready to follow Thy holy commandments; through. [1549.]

Or this.

BE Thou, O Lord, the Sanctifier and Guardian of Thy people; that defended by the prayers of Thy apostle James, they may please Thee in all manner of conversation, and serve Thee without fear; through.

At Second Evensong a memorial is made of St. Anne.

ST. ANNE, THE MOTHER OF MARY.

July 26.

ST. ANNE, THE MOTHER OF MARY.

Feast of nine Lessons. When a church, or chapel, or altar is dedicated in honour of St. Anne, then First Evensong is of St. Anne, with a memorial of St. James. Otherwise Evensong is of St. James, with memorial of St. Anne.

At Compline.

All as on Trinity Sunday. Compl. xviii.

At Prime.

Antiphon.

Lo, the choir of saints her praises
Sing, who bore the maiden mild,
Of whose virgin womb proceeding
Sprang the wondrous Child.

Antiphon. — Thanks be to Thee.

At Terce.

Antiphon.

She for offspring now devoutly
Asketh of the God of light;
God be praiséd! she conceiveth
Mary, Virgin bright.

Chapter, Responsory, and Verse, as at Terce on the Feast of St. Mary Magdalene, p. 149.

Collect.

O GOD, Who on this day didst exalt blessed Anne, who gloriously bare Thy well-beloved Mother, to the bliss of the heavenly life; Grant us, we pray Thee, by the assistance of her prayers to attain to eternal blessedness, of whose offspring Thou didst will to take human flesh for the world's salvation, Who livest and reignest.

At Sext.

Antiphon.

Joachim is Mary's father,
Anna is the mother mild,
And the Lord of life and glory
Mary's holy Child.

Chapter. Proverbs xxxi. 29.

Many daughters have laid up riches, but thou excellest them all; favour is deceitful, and beauty is vain, but a woman that feareth the Lord she shall be praised.

R. With thy glory, etc.

R. and V. as on the Feast of St. Mary Magdalene.

At None.

Antiphon.

Anna shineth as a lily
In the heavenly palace bright;
She hath gained a throne of glory
'Mid the immortal light.

Chapter. Proverbs xxxi. 20.

She stretcheth out her hand to the poor; yea, she reacheth forth her hands to the needy; strength and honour are her clothing, and she shall rejoice in time to come.

R. God hath given her the help of His countenance. V. God is in the midst of her, therefore shall she not be removed. R. The help of His countenance. V. Glory be. R. God hath given.

V. God hath elected her and pre-elected her. R. He hath made her to dwell in His tabernacle.

August 1.
ST. PETER'S CHAINS.
[Lammas Day.]

Feast of nine Lessons.

At Prime.

Antiphon.—The angel of the Lord came upon him, and a light shined in the prison: and he smote Peter on the side, and raised him up, saying, Arise up quickly.

Antiphon. — Thee all Thy creatures.

At Terce.

Antiphon. — The angel said unto Peter: Cast thy garment about thee, and follow me.

Chapter. Acts xii. 5.

Peter therefore was kept in prison: but prayer was made without ceasing of the Church unto God for him.

R. Their sound is gone out into all lands. V. And their words into the ends of the world. R. Into all lands. V. Glory be. R. Their sound.

V. Thou shalt make them princes in all lands. R. They shall remember Thy Name, O Lord.

Collect.

O GOD, Who didst loose Thy blessed Apostle Peter from his chains, and madest him to depart without hurt; Loose us, we beseech Thee, from the chain of our sins, and of Thy mercy deliver us from all evil; through.

At Sext.

Antiphon. — Peter went out and followed him: and wist not that it was true which was done by the angel.

Chapter. Acts xii. 7.

The angel of the Lord came upon him, and a light shined in the prison: and he smote Peter on the side, and raised him up, saying, Arise up quickly. And his chains fell off from his hands.

R. Thou shalt make them princes in all lands. V. They shall remember Thy Name, O Lord. R. In all lands. V. Glory be. R. Thou shalt make.

V. Great is the honour of Thy friends, O Lord. R. Great is the might of their dominion.

At None.

Antiphon. — Peter, at God's commanding, break the bondage of this world; Thou that dost open the gates of heavenly realms to the blessed.

Chapter. Acts xii. 9.

Peter went out, and followed the angel; and wist not that it was true which was done by him; but thought he saw a vision.

R. Great is the honour of Thy friends, O Lord. V. Great is the might of their dominion. R. Of Thy friends, O Lord. V. Glory be. R. Great is.

V. They have declared the marvellous acts of God. R. They have also told of His greatness.

TRANSFIGURATION OF JESUS CHRIST OUR LORD.

August 6.
THE TRANSFIGURATION OF JESUS CHRIST OUR LORD.
LESSER DOUBLE.

At Prime.

Antiphon.—The disciples fell on their face, and were sore afraid at the Divine Voice: and Jesus came and touched them, and said, Arise, be not afraid.

At Terce.

Antiphon. — Jesus came and touched His disciples as they lay, and said, Arise, be not afraid: and when they had lifted up their eyes, they saw no man, save Jesus only.

Chapter. Philippians iii. 20.

We look for the Saviour, the Lord Jesus Christ: who shall change our vile body, that it may be fashioned like unto His glorious Body, according to His working whereby He is able even to subdue all things unto Himself.

R. Let us adore the Father and the Son with the Holy Ghost. Alleluia! Alleluia! V. Reigning in His majesty. R. Alleluia! Alleluia! V. Glory be. R. Let us adore.

V. A blessed day hath shined unto us. R. O come, all ye nations, and worship the Lord.

Collect.

O GOD, Who on this day didst from heaven reveal Thine only begotten Son, wonderfully transfigured, to the fathers of both Covenants; Grant us, we beseech Thee, that all our actions being made well-pleasing unto Thee, we may attain to the eternal contemplation of His glory, in whom Thou hast declared Thyself well-pleased; through the same.

At Sext.

Antiphon. — The Lord hath manifested Himself in His Transfiguration betwixt Moses and Elias: that He might receive witness from the Law and the Prophets.

Chapter. 2 Peter i. 16.

We made known unto you the power and coming of our Lord Jesus Christ, having been eye-witnesses of His majesty.

R. A blessed day hath shined unto us. Alleluia! Alleluia!
V. O come, all ye nations, and worship the Lord. R. Alleluia! Alleluia! V. Glory be. R. A blessed day.

V. Let us worship the Lord. R. In His holy temple.

At None.

Antiphon. — As they came down from the mountain, Jesus charged them, saying, Tell the vision to no man, until the Son of man be risen again from the dead.

Chapter. 2 Peter i. 17.

The Lord Jesus received from God the Father honour and glory, when there came such a voice to Him from the excellent glory, This is My beloved Son, in whom I am well pleased.

R. Let us worship the Lord.

Alleluia! Alleluia! *V.* In His holy temple. *R.* Alleluia! Alleluia! *V.* Glory be. *R.* Let us worship.
V. Worship the Lord. *R.* All ye angels of His.

AUGUST 7.

THE FEAST OF THE MOST SWEET NAME OF JESUS.
GREATER DOUBLE.

Octaves with rulers.

First Ebensong of the Holy Name, with solemn memorial of the Transfiguration.

At Compline.

Antiphon over the Psalms.—Have mercy upon me, O Lord: as Thou usest to do unto those that love Thy Name.

Hymn.

Now let the choir of the Lord, etc., *with the following doxology:*

These sacred titles
To Jesus belong.
All praise to the Saviour.
Amen.

Antiphon over Nunc Dimittis.—O King, glorious amid Thy saints, Who art ever to be adored, yet of majesty ineffable; Thou, Lord, art in the midst of us, and we are called by Thy Name; leave us not, O our God: and in the day of judgment vouchsafe to number us among Thy saints, O King most blessed.

Compline is said thus throughout the Octaves, whenever the Service is of the Holy Name.

At Prime.

Doxology.

All glory, Virgin born, to Thee,
Jesus, Incarnate Deity,
Whom with the Father we adore,
And Holy Ghost for evermore.

And so shall all the Hymns end throughout the Octaves, when the service is of the Holy Name, except at Compline.

Antiphon.—His Name was called Jesus: which was so named of the angel before He was conceived in the womb. Alleluia!

Chapter. 1 *Timothy* i. 17.

Now unto the King, Eternal, Immortal, Invisible, the only wise God, be honour and glory for ever and ever. Amen.

R. Jesu Christ, Son of the living God, have mercy upon us. Alleluia! Alleluia! *V.* Thou that didst not abhor the Virgin's womb. *R.* Have mercy upon us. Alleluia! Alleluia! *V.* Glory be to the Father, and to the Son, and to the Holy Ghost. *R.* Jesu Christ, Son of the living God, have mercy upon us. Alleluia! Alleluia!

V. O Lord, arise, help us. *R.* And deliver us for Thy Name's sake.

Petitions as usual.

At Terce.

Antiphon.—O praise the Name of our Lord Jesus Christ, because it is lovely: and His mercy endureth for ever. Alleluia!

Chapter. 1 *Corinthians* i. 2.

To all that in every place call upon the Name of Jesus Christ

THE FEAST OF THE MOST SWEET NAME OF JESUS.

our Lord, both theirs and ours; grace be unto you, and peace, from God our Father, and from the Lord Jesus Christ.

R. I will praise the Name of the Lord: with a song. Alleluia! Alleluia! V. And magnify it with thanksgiving. R. Alleluia! Alleluia! V. Glory be. R. I will praise.

V. Praise the Lord, O my soul. R. And all that is within me, praise His holy Name.

Collect.

O GOD, who hast made the most glorious Name of Thy only begotten Son, Jesus Christ, to be sweet and lovely to Thy faithful people, but full of terror to evil spirits; Mercifully grant that all who devoutly venerate this Name of Jesus upon earth, may enjoy the sweetness of holy consolation in this present world, and in the world to come may attain glory of everlasting bliss; through the same.

At Sext.

Antiphon.—As long as I live will I magnify Thee, O Lord Jesus: and lift up my hands in Thy Name. Alleluia!

Chapter. Colossians iii. 17.

Whatsoever ye do in word or deed, do all in the Name of the Lord Jesus, giving thanks to God and the Father by Him.

R. Praise the Lord: O my soul. Alleluia! Alleluia! V. And all that is within me, praise His holy Name. R. Alleluia! Alleluia! V. Glory be. R. Praise.

V. Not unto us, O Lord, not unto us. R. But unto Thy Name give the praise.

At None.

Antiphon.—Young men and maidens, old men and children, praise the Name of the Lord: for His Name only is excellent. Alleluia!

Chapter. 2 Thessalonians iii. 6.

Now we command you, brethren, in the Name of our Lord Jesus Christ, that ye withdraw yourselves from every brother that walketh disorderly, and not after the tradition which he received of us.

R. Not unto us, O Lord: not unto us. Alleluia! Alleluia! V. But unto Thy Name give the praise. R. Alleluia! Alleluia! V. Glory be. R. Not unto us.

V. Blessed be the Name of the Lord Jesus. R. From this time forth for evermore.

The Octaves of the Holy Name should be kept as follows: **Second Day,** Of the Constitution of the Name Jesus: *i.e. the mystical significance of the syllables and letters of the Holy Name.* **Third Day,** Of the Hallowing of the Name Jesus. **Fourth Day,** Feast of St. Laurence, Martyr. **Fifth Day,** Of the Delineation of the Name Jesus: *i.e. the mystery of its inscription on the foreheads of the elect, etc.* **Sixth Day,** Of the Pre-announcement of the Name Jesus. **Seventh Day,** Feast of St. Hippolytus and his companions. **Octave** of the Holy Name.

During the Octaves, when the service is of the Holy Name, all is said as on the Festival, except that at Prime the Antiphon to the Creed of St. Athanasius and the chapter are said as within Octaves.

No Common Memorials are made, because the Octaves have rulers.

On the Sunday within the Octaves, if no other Feast fall on that day, the service is of the Holy Name with memorial of the Sunday.

On the Octave-day all the service is as on the Festival, with memorial of St. Laurence.

AUGUST 10.
ST. LAURENCE, MARTYR.

Feast of nine Lessons.
First Evensong of St. Laurence, with memorial of the Holy Name.
Memorial of the Holy Name is made at both Evensongs, Mattins, and Mass.

At Prime.

Antiphon.—Laurence the martyr entered into the fire: and confessed the Name of our Lord Jesus Christ.

At Terce.

Antiphon.—Laurence wrought a good work: who by the cross of Christ enlightened the blind.

Chapter. 2 Corinthians ix. 6.

He which soweth sparingly shall reap also sparingly; and he which soweth bountifully shall reap also bountifully.

R. With glory and worship: Thou hast crowned him, O Lord. *V.* Thou makest him to have dominion of the works of Thy hands. *R.* Thou hast crowned him, O Lord. *V.* Glory be. *R.* With glory.

V. Thou hast set upon his head, O Lord. *R.* A crown of pure gold.

Collect.

GRANT us, we beseech Thee, Almighty God, to extinguish the flames of our evil passions; like as Thou didst enable blessed Laurence to overcome the fires of torture; through.

At Sext.

Antiphon.—My soul cleaveth unto Thee: for my flesh is burned in the fire for Thee, my God.

Chapter. 2 Corinthians ix. 8.

God indeed is able to make all grace abound toward you; that ye always having all sufficiency in all things, may abound to every good work; as it is written, He hath dispersed abroad; he hath given to the poor: his righteousness remaineth for ever.

R. Thou hast set: upon his head, O Lord. *V.* A crown of pure gold. *R.* Upon his head, O Lord. *V.* Glory be. *R.* Thou hast set.

V. The righteous shall flourish like a palm tree, in the house of the Lord. *R.* And shall spread abroad like a cedar in Libanus.

At None.

Antiphon.—Blessed Laurence prayed: saying, Thanks be to Thee, O Lord, for that Thou hast counted me worthy to enter into Thy gates.

Chapter. 2 Corinthians ix. 10.

Now he that ministereth seed to the sower, both minister bread for your food, and multiply your seed sown, and increase the fruits of your righteousness.

R. The righteous shall flourish like a palm-tree : in the house of the Lord. *V.* He shall spread abroad like a cedar in Libanus. *R.* In the house of the Lord. *V.* Glory be. *R.* The righteous.
V. The righteous shall blossom as a lily. *R.* He shall flourish for ever before the Lord.

At Second Evensong a memorial of the Holy Name is made; and if it be Sunday, a memorial of Sunday and of the Trinity.
The Octave of St. Laurence is observed with a memorial only.

AUGUST 14.
OCTAVE OF THE HOLY NAME JESUS.

All as on the Festival, with memorial of St. Laurence; and if it fall on Sunday, then memorials of Sunday and of the Trinity are made.

AUGUST 24.
ST. BARTHOLOMEW, APOSTLE.
DOUBLE FEAST.

All of the Common of Apostles, p. 113.

Collect.

O ALMIGHTY and everlasting God, Who didst give to Thine apostle Bartholomew grace truly to believe and to preach Thy Word ; Grant, we beseech Thee, unto Thy Church to love that Word which he believed, and both to preach and receive the same ; through.

AUGUST 28.
ST. AUGUSTINE, BISHOP, CONFESSOR, AND DOCTOR.
INFERIOR DOUBLE.

All of the Common of a Confessor and Bishop, p. 117, with the following Chapters and Collect.

AT TERCE. *Ecclus.* xlvii. 8. In all his works he praised the Holy One most High with words of glory; with his whole heart he sang songs and loved Him that made him.

AT SEXT. *Chapter. Ecclus.* xlvii. 9. The Lord gave him strength against his enemies; he set singers also before the altar, that by their voices they might make sweet melody.

AT NONE. *Chapter. Ecclus.* xxiv. 1. Wisdom shall praise herself, and shall glory in the midst of her people. In the congregation of the Most High shall she open her mouth, and triumph before His power.

Collect.

O GOD, Who didst give blessed Augustine to be to Thy Church a catholic doctor in expounding the mysteries of Holy Writ ; Grant to us both to be instructed by his doctrine and strengthened by his prayers evermore ; through.

At Second Evensong solemn memorial of St. John is made.
But if the Church be dedicated in honour of the Beheading of St. John, then Evensong is of St. John with memorial of St. Augustine.

August 29.
BEHEADING OF ST. JOHN THE BAPTIST.
Feast of nine Lessons.

At Prime.

Antiphon.—Herod laid hold on John and bound him, and put him in prison for Herodias' sake.

At Terce.

Antiphon.—Her mother commanded the dancing girl: ask for nothing but the head of John.

Chapter. Proverbs x. 28.

The hope of the righteous shall be gladness: but the expectation of the wicked shall perish. The way of the Lord is strength to the upright: but destruction shall be to the workers of iniquity.

R. With glory and worship Thou hast crowned him, O Lord. *V.* Thou makest him to have dominion of the works of Thy hands. *R.* Thou hast crowned him, O Lord. *V.* Glory be. *R.* With glory.

V. Thou hast set upon his head, O Lord. *R.* A crown of pure gold.

Collect.

GRANT, O Lord, we pray Thee, that as we celebrate the Feast of St. John Baptist Thy martyr, so we may by his assistance attain to everlasting salvation; through.

At Sext.

Antiphon.—My Lord King: give me here John Baptist's head in a charger.

Chapter. Proverbs x. 30.

The righteous shall never be removed: but the wicked shall not inhabit the earth.

R. Thou hast set: upon his head, O Lord. *V.* A crown of pure gold. *R.* Upon his head, O Lord. *V.* Glory be. *R.* Thou hast set.

V. The righteous shall flourish like a palm-tree in the house of the Lord. *R.* And shall spread abroad like a cedar in Libanus.

At None.

Antiphon.—The king sent: and beheaded John Baptist.

Chapter. Proverbs xi. 8.

The righteous is delivered out of trouble, and the wicked cometh in his stead.

R. The righteous shall flourish like a palm-tree: in the house of the Lord. *V.* He shall spread abroad like a cedar in Libanus. *R.* In the house of the Lord. *V.* Glory be. *R.* The righteous.

V. The righteous shall blossom as a lily. *R.* He shall flourish for ever before the Lord.

September 1.
ST. GILES, ABBAT.

Feast of nine Lessons. All of the Common of a Confessor and Abbat (see p. 117).

Collect.

O GOD, Who on this day didst vouchsafe to blessed Giles Thy confessor and abbat to enter the courts of Thy heavenly kingdom; Grant, we pray Thee, that we who rejoice in his merits, may ever be strengthened by his prayers; through.

If this Festival fall on a Sunday, it is transferred to the morrow.

NATIVITY OF THE BLESSED VIRGIN MARY. 159

SEPTEMBER 7.
ST. EVURTIUS, BISHOP AND CONFESSOR.
All of the Common of a Bishop and Confessor, p. 117.

SEPTEMBER 8.
NATIVITY OF THE BLESSED VIRGIN MARY.
GREATER DOUBLE.

At Compline.

All as in Compl. xxii.
This Compline is said daily throughout the Octaves, except on the Feast of the Exaltation of the Holy Cross.

At Prime.

Antiphon.—To-day is the Nativity of holy Mary the Virgin: whose glorious life doth lighten all the churches.

At Terce.

Antiphon.—The Nativity of the glorious Virgin Mary born of the seed of Abraham, of the tribe of Judah, of the mighty stock of David.

Chapter. Ecclus. xxiv. 17.

As the vine brought I forth pleasant savour, and my flowers are the fruit of honour and riches.

R. Holy mother of God ever Virgin Mary. V. Intercede for us with the Lord our God. R. Ever Virgin Mary. V. Glory be. R. Holy mother.

V. After child-bearing thou remainedst a pure virgin. R. O mother of God, pray for us.

Collect.

O GOD of all mercy, hear the supplication of us Thy servants: and grant that we, who are gathered together on this feast of the Nativity of the virgin mother of God, at her intercession may by Thee be delivered from all dangers that beset us; through the same.

At Sext.

Antiphon.—Glorious is Mary, born of a royal house: by whose prayers, with heart and soul's devotion, we beseech protection.

Chapter. Ecclus. xxiv. 19.

Come unto me, all ye that be desirous of me, and fill yourselves with my fruits: for my memorial is sweeter than honey, and mine inheritance than the honeycomb.

R. After child-bearing thou remainedst a pure virgin. V. O mother of God, pray for us. R. Thou remainedst a pure virgin. V. Glory be. R. After child-bearing.

V. Thou art become fair and pleasant. R. In thy delights, O holy mother of God.

At None.

Antiphon. — With joyfulness we celebrate the Nativity of blessed Mary: that she may pray for us with Jesus Christ the Lord.

Chapter. Ecclus. xxiv. 22.

He that obeyeth me shall never be confounded, and they that work by me shall not do amiss, and they that seek me shall have life eternal.

R. Thou art become fair and pleasant. V. In thy delights, O holy mother of God. R. Fair and pleasant. V. Glory be. R. Thou art become.
V. God hath elected her and pre-elected her. R. He hath made her to dwell in His tabernacle.

And so the service is performed throughout the Octaves, except on the Exaltation of the Holy Cross.
On Sunday within the Octaves memorials are made of the Sunday and of the Trinity.

SEPTEMBER 14.
EXALTATION OF THE HOLY CROSS.
LESSER DOUBLE.

At Compline.

All as on Trinity Sunday Compl. xviii.

At Prime.

Antiphon.—O mighty work of love: death then was done to death, when Life hung dead upon the tree.
Antiphon. — Thanks be to Thee.
Chapter. Now unto the King eternal.
R. Jesu Christ, Son of the living God: have mercy upon us. Alleluia! Alleluia! V. Thou that sittest at the right hand of the Father. R. Have mercy upon us. Alleluia! Alleluia! V. Glory be. R. Jesu Christ.
V. O Lord, arise, help us. R. And deliver us for Thy mercy's sake.
Petitions as usual.

At Terce.

Antiphon.—Behold the Cross of the Lord; flee away, ye adversaries: the Lion of the tribe of Judah, the Root of David, hath conquered. Alleluia!
Chapter. Galatians vi. 14.
God forbid that I should glory save in the Cross of our Lord Jesus Christ, by Whom the world is crucified unto me, and I unto the world.
R. This sign of the Cross shall be in heaven: Alleluia! Alleluia! V. When the Lord shall come to judgment. R. Alleluia! Alleluia! V. Glory be. R. This sign.
V. Tell it out among the heathen. R. That the Lord hath reigned from the tree. Alleluia!

Collect.

O GOD, Who by the precious blood of Thine only begotten Son, Jesus Christ our Lord, hast vouchsafed to redeem the human race; Mercifully grant, that they who venerate the life-giving Cross may be freed from the bands of their sins; through the same.

At Sext.

Antiphon.—O wondrous Cross: healer of wounds, restorer of health.
Chapter. 1 *Corinthians* i. 18.
The preaching of the Cross is to them that perish foolishness; but unto us which are saved it is the power of God.

ST. MATTHEW, APOSTLE AND EVANGELIST.

R. Tell it out among the heathen: Alleluia! Alleluia! *V.* That the Lord hath reigned from the tree. *R.* Alleluia! Alleluia! *V.* Glory be. *R.* Tell it out.

V. We adore Thee, O Christ, and we bless Thee. *R.* Because by Thy cross Thou hast redeemed the world. Alleluia!

At None.

Antiphon.—The blessed Cross shines forth, whereon hung the Incarnate Lord: and with His own Blood washed our wounds.

Chapter. 1 *Corinthians* i. 23.

Now we preach Christ crucified, unto the Jews a stumbling-block, and unto the Greeks foolishness; but unto them which are called, both Jews and Greeks, Christ the power of God and the wisdom of God.

R. We adore Thee, O Christ, and we bless Thee: Alleluia! Alleluia! *V.* Because by Thy cross Thou hast redeemed the world. *R.* Alleluia! Alleluia! *V.* Glory be. *R.* We adore.

V. Let all the earth worship Thee, O God. *R.* Sing of Thee, and praise Thy Name. Alleluia!

If this Feast fall on Sunday, then at both Evensongs and at Mattins, the memorial of the Sunday is made silently, with Mass in Chapter on the morrow. Also at the same the memorial of the Trinity is made silently.

At Mattins and Second Evensong a solemn memorial of holy Mary is made.

At Compline, all as on Trinity Sunday.

SEPTEMBER 15.
OCTAVE OF THE NATIVITY.

SEPTEMBER 17.
ST. LAMBERT, BISHOP AND MARTYR.

Feast of three Lessons. All of the Common of a Martyr and Bishop (see p. 114).

Collect.

O LORD, we pray Thee, hear the prayers which Thy Martyr and Bishop St. Lambert offers before Thee for us; and as on this day are celebrated his glorious sufferings, so grant us ever to be defended by his prayers; through.

If the Feast of St. Lambert fall on a Sunday, a memorial is made of him at First Evensong and Mattins.
If this Feast or any other of Three Lessons fall on any Feria in Embertide, then Mattins is of the Feast and Mass of the Fast.
If the Feast of St. Lambert fall on a Saturday, then on Sunday Evensong is of St. Mary, with her full service on the morrow.

SEPTEMBER 21.
ST. MATTHEW, APOSTLE AND EVANGELIST.
INFERIOR DOUBLE.

At Compline.

All as on the Feast of the Holy Trinity. Compl. xviii.

At Prime.

Antiphon. — Beloved of God and men are the holy evangelists: who all their lives through with sweet savour adorned the times of Christ.

Antiphon.—Thanks be to Thee.

At Terce.

Antiphon. — The saints have made the glory of their work to be celebrated: therefore their memory is blessed for evermore.

Chapter. Ezekiel i. 10.

As for the likeness of their faces, they four had the face of a man, and the face of a lion on the right side: and they four had the face of an ox on the left side; they four also had the face of an eagle.

R. Their sound is gone out into all lands. *V.* And their words into the ends of the world. *R.* Into all lands. *V.* Glory be. *R.* Their sound.

V. Thou shalt make them princes in all lands. *R.* They shall remember Thy Name, O Lord.

Collect.

O ALMIGHTY GOD, Who by Thy blessed Son didst call Matthew from the receipt of custom to be an Apostle and Evangelist; Grant us grace to forsake all covetous desires, and inordinate love of riches, and to follow the same; Who liveth.

[1549]

Or this.

LORD, grant us Thy aid at the prayers of Thy blessed Apostle and Evangelist Matthew; and what we for our unworthiness cannot obtain, vouchsafe to give us at his intercession; through.

At Sext.

Antiphon.—With their whole heart they praised the holy Name of the Lord: to magnify the Name of His holiness.

Chapter. Ezekiel i. 13.

As for the likeness of the living creatures, their appearance was like burning coals of fire, and like the appearance of lamps.

R. Thou shalt make them princes in all lands. *V.* They shall remember Thy Name, O Lord. *R.* In all lands. *V.* Glory be. *R.* Thou shalt.

V. Great is the honour of Thy friends, O Lord. *R.* Great is the might of their dominion.

At None.

Antiphon.—Their work was wrought in truth: therefore in their land they shall possess double; and they shall have everlasting joy in Christ.

Chapter. Ezekiel i. 13.

The likeness went up and down among the living creatures; and the fire was bright, and out of the fire went forth lightning. And the living creatures ran and returned as the appearance of a flash of lightning.

R. Great is the honour: of Thy friends, O Lord. *V.* Great is the might of their dominion. *R.* Of Thy friends, O Lord. *V.* Glory be. *R.* Great is.

V. They have declared the marvellous acts of God. *R.* They have also told of His greatness.

SEPTEMBER 26.

ST. CYPRIAN AND ST. JUSTINA, MARTYRS.

Feast of three Lessons. All of the Common of Many Martyrs, p. 115.

ST. MICHAEL, ARCHANGEL.

SEPTEMBER 29.
ST. MICHAEL, ARCHANGEL.
INFERIOR DOUBLE.

At Compline.

All as on the Feast of the Holy Trinity. Compline xviii.

At Prime.

Antiphon. — While Michael the Archangel fought with the Dragon: a voice was heard, saying, Salvation to our God. Alleluia!

Antiphon. — Thanks be to Thee.

Chapter. 1 *Timothy* i.
Now unto the King eternal.

V. Jesu Christ, Son of the living God, have mercy upon us. Alleluia! Alleluia! *V.* Thou that sittest at the right hand of God. *R.* Have mercy upon us. Alleluia! Alleluia! *V.* Glory be. *R.* Jesu Christ.

V. O Lord, arise, help us. *R.* And deliver us for Thy Name's sake.

At Terce.

Antiphon.—While the Dragon did battle with Michael the Archangel: the voice of thousands of thousands was heard saying, Salvation to our God.

Chapter. Revelation i. 1.
God sent and signified by His angel what must shortly come to pass, unto His servant John: who bare record of the Word of God, and of the testimony of Jesus Christ, and of all things that he saw.

R. An angel stood by the altar of the temple : Alleluia! Alleluia! *V.* Having a golden censer in his hand. *R.* Alleluia! Alleluia! *V.* Glory be. *R.* An angel.

V. The smoke of the incense ascended up. *R.* Before God out of the angel's hand.

Collect.

O EVERLASTING GOD, Who hast ordained and constituted the services of Angels and men in a wonderful order; Mercifully grant, that as Thy holy Angels alway do Thee service in heaven, so by Thy appointment they may succour and defend us on earth; through.

At Sext.

Antiphon.—O Archangel Michael, I have constituted thee chief over all souls that need succour.

Chapter. Revelation xii. 7.
There was war in heaven: Michael and his angels fought against the Dragon; and the Dragon fought and his angels, and prevailed not; neither was their place found any more in heaven.

R. The smoke of the incense ascended up: Alleluia! Alleluia! *V.* Before God out of the angel's hand. *R.* Alleluia! Alleluia! *V.* Glory be. *R.* The smoke.

V. In the presence of the angels will I sing praise unto Thee, my God. *R.* I will worship toward Thy holy temple, and praise Thy Name.

At None.

Antiphon. — Angels, Archangels, Thrones, and Dominions, Principalities, and Powers, Virtues of heaven: praise ye the Lord from heaven. Alleluia!

Chapter. Rev. viii. 1; xii. 7.

There was silence in heaven, while the Dragon did battle, and Michael fought with him and gained the victory.

R. In the presence of the angels will I sing praise unto Thee, my God: Alleluia! Alleluia! *V.* I will worship toward Thy holy temple, and will praise Thy Name. *R.* Alleluia! Alleluia! *V.* Glory be to the Father, and to the Son, and to the Holy Ghost. *R.* In the presence of the angels will I sing praise unto Thee, my God. Alleluia! Alleluia!

V. Praise the Lord, all ye angels of His. *R.* Praise Him, all His host.

On this day Evensong shall be of St. Jerome, Confessor and Doctor, with solemn memorial of St. Michael: unless the Church be dedicated to St. Michael, in which case only a solemn memorial shall be made of St. Jerome.

At Compline.

All as on the Feast of the Holy Trinity. Compl. xviii.

SEPTEMBER 30.

ST. JEROME, PRIEST, CONFESSOR, AND DOCTOR.

INFERIOR DOUBLE.

All of the Common of a Confessor and Doctor (see p. 117), with antiphon to the Creed of Athanasius, Thanks be to Thee.

Collect.

O GOD, Who didst give us blessed Jerome, Thy Confessor and Priest, to set forth the verities of Holy Writ and its sacred mysteries; Grant, we pray Thee, that as we keep his solemnity, so we may ever be instructed by his teaching, and helped by his merits; through.

OCTOBER 1.

SS. REMIGIUS, GERMANUS, VEDASTUS, AND BAVO, BISHOPS AND CONFESSORS.

Feast of nine Lessons. All of the Common of Many Confessors and Bishops (see p. 115).

Collect.

HEAR the prayer of Thy people, O Lord, who invoke Thy holy Confessors and Bishops, Remigius, Germanus, Vedastus, and Bavo; and grant us both to enjoy peace in our earthly life, and rest in the life to come; through.

OCTOBER 6.

ST. FAITH, VIRGIN AND MARTYR.

Feast of three Lessons. All of the Common of a Virgin and Martyr (see p. 119).

Collect.

O GOD, Who hast consecrated this day by the martyrdom of Thy blessed Virgin Faith; Grant to Thy Church both to rejoice in her merits, and to profit by her prayers; through.

October 9.
ST. DENYS AND HIS COMPANIONS, MARTYRS.

Feast of nine Lessons. All of the Common of Many Martyrs (see p. 115), with the following Antiphons and Collect.

At Prime.

Antiphon.—These holy men would never brook to be out of the presence of blessed Denys: the questions of the persecutor found them all of one mind.

At Terce.

Antiphon.—Abiding therefore constant in the faith, they committed their bodies to the earth, and for their blessed souls won an entrance into heaven.

At Sext.

Antiphon.—By so mighty a confession did they win grace to depart to the Lord, that even after they had been beheaded their tongues did seem to confess His name.

At None.

Antiphon.—And the multitude of the heavenly host did accompany the lifeless body of blessed Denys carrying his own head, praising God, and saying, Glory be to Thee, O Lord.

Collect.

O GOD, Who on this day didst strengthen blessed Denys with the virtue of constancy under suffering, and didst vouchsafe to associate with him Rusticus and Eleuthesius in declaring Thy glory to the Gentiles; Grant us, we beseech Thee, grace so to follow their examples, that for love of Thee we may neither fear the enmity of the world nor court its favour; through.

October 13.
TRANSLATION OF ST. EDWARD, KING AND CONFESSOR.
INFERIOR DOUBLE.

At Compline.

All as on the Feast of the Holy Trinity. Compl. xviii.

At the Hours the service is all as on the Feast of a Confessor and Abbot (see p. 117), but the alternative chapters are said.

Collect.

O GOD, Who hast crowned Thy blessed Confessor King Edward with eternal glory; Grant that we who venerate him on earth may attain to reign with him in heaven; through.

October 17.
TRANSLATION OF ST. ETHELDREDA, VIRGIN NOT A MARTYR.

All of the Common of a Virgin not a Martyr (see p. 119).

Collect.

O GOD, Who art the Spouse of virgin souls, the refreshment of the pure in heart, and the salvation of all who love Thee; Mercifully grant, that we who celebrate the feast of the

PROPER OF SAINTS.

Translation of Thy blessed Virgin Etheldreda, may by her prayers win pardon of Thy Divine Majesty; through.

OCTOBER 18.
ST. LUKE, EVANGELIST.
INFERIOR DOUBLE.

At Compline.

All as on the Feast of the Holy Trinity. Compl. xviii.
At the Hours all as on the Feast of St. Matthew, Apostle and Evangelist (see p. 161).

Collect.

ALMIGHTY GOD, Who calledst Luke the Physician, whose praise is in the Gospel, to be an Evangelist, and Physician of the soul; May it please Thee, that, by the wholesome medicines delivered by him, all the diseases of our souls may be healed; through. [1549]

Or this.

WE beseech Thee, O Lord, to hear the prayers of Thy holy Evangelist Luke for us: who for the honour of Thy Name carried about continually in his body the dying of the Lord Jesus; through the same.

OCTOBER 25.
ST. CRISPIN AND
ST. CRISPINIAN, MARTYRS.

Feast of nine Lessons. All of the Common of Many Martyrs, p. 115.

Collect.

O GOD, Who didst endue St. Crispin and St. Crispinian with so great a gift of grace that they should win the glory of martyrdom; Grant to us Thy servants pardon of all our sins, that by the merits and prayers of these Thy saints we may be delivered from all adversity; through.

OCTOBER 28.
THE HOLY APOSTLES SIMON AND JUDE.
INFERIOR DOUBLE.

At Compline.

All as on the Feast of the Holy Trinity. Compl. xviii.

At Terce.

Chapter. Romans viii. 28.

We know that all things work together for good to them that love God, who are the called according to His purpose.

All the rest is of the Common of Apostles (see p. 113), with Collect of the Proper.

Collect.

O ALMIGHTY GOD, Who hast built Thy Church upon the foundation of the Apostles and Prophets, Jesus Christ Himself being the head corner-stone; Grant us so to be joined together in unity of spirit by their doctrine, that we may be made an holy temple, acceptable unto Thee; through the same. [1549]

Or this.

O GOD, Who by Thy holy Apostles Simon and Jude hast brought us to the knowledge of Thy name; Grant us, we pray

ALL SAINTS' DAY. 167

Thee, so to celebrate their eternal glory, that we may profit by their examples; through.

NOVEMBER 1.
ALL SAINTS' DAY.
GREATER DOUBLE.

At First Evensong no memorials are made, nor at Mattins, nor at Second Evensong, except when this Feast falls on a Sunday: in which case memorials are made privately of the Sunday and of the Trinity. In like manner is done at Second Evensong when this Feast falls on a Saturday.

At Compline.

Antiphon.—At the prayers of all saints, grant, O Christ, to Thy servants health of body and soul.

Hymn.—Saviour, who didst the ransom pay.

Antiphon over Nunc Dimittis.—Lord, grant us Thy light, that, being freed from the darkness of our hearts, we may come to the true Light, which is Christ.

At Prime.

Antiphon.—I beheld, and lo, a great multitude which no man could number, of all nations, stood before the throne.

At Terce.

Antiphon.—And all the angels stood round about the throne: and fell before the throne on their faces, and worshipped God.

Chapter. Revelation vii. 2.

Behold, I, John, saw another angel ascending from the east, having the seal of the living God; and he cried with a loud voice to the four angels, to whom it was given to hurt the earth and the sea, saying, Hurt not the earth, neither the sea, nor the trees, till we have sealed the servants of our God in their foreheads.

R. Be glad, O ye righteous: and rejoice in the Lord. V. And be joyful, all ye that are true of heart. R. And rejoice in the Lord. V. Glory be. R. Be glad.

V. Let the righteous be glad, and rejoice before God. R. Let them also be merry and joyful.

Collect.

O ALMIGHTY GOD, Who hast knit together Thine elect in one communion and fellowship, in the mystical body of Thy Son Christ our Lord; Grant us grace so to follow Thy blessed Saints in all virtuous and godly living, that we may come to those unspeakable joys, which Thou hast prepared for them that unfeignedly love Thee; through the same. [1549]

Or this.

O ALMIGHTY and everlasting God, Who hast given us grace to celebrate the merits of all saints in one solemnity; Multiply upon us, we beseech Thee, through their united intercessions, the abundance of Thy mercy; through.

At Sext.

Antiphon. — Thou hast redeemed us, O Lord God, by Thy blood out of every kindred, and tongue, and people, and nation: and hast made us unto our God kings.

Chapter. Revelation vii. 4.

I heard the number of them which were sealed: and there were sealed an hundred and forty and four thousand of all the tribes of the children of Israel.

R. Let the righteous be glad: and rejoice before God. *V.* Let them also be merry and joyful. *R.* And rejoice before God. *V.* Glory be. *R.* Let the righteous.

V. The souls of the righteous are in the hand of God. *R.* And there shall no torment touch them.

At None.

Antiphon. — All His saints shall praise Him, even the children of Israel, even the people that serveth Him: such honour have all His saints.

Chapter. Revelation vii. 9.

I beheld, and, lo, a great multitude, which no man could number, of all nations, and kindreds, and people, and tongues, stood before the throne, and before the Lamb, clothed with white robes, and palms in their hands.

R. The souls of the righteous are: in the hand of God. *V.* And there shall no torment touch them. *R.* In the hand of God. *V.* Glory be. *R.* The souls.

V. Wonderful art Thou in Thy saints, O God. *R.* And glorious in Thy majesty.

NOVEMBER 6.
ST. LEONARD, ABBAT AND CONFESSOR.

Feast of nine Lessons. All of the Common of a Confessor and Abbat, p. 117.

Collect.

CROWN our prayers, we beseech Thee, O Lord, with Thy heavenly grace; that we who rejoice in the patronage of Leonard, Thy blessed Confessor and Abbat, may be worthy of the aid of his intercessions; through.

NOVEMBER 11.
ST. MARTIN, BISHOP AND CONFESSOR.

Feast of nine Lessons.

At Prime.

Antiphon.—Quoth his disciples to blessed Martin, Why dost thou desert us, father? or to whom dost thou leave us desolate ones? Now shall grievous' wolves enter in among thy flock.

Antiphon. — Thee, all Thy creatures.

At Terce.

Antiphon.—Lord, if I am still necessary to Thy people: I refuse not toil; Thy will be done.

Chapter. Ecclus. xliv. 17.

Behold, a great priest, who in his days feared God, and was found righteous: and in time of wrath made reconciliation.

ST. BRITIUS, BISHOP AND CONFESSOR.

R. The Lord loved him, and beautified him with comely ornaments. *V.* He clothed him with a robe of glory. *R.* And beautified him with comely ornaments. *V.* Glory be. *R.* The Lord.

V. The Lord guided the righteous man in right paths. *R.* And showed him the kingdom of God.

Collect.

O GOD, Who seest that we put not our trust in anything that we do; Mercifully grant, that through the intercession of Thy blessed Confessor and Bishop Martin, we may be defended against all adversities; through.

At Sext.

Antiphon.—O man most marvellous! whom toil hath not conquered, whom death cannot vanquish: who fearest not to die, nor yet dost refuse to live!

Chapter. Ecclus. xliv. 22.

With him did the Lord establish the blessing of all men, and the covenant, and made it rest upon his head.

R. The Lord guided the righteous man in right paths. *V.* And showed him the kingdom of God. *R.* In right paths. *V.* Glory be. *R.* The Lord.

V. The righteous shall flourish like a palm tree in the house of the Lord. *R.* And spread abroad like a cedar in Libanus.

At None.

Antiphon. — Joyfully Martin attaineth unto the bosom of Abraham. Martin, the beggar here on earth, entereth heaven a rich man, and is greeted with celestial songs.

Chapter. Ecclus. xliv. 23.

The Lord acknowledged him in His blessing. He kept His mercy for him, and he found favour in the sight of the Lord.

R. The righteous shall flourish like a palm tree in the house of the Lord. *V.* He shall spread abroad like a cedar in Libanus. *R.* In the house of the Lord. *V.* Glory be. *R.* The righteous.

V. The righteous shall blossom as a lily. *R.* He shall flourish for ever before the Lord.

During the Octaves all is said at the Hours as on the Festival, whenever the Service is of St. Martin; but Prime is said as within Octaves without rulers.

The ordinary memorials are said, as the choir is not ruled.

NOVEMBER 13.
ST. BRITIUS, BISHOP AND CONFESSOR.

Feast of three Lessons: without Rulers.

At First Evensong memorial of St. Martin is made, followed by the ordinary memorials, unless it be Sunday: and so at Mattins.

Chapters as on the Feast of St. Martin; all the rest of the Common, p. 117, with this Collect.

Collect.

KEEP, we beseech Thee, O Lord, Thy people who trust in Thy love, at the intercession of Thy blessed Confessor and Bishop, Britius; that we may be made worthy to enjoy with him eternal happiness; through.

November 15.
ST. MACHUTUS, BISHOP AND CONFESSOR.

Feast of nine Lessons. All of the Common of a Confessor and Bishop (see p. 117).

Collect.

ALMIGHTY and everlasting God, mercifully hear the prayers of Thy people; and at the intercession of Thy blessed Confessor and Bishop Machutus, whose festival we celebrate to-day, grant that we may so pass through things temporal, that we finally lose not the things eternal; through.

Memorial is made of St. Martin.

November 17.
ST. HUGH, BISHOP AND CONFESSOR.

Feast of nine Lessons. All of the Common of a Confessor and Bishop (see p. 117).

Collect.

O GOD, Who hast adorned Thy Confessor and Bishop St. Hugh with many excellent virtues and deeds of renown; Mercifully grant that we may both emulate his example and strive after the attainment of the same virtues; through.

Memorial is made of St. Martin.

November 18.
OCTAVE OF ST. MARTIN, BISHOP AND CONFESSOR.

November 20.
ST. EDMUND, KING AND MARTYR.

Feast of nine Lessons. All of the Common of a Martyr, p. 114.

Collect.

O GOD of ineffable pity, Who didst grant the blessed King Edmund to overcome the enemy by dying for Thy Name; Mercifully behold this Thy family, and grant, that through his prayers we may be enabled to quench all the fiery darts of the evil one, and to win the victory at last; through.

November 22.
ST. CECILIA, VIRGIN AND MARTYR.

Feast of nine Lessons. All of the Common of a Virgin and Martyr (see p. 119), except as follows:

Collect.

O GOD, Who makest us glad with the yearly solemnity of Thy blessed Virgin and Martyr Cecilia; Grant that as we devoutly venerate her holy life, so may we ever follow her glorious example; through.

At Prime.

Antiphon.—Cecilia would play upon the organ, and sing unto the

ST. KATHERINE, VIRGIN AND MARTYR.

Lord, saying, O let my heart be sound in Thy statutes, that I be not ashamed.

At Terce.

Antiphon.—A secret I have to tell thee, O Valerian: the angel of God is my lover, and he guardeth me with exceeding love.

At Sext.

Antiphon. — Valerian found Cecilia praying in her chamber with the angel.

At None.

Antiphon.—Cecilia Thy servant, O Lord, serveth Thee busily.

NOVEMBER 23.
ST. CLEMENT, POPE AND MARTYR.

Feast of nine Lessons. All of the Common of a Martyr and Bishop, p. 114, except as follows:

At First Evensong memorial is made of St. Cecilia.

At Prime.

Antiphon.—'Tis not by my merits that the Lord hath sent me to you, that I should receive with you the crown.

At Terce.

Antiphon.—As holy Clement prayed, there appeared to him the Lamb of God.

At Sext.

Antiphon.—I beheld standing upon the mountain the Lamb, from beneath whose feet floweth forth a living stream.

At None.

Antiphon.—By means of the miraculous circle all nations believed Christ to be the Lord.

Collect.

O GOD, Who makest us glad with the yearly solemnity of Thy blessed Martyr and Bishop St. Clement; Mercifully grant, that as we venerate his festival, so we may ever follow the example of his godly conversation and sufferings; through.

NOVEMBER 25.
ST. KATHERINE, VIRGIN AND MARTYR.

Feast of nine Lessons. All of the Common of a Virgin and Martyr, p. 119, except as follows:

At Prime.

Antiphon.—The sufferings of the glorious Virgin Katherine all faithful people devoutly celebrate: whose prayers and merits commend to God all who keep the feast.

At Terce.

Antiphon. — After manifold tortures, the blessed Martyr was led to execution; raising her hands and eyes to heaven in prayer, she gives glory to God.

At Sext.

Antiphon.—For Thee, O Jesu, blessed King, I await the sword; grant Thou my spirit to enter paradise, and to those who honour my memory grant Thy mercy.

At None.

Antiphon.—Pray for us, O blessed Katherine, who with holy praises venerate thy memory.

Collect.

ALMIGHTY and everlasting God, Who didst command the body of Thy glorious virgin and Martyr Katherine to be borne by angels to Mount Sinai; Grant, we pray Thee, at her entreaty, that we may be borne to heights of virtue, whence we may attain to the vision of Thy glory; through.

APPENDIX.

December 29.
ST. THOMAS OF CANTERBURY, MARTYR.
LESSER DOUBLE.

At Mattins *memorial* (1) *of the Nativity,* (2) *of St. Stephen,* (3) *of St. John,* (4) *of the Holy Innocents.*

At Prime.

Antiphon.—
Falls to earth the corn of wheat,
    springs the harvest golden:
Sweetest scent distilleth from alabaster broken.

At Terce.

Antiphon.—
Now the nations vie in love at the
    martyr's story:
Signs and wonders marvellous witness to his glory.

Chapters, Responsories, and Verses, all of the Common of a Martyr and Bishop, p. 114, only that the Responsories are said with Alleluia.

Collect.

O GOD, forasmuch as the glorious Bishop Thomas fell by the swords of wicked men in defending Thy Church; Grant, we beseech Thee, that all who seek his protection may perceive in themselves the saving efficacy of his prayers; through.

At Sext.

Antiphon.—
Five times Thomas' sacred fount
    changing colours showeth:
Once with milk, four times with
    blood, wondrously it floweth.

At None.

Antiphon.—
Four times on St. Thomas' Day
    light from heaven is streaming:
Now glory to the Saint! the lamps
    kindle at its gleaming.

At Evensong *memorials as noted on* p. 12.

June 30.
COMMEMORATION OF ST. PAUL, APOSTLE.

Feast of nine Lessons.
At Mattins *Memorials* (1) *of St. Peter,* (2) *of St. John Baptist.*

At Prime.

*Antiphon.—*I planted, Apollos watered: but God gave the increase. Alleluia.

At Terce.

*Antiphon.—*Most gladly will I glory in my infirmities: that the power of Christ may rest upon me.

THE FEAST OF RELICS.

Chapter. Galatians i. 11.

I certify you that the gospel which was preached of me is not after man. For I neither received it of man, neither was I taught it, but by the revelation of Jesus Christ.

RR., VV. *of the Common of an Apostle at all the Hours.*

Collect.

GOD, Who didst teach the multitude of the Gentiles by the preaching of Thy blessed Apostle St. Paul; Grant, we beseech Thee, that we who celebrate his festival may be ever protected by his prayers; through.

At Sext.

Antiphon.—The grace of God which was bestowed upon me was not in vain: but His grace is with me alway.

Chapter. Philippians i. 21.

For to me to live is Christ, and to die is gain. God forbid that I should glory, save in the cross of our Lord Jesus Christ, by Whom the world is crucified unto me, and I unto the world.

At None.

Antiphon.—Holy Paul the Apostle, preacher of truth and teacher of the nations: intercede for us with the Lord Who chose thee.

Chapter. 2 *Timothy* iv. 7.

I have fought a good fight, I have finished my course, I have kept the faith: henceforth there is laid up for me a crown of righteousness, which the Lord, the righteous Judge, shall give me at that day.

Evensong is of both Apostles with memorial of St. John Baptist. If this Commemoration fall on a Saturday, Evensong on that day shall be of the Sunday following, with a solemn memorial of the Apostles. Then follows the memorial of the Octave of St. John Baptist, and afterwards of the Holy Trinity.

JULY 7.

TRANSLATION OF ST. THOMAS, MARTYR.

LESSER DOUBLE.

At First Evensong *solemn memorial of the Apostles. Memorial of the Visitation at both Evensongs and at Mattins.*

At Compline *all as on Trinity Sunday.*

At the Hours *all is done as upon his other festival, but without Alleluia at the* RR.

Here it is to be noted, that always on the next Sunday after the feast of the Translation of St. Thomas, Martyr, is celebrated the Feast of Relics *according to the use of the Church of Sarum: which of old time was celebrated on the Octave of the Nativity of blessed Mary, and is to be celebrated as a Greater Double, wherever there are relics, or the bodies of the dead are buried; for although holy Church and the clergy keep no solemnity in their honour, yet we cannot say what glory may not be theirs in the sight of God.*

THE FEAST OF RELICS.

GREATER DOUBLE.

At First Evensong. *No memorial is made of any Feast of three Lessons falling on this day.*

At Compline.

All as in Compl. xix.

At Prime.

Antiphon.—But the souls of the righteous are in the hand of God: and there shall no torment touch them.

At Terce.

Antiphon. — With the palm have the saints attained to the kingdom: crowns of glory have they merited at the hand of the Lord.

Chapter. Ecclus. xliv. 10.

These were merciful men, whose righteousness hath not been forgotten: with their seed shall continually remain a good inheritance, and their children are within the covenant.

RR., VV., *of the Common of Many Martyrs at all the Hours.*

Collect.

GRANT, we beseech Thee, Almighty God, that the merits of the holy Mother of God and ever Virgin Mary, and of Thy saints whose relics are preserved in this church, may protect us Thy servants; and so by their prayers we may continually rejoice in Thy service with all godly quietness; through the same.

At Sext.

Antiphon.—The bodies of the saints are buried in peace, and their names shall live for evermore.

Chapter. Ecclus. xliv. 15.

All nations will tell of the wisdom of the saints, and the whole Church of God will show forth their praise.

At None.

Antiphon.—The saints shall exult in glory: they shall rejoice in their beds.

Chapter. Ecclus. xliv. 14.

The bodies of the saints are buried in peace: and their names shall live for evermore.

Compline *as above.*

Any feast of nine Lessons falling on this day is transferred to the morrow; and no memorial is made audibly of such feasts at the Second Evensong of Relics; nor if one fall on Monday, unless it be a double feast. But if a Greater Double, such as the Dedication of the church, or the Feast of the place, fall on Monday, then Evensong on Sunday shall be of such feast with a solemn memorial of Relics.

No feast of three Lessons is observed on this day.

Daily within the Octaves, and on the Octave day, is made a Memorial of Relics at Evensong, Mattins, and Mass, both on Ferias and Feasts of saints.

August 15.

THE ASSUMPTION OF THE BLESSED VIRGIN MARY.

PRINCIPAL FEAST.

At Compline.

All as in Compl. xxi., *and so daily throughout the Octaves.*

At Prime.

Antiphon.—Mary is taken up into heaven: angels rejoice, praise, and bless the Lord.

At Terce.

Antiphon.—Mary the Virgin is taken up into the celestial palace, wherein sitteth the King of kings upon His starry throne.

Chapter. Ecclus. xxiv. 7.

With all these I sought rest, and in the inheritance of the Lord I shall abide. So the Creator of all things gave me a commandment, and He that made me caused my tabernacle to rest.

RR., VV. as on the Purification at all the Hours.

Collect.

GRANT, O Lord, that the worshipful solemnity of this day may bring us everlasting aid; wherein the holy Mother of God did endure the death of the body, who nevertheless could not be holden of the bands of death, seeing that of her flesh undefiled Thy Son our Lord became incarnate; Who liveth and reigneth.

At Sext.

Antiphon.—We haste unto the sweet savour of Thine ointments: the maidens loved Thee exceedingly.

Chapter. Ecclus. xxiv. 10.

And so was I established in Syon, likewise in the beloved city He gave me rest, and in Jerusalem was my power.

At None.

Antiphon.—Thou art beautiful and comely, O daughter of Jerusalem: terrible as an army with banners.

Chapter. Ecclus. xxiv. 11.

And I took root in an honourable people, even in the portion of the Lord's inheritance: and my resting-place was in the heritage of the saints.

Throughout the Octaves no memorial of the Holy Cross is made, nor of All Saints, since the Octaves have Rulers.

At Prime and the other Hours all is done as within Octaves.

On Sunday within the Octaves all the Service is of holy Mary, with memorials of the Sunday and of the Trinity at first Evensong and at Mattins.

If the Octave of the Assumption fall on a Saturday, the last Evensong of the Octave is said, with memorial of the following Sunday; and on Sunday shall be said Evensong of St. Bartholomew, with memorial of the Sunday.

NOVEMBER 2.
ALL SOULS' DAY.
INFERIOR DOUBLE.

The Second Evensong of All Saints being finished, immediately is begun Evensong of the Dead.

At Compline all as in Compl. xix.

At Prime and at the other Hours is not said O God, make speed, *nor the Hymn, but immediately is begun the Antiphon over the Psalms, as follows:*

Antiphon.—Eternal rest grant them, O Lord: and let light perpetual shine upon them.

Ps. Save me, O God.
Ps. Blessed are those.
Ps. O do well.

The Psalms being finished, after Glory be to the Father, *the whole Antiphon is said; which done, there follows* Kyrie, eleyson; Christo, eleyson, Kyrie, eleyson; Our Father; Hail, Mary. *Afterwards let the Priest say:*

And lead us not into temptation. R. But deliver us from evil.

V. Eternal rest grant them, O Lord. R. And let light perpetual shine upon them.

V. From the gates of hell. R. Deliver their souls, O Lord.

V. I believe verily to see the goodness of the Lord. R. In the land of the living.

V. The Lord be with you. R. And with thy spirit.

Let us pray.

Collect.

O GOD of Thy faithful people, the Maker and Redeemer of all; Grant to the souls of all the faithful departed remission of all their sins, that the pardon which they ever desired, by our pious supplications they may obtain; Who livest and reignest with the Father and the Holy Ghost, God, world without end. Amen.

V. May they rest in peace.
R. Amen.

In this manner are said all the other Hours of this day (with their own Psalms).
If this Commemoration of All Souls happen to fall on a Sunday, it is transferred to the morrow.

CORPUS CHRISTI.
GREATER DOUBLE.

At First Evensong no memorials are made audibly, unless some double feast has been celebrated on this Wednesday, and unless the Octaves of the Holy Trinity are observed with Rulers of the Choir.
At Compline everything as on Trinity Sunday, except that the Doxology to the Hymn is:

All glory, Virgin-born, to Thee,
Jesu, Incarnate Deity,
Whom with the Father we adore
And Holy Spirit evermore.

This verse is said at the end of all Hymns of the same metre daily throughout the Octaves, when the Service is of Corpus Christi.

At Prime.

Antiphon. — Wisdom hath builded her house: she hath mingled her wine, she hath also furnished her table. Alleluia.

Antiphon.—O holy, blessed, and glorious Trinity: Father, Son, and Holy Ghost.

Chapter. 1 Tim. i. 17.

Now unto the King eternal, immortal, invisible, the only wise God, be honour and glory for ever and ever. Amen.

R. Jesu Christ, Son of the living God, have mercy upon us. Alleluia, Alleluia. V. Thou that didst not abhor the Virgin's womb. R. Have mercy upon us. Alleluia, Alleluia. V. Glory be. R. Jesu Christ.

The rest as on Double Feasts.

At Terce.

Antiphon.—Thou hast fed Thy people with angel's food: Thou hast given them bread from heaven. Alleluia.

Chapter. 1 Cor. xi. 23.

The Lord Jesus the same night in which He was betrayed took bread: and when He had given thanks, He brake it, and said, Take, eat: this is My Body, which is given for you.

R. Thou gavest them bread from heaven. Alleluia, Alleluia.
V. Man did eat angel's bread. R. Alleluia, Alleluia. V. Glory be. R. Thou gavest.
V. He fed them with the finest wheat flour. R. And with honey out of the stony rock did He satisfy them.

Collect.

O GOD, Who in Thy wonderful sacrament hast loft us a memorial of Thy Passion; Grant us, we beseech Thee, so to venerate the sacred mysteries of Thy Body and Blood, that we may ever perceive in ourselves the fruit of Thy redemption; Who livest and reignest.

At Sext.

Antiphon.—Rich is the Bread of Christ: yielding dainties for princes. Alleluia! Alleluia! Alleluia!

Chapter. 1 Cor. xi. 26.

As oft as ye eat this bread, and drink this cup, ye do show the Lord's death till He come.

R. He fed them with the finest wheat-flour. Alleluia! Alleluia! V. And with honey out of the stony rock did He satisfy them. R. Alleluia! Alleluia!
V. Glory be. R. He fed them.
V. Thou bringest bread out of the earth. R. And wine to make glad the heart of man.

At None.

Antiphon.—To him that overcometh will I give the hidden manna and a new name. Alleluia!

Chapter. 1 Cor. xi. 27.

Whosoever shall eat this bread, and drink this cup of the Lord, unworthily, shall be guilty of the body and blood of the Lord.

R. Thou bringest bread out of the earth. Alleluia! Alleluia!
V. And wine to make glad the heart of man. R. Alleluia! Alleluia! V. Glory be. R. Thou bringest.
V. He hath made peace in thy borders. R. And He filleth thee with the flour of wheat.

If the Feast of St. Barnabas fall on the Feast of Corpus Christi, it is transferred to the morrow, and at Second Evensong, which shall be of Corpus Christi, is made a memorial of St. Barnabas silently.

Throughout the Octaves, the service is of Corpus Christi without rulers of the Choir, unless some Feast intervene, or commemoration of blessed Mary has to be observed.

On Saturday there is full service of holy Mary, unless some Feast of nine Lessons prevent it, or unless the Octaves be observed with rulers. And if some Feast intervene, the service shall be performed in every respect by the same rule as within the Octaves of the Holy Trinity; so that there be made first of all memorial of Corpus Christi, then of the Trinity.

Whenever a Feast of nine Lessons falls on the Feast of Corpus Christi, it is transferred to the morrow or further if necessary, as in case of some Feast of nine Lessons occupying the morrow of this day.

If the Feast of Corpus Christi fall on the day of the Nativity of St. John Baptist, the latter is transferred to the morrow; and at Second Evensong, which shall be of Corpus Christi, solemn memorial is made of St. John. Then let the Procession go to the altar

OCTAVE OF CORPUS CHRISTI.

of St. John, if there be one, and the rest is done as is set forth on the Feast of the same; and then nothing is done of Corpus Christi throughout the Octaves, except a memorial, until the Octave day; and then the whole service is of Corpus Christi, with solemn memorial of St. John, and Mass in chapter; and at First Evensong, which shall be of Corpus Christi, solemn memorial is made of the Apostles, viz. on the day of the Commemoration of St. Paul, and afterwards is made solemn memorial of the Octaves of St. John Baptist.

If the Feast of Corpus Christi fall on that of St. Alban the Martyr, the latter is transferred to the morrow; and at Second Evensong, which is of Corpus Christi, shall be made silently memorial of St. Alban.

When this aforesaid Feast of Corpus Christi falls on the Eve of St. John the Baptist, it is celebrated on the same. Mass of Corpus Christi is said after Terce, and after Sext the Mass of the Eve is sung in choir at the high altar. Evensong is of Corpus Christi, with solemn memorial of St. John, and Procession to his altar, if there be one.

If the Feast of St. John Baptist fall on the solemnity of Corpus Christi, the former is transferred to the morrow, though it be the Feast of the place; and then at First Evensong, which shall be of St. John, is made a solemn memorial of Corpus Christi only, and then on the Octave of Corpus Christi is made solemn memorial of the Octave of St. John Baptist at First Evensong and at Mattins, with Mass in Chapter of St. John Baptist.

WITHIN THE OCTAVES.

At the Hours all is done as on the Festival, after the manner of a simple Feast without rulers. However on the Ferias within the Octaves after Sunday, the Antiphon over the Creed of Athanasius at Prime shall be Glory to Thee, Co-equal Trinity.

Compline is said as on the preceding Ferias within the Octaves of the Holy Trinity; but the hymn, To Thee, Creator Lord, ends with the doxology, All glory, Virgin-born, to Thee; except that when the Octaves of Corpus Christi have rulers of the choir, then Compline is said as on the Festival.

OCTAVE OF CORPUS CHRISTI.

At Compline, all as within the Octave.

At Mattins, if any Feast of three Lessons fall on this day, a memorial only is made of it; and the same at Evensong and Mass.

At Prime.

Antiphon. — Wisdom hath builded, etc.

Antiphon.—Thee all Thy creatures.

At the other Hours all is done as on the Festival.

If a simple Feast of nine Lessons fall on this day, it is transferred to the morrow, and Evensong shall be of the Feast, with solemn memorial of the Octave; except when the Commemoration of St. Paul falls on this day, for it is transferred to the morrow, and then there shall be a Second Evensong of the Octave, and at Mattins of the Commemoration of St. Paul is made solemn memorial of the Octaves of St. John Baptist, with Mass in Chapter.

But if a double Feast fall on this day it is not transferred; but the whole service is of the Feast, and only a solemn memorial of the Octave at both Evensongs, and at Mattins and at Mass in that year, although it be the Feast of the place.

When Octaves of Corpus Christi fall on the Eve of St. John Baptist, or on the Eve of the Apostles Peter and Paul, the whole service is of the Octaves, with memorial of the Saints. The Mass of the Octaves is said after Terce, and the Mass of the Eve after Sext, both at the principal altar.

When the Octaves of Corpus Christi have rulers of the choir, the service is as follows: On the first day, both at Evensong and Matlins, and at the other hours, all is done as on the first day when the Octaves are without rulers.

With respect to the occurrence of two Feasts the above rules hold good.

Throughout the Octaves the service is of Corpus Christi, also on the Sunday, unless a Feast of nine Lessons intervene.

No memorial is made throughout the Octaves, because the choir is ruled, except some Feast without rulers intervene, and except on the Sunday, when the morrow of the Octaves, being a Friday, is unoccupied, as is noted below.

At Prime and the other Hours, all is done as on the first day.

Everything else at Evensong and Compline is done as on the Festival.

On the Sunday within the Octaves, if it be not occupied with a Feast of nine Lessons, at First Evensong all is done as on other days within the Octaves. No memorial is made of the Sunday, nor of the Trinity, unless it happens that on the morrow of the Octaves the services of Friday have to be performed; for then is made memorial of the Sunday and of the Trinity, and then the Sunday Mass is said on the Friday after the Octaves.

At Mattins, everything as on the Festival.

At Prime and the other Hours, all as on the other days within the Octaves, except the Antiphon over the Creed of Athanasius, which shall be Thee all Thy creatures. And this Antiphon is said on the following Ferias within the Octaves, unless a double Feast intervene.

At Second Evensong and at Compline, everything as on the other days within the Octaves.

If a double Feast fall within the Octaves, or on the Octave Day, the whole service is of the Feast, and a memorial only of the Octaves. If a Feast of nine Lessons, not a double, fall within the Octaves, or on Sunday, all the service is of the Feast, and a memorial only of the Sunday.

Feasts of three Lessons, without rulers, falling within the Octaves, have only a memorial.

FULL SERVICE OF BLESSED MARY.

During Advent.

At Compline.

All is of the Compline of the season, except the following:

Doxology to the Hymn.

All glory, Virgin-born, to Thee,
Jesu, Incarnate Deity,
Whom with the Father we adore
And Holy Spirit evermore.

Antiphon to Nunc Dimittis.—We glorify thee, O mother of God, etc. (p. 108).

At Prime.

Antiphon.—Prophets did predict that the Saviour should be born of the Virgin Mary.

Psalms.—Save me, O God.
Blessed are those.
O do well.

Antiphon.—Thee all Thy creatures.

Chapter.—Now unto the King eternal.

Responsory as on Christmas Day.

At Terce.

Antiphon.—The angel Gabriel was sent to Mary, a virgin, espoused to Joseph.

Chapter. Isaiah vii. 14.

Behold, a virgin shall conceive, and bear a Son, and shall call His name Emmanuel. Butter and honey shall He eat, that He may know to refuse the evil and choose the good.

RR., VV., and Collect at all the Hours, as on the Feast of the Annunciation, p. 135.

At Sext.

Antiphon.—The angel of the Lord announced unto Mary, and she conceived by the Holy Ghost. Alleluia.

Chapter. Isaiah xi. 1.

There shall come forth a Rod out of the stem of Jesse, and a Branch shall grow out of his roots: and the Spirit of the Lord shall rest upon Him.

At None.

Antiphon. — Hail, Mary, full of grace, the Lord is with thee: blessed art thou among women, Alleluia.

Chapter. Isaiah xi. 3.

He shall not judge after the sight of His eyes, neither reprove after the hearing of His ears: but with righteousness shall He judge the poor, and reprove with equity for the meek of the earth.

FULL SERVICE OF BLESSED MARY.

FROM THE OCTAVE OF EPIPHANY TO THE PURIFICATION.

At Compline.

All is done as is directed above at Full Service during Advent.

At Prime.

All as above, except the Antiphon to the Psalms, which is as follows:

Antiphon.—O marvellous exchange! the Creator of mankind, taking to Himself a living body, hath deigned to be born of a Virgin: and proceeding forth as Man by an immaculate conception, hath made us co-heirs of His Godhead.

At Terce.

Antiphon.—When Thou wast born ineffably of a Virgin, then were the Scriptures fulfilled: Thou shalt come down as rain into a fleece of wool, to accomplish the salvation of mankind. We praise Thee, O our God.

Chapter. Titus iii. 4.

The kindness and love of God our Saviour toward man appeared, not by works of righteousness which we have done, but according to His mercy He saved us.

R. Holy mother of God, ever Virgin Mary. V. Intercede for us with the Lord our God. R. Ever Virgin Mary. V. Glory be. R. Holy mother.

V. After child-bearing thou remainedst a pure Virgin. R. O mother of God, pray for us.

Collect.

O GOD, Who, through the fruitful virginity of blessed Mary, hast bestowed upon the race of man rewards of eternal salvation; Grant, we pray Thee, that as we have received through her the Author of life, so she may ever intercede for us in the heavens; through the same.

At Sext.

Antiphon.—In the bush which Moses beheld burning but unconsumed, we recognise Thy glorious virginity: O mother of God, pray for us.

Chapter.

Thee do the angels praise, O holy mother of God, who knewest no man: and in thy womb barest the Lord.

R. After child-bearing thou remainedst a pure Virgin. *V.* O mother of God, pray for us. *R.* Thou remainedst a pure Virgin. *V.* Glory be. *R.* After child-bearing.

V. Thou art become fair and pleasant. *R.* In thy delights, O holy mother of God.

At None.

Antiphon.—The root of Jesse hath budded: a Star hath risen out of Jacob, a Virgin hath borne the Saviour: we praise Thee, O our God.

Chapter.

A Virgin hath conceived by a word, a Virgin remained she, a Virgin brought she forth the King of all kings.

R. Thou art become fair and pleasant. *V.* In thy delights, O holy mother of God. *R.* Fair and pleasant. *V.* Glory be. *R.* Thou art.

V. God hath elected her and pre-elected her. *R.* He hath made her to dwell in His tabernacle.

Between the Purification and Advent all is said as above, except the Chapters, which are as follows:

AT TERCE. *Chapter. Ecclus.* xxiv. 9. He created me from the beginning before the world, and I shall never fail. In the holy tabernacle I served before Him.

AT SEXT. *Chapter. Ecclus.* xxiv. 10. And so was I established in Syon, and in the holy city He gave me rest, and in Jerusalem was my power.

AT NONE. *Chapter. Ecclus.* xxiv. 12. And I took root in an honourable people, even in the portion of the Lord's inheritance: and in the fulness of the saints is my habitation.

Notandum quod omni feriali die per totam Quadragesimam dicitur Letania sicut in secunda feria usque ad ordinem martyrum. Et a Propitius esto, *usque ad finem. Et quicquid sacerdos dicit de Letania, chorus idem repetat plene et integre usque ad prolationem* Ut pacem nobis dones, *tunc respondeat chorus* Te rogamus audi nos, *tantum: et sic de singulis usque ad* Fili Dei, Te rogamus audi nos, *tunc respondeat chorus idem: et sic de singulis usque ad* Kyri, eleyson; Christe, eleyson; Kyri, eleyson.

LETANIA.

Feria Secunda.

Kyri, eleyson. Christe eleyson.
  Christe, audi nos.
Pater de cœlis Deus, ⎫
Fili Redemptor mundi ⎪
  Deus, ⎬ *Miserere*
Spiritus Sancte Deus, ⎪ *nobis.*
Sancta Trinitas, unus ⎭
  Deus,
Sancta Maria,   Ora pro nobis.
Sancta Dei Genitrix,   Or.
Sancta Virgo virginum,   Or.
Sancte Michael,   Or.
Sancte Gabriel,   Or.
Sancte Raphael,   Or.
Omnes sancti Angeli et Archangeli,   Orate pro nobis.
Omnes sancti beatorum Spirituum ordines,   Orate pro nobis.
Sancte Johannes Baptista,
  Ora pro nobis.
Omnes sancti Patriarchæ et Prophetæ,   Orate pro nobis.
Sancte Petre,   Ora pro nobis.
Sancte Paule,   Or.
Sancte Andrea,   Or.
Sancte Johannes,   Or.
Sancte Jacobe,   Or.
Sancte Thoma,   Or.
Sancte Philippe,   Or.
Sancte Jacobe,   Or.
Sancte Matthæe,   Or.
Sancte Bartholomæe,   Or.
Sancte Symon,   Or.
Sancte Thadæe,   Or.
Sancte Mathia,   Or.
Sancte Barnaba,   Or.
Sancte Marce,   Or.
Sancte Luca,   Or.
Omnes sancti Apostoli et Evangelistæ,   Orate pro nobis.
Omnes sancti Discipuli Domini et Innocentes,   Orate pro nobis.

Hucusque dicitur in Singulis Letaniis.

Sancte Stephane, Ora pro nobis.
Sancte Line,   Or.
Sancte Clete,   Or.
Sancte Clemens,   Or.
Sancte Fabiane,   Or.
Sancte Sebastiane,   Or.
Sancte Cosma,   Or.
Sancte Damiane,   Or.
Sancte Prime,   Or.
Sancte Feliciane,   Or.
Sancte Dionysi cum sociis tuis,
  Or.

Sancte Victor, cum sociis tuis,
  Ora pro nobis.
Omnes sancti Martyres,
  Orate pro nobis.
Sancte Silvester, *Ora pro nobis.*
Sancte Leo,   *Or.*
Sancte Hieronyme,   *Or.*
Sancte Augustine,   *Or.*
Sancte Ysidore,   *Or.*
Sancte Juliane,   *Or.*
Sancte Gildarde,   *Or.*
Sancte Medarde,   *Or.*
Sancte Albine,   *Or.*
Sancte Eusebi,   *Or.*
Sancte Swithune,   *Or.*
Sancte Birine,   *Or.*
Omnes sancti Confessores,
  Orate pro nobis.
Omnes sancti Monachi et Heremitæ,   *Orate pro nobis.*
Sancta Maria Magdalene,
  Ora pro nobis.
Sancta Maria Ægyptiaca, *Or.*
Sancta Margareta,   *Or.*
Sancta Scholastica,   *Or.*
Sancta Petronilla,   *Or.*
Sancta Genovefa,   *Or.*
Sancta Praxedis,   *Or.*
Sancta Sotheris,   *Or.*
Sancta Prisca,   *Or.*
Sancta Tecla,   *Or.*
Sancta Afra,   *Or.*
Sancta Editha,   *Or.*
Omnes sanctæ Virgines,
  Orate pro nobis.
Omnes Sancti,   *Or.*

———

Propitius esto;
  Parce nobis, Domine.
Ab omni malo,
  Libera nos, Domine.
Ab insidiis diaboli,   *Libera.*
A damnatione perpetua, *Libera.*
Ab imminentibus peccatorum nostrorum periculis, *Libera.*

Ab infestationibus dæmonum,
  Libera.
A spiritu fornicationis, *Libera.*
Ab appetitu inanis gloriæ,
  Libera.
Ab omni immunditia mentis et corporis,   *Libera.*
Ab ira et odio, et omni mala voluntate,   *Libera.*
Ab immundis cogitationibus.
  Libera.
A cæcitate cordis, *Libera.*
A fulgure et tempestate, *Libera.*
A subitanea et improvisa morte,
  Libera.
Per mysterium sanctæ Incarnationis tuæ,   *Libera.*
Per Nativitatem tuam, *Libera.*
Per sanctam Circumcisionem tuam,   *Libera.*
Per Baptismum tuum, *Libera.*
Per Jejunium tuum, *Libera.*
Per Passionem et Crucem tuam,
  Libera.
Per pretiosam Mortem tuam,
  Libera.
Per gloriosam Resurrectionem tuam,   *Libera.*
Per admirabilem Ascensionem tuam,   *Libera.*
Per gratiam Sancti Spiritus Paraclyti,   *Libera.*
In hora mortis,
  Succurre nobis, Domine.
In die judicii,
  Libera nos, Domine.
Peccatores, *Te rogamus audi nos.*
Ut pacem nobis dones,
  Te rogamus.
Ut misericordia et pietas tua nos custodiat,
  Te rogamus audi nos.
Ut Ecclesiam tuam regere et defensare digneris,
  Te rogamus audi nos.
Ut dominum Apostolicum et omnes gradus Ecclesiæ in

LETANIA.

sancta religione conservare digneris, *Te rogamus audi nos.*
Ut Episcopos et Abbates nostros: in sancta religione conservare digneris, *Te rogamus audi nos.*
Ut Regi nostro et Principibus nostris pacem et veram concordiam atque victoriam donare digneris,
Te rogamus audi nos.
Ut congregationes omnium sanctorum in tuo sancto servitio conservare digneris,
Te rogamus audi nos.
Ut cunctum populum Christianum pretioso Sanguine tuo redemptum conservare digneris, *Te rogamus audi nos.*
Ut omnibus benefactoribus nostris sempiterna bona retribuas, *Te rogamus audi nos.*
Ut animas nostras et parentum nostrorum ab æterna damnatione eripias,
Te rogamus audi nos.
Ut fructus terræ dare et conservare digneris,
Te rogamus audi nos.
Ut oculos misericordiæ tuæ super nos reducere digneris,
Te rogamus audi nos.
Ut obsequium servitutis nostræ rationabile facias,
Te rogamus audi nos.
Ut mentes nostras ad cœlestia desideria erigas,
Te rogamus audi nos.
Ut miserias pauperum et captivorum intueri et relevare digneris,
Te rogamus audi nos.
Ut omnibus fidelibus defunctis requiem æternam dones,
Te rogamus audi nos.
Ut nos exaudiri digneris,
Te rogamus audi nos.
Fili Dei, *Te rogamus audi nos.*

Agnus Dei, qui tollis peccata mundi, *Exaudi nos, Domine.*
Agnus Dei, qui tollis peccata mundi, *Parce nobis, Domine.*
Agnus Dei, qui tollis peccata mundi, *Miserere nobis.*
Kyri, eleyson. *Christe, eleyson.*
Kyri, eleyson.
Pater noster.
Et ne nos inducas in tentationem,
Sed libera nos a malo.
Ostende nobis, Domine, misericordiam tuam.
Et salutare tuum da nobis.
Et veniat super nos misericordia tua, Domine.
Salutare tuum secundum eloquium tuum.
Peccavimus cum patribus nostris.
Injuste egimus, iniquitatem fecimus.
Domine, non secundum peccata nostra facias nobis.
Neque secundum iniquitates nostras retribuas nobis.
Oremus pro omni gradu Ecclesiæ.
Sacerdotes tui induantur justitiam, et sancti tui exultent.
Pro fratribus et sororibus nostris.
Salvos fac servos tuos et ancillas tuas: Deus meus sperantes in te.
Pro cuncto populo Christiano.
Salvum fac populum tuum, Domine, et benedic hereditati tuæ: et rege eos et extolle illos usque in æternum.
Domine, fiat pax in virtute tua.
Et abundantia in turribus tuis.
Animæ famulorum famularumque tuarum requiescant in pace.
Amen.
Domine, exaudi orationem meam.
Et clamor meus ad te veniat.
Dominus vobiscum.
Et cum spiritu tuo.

Oremus.

Deus, cui proprium est misereri semper, et parcere ; Suscipe deprecationem nostram ; ut quos delictorum catena constringit, miseratio tuæ pietatis absolvat ; Per Christum Dominum nostrum.

Oremus.

Omnipotens, sempiterne Deus, qui facis mirabilia magna solus ; Prætende super famulos tuos Pontifices et super cunctas congregationes illis commissas spiritum gratiæ salutaris ; et ut in veritate tibi complaceant, perpetuum eis rorem tuæ benedictionis infunde.

Oratio.

Deus, qui charitatis dona per gratiam Sancti Spiritus tuorum cordibus fidelium infundis ; Da famulis et famulabus tuis ; fratribus et sororibus nostris pro quibus tuam deprecamur clementiam salutem mentis et corporis ; ut te tota virtute diligant, et quæ tibi placita sunt tota dilectione perficiant.

Oratio.

Deus, a quo sancta desideria, recta consilia, et justa sunt opera ; Da servis tuis illam quam mundus dare non potest pacem ; ut et corda nostra mandatis tuis dedita, et, hostium sublata formidine, tempora sint tua protectione tranquilla.

Oratio.

Ineffabilem misericordiam tuam nobis quæsumus, Domine, clementer ostende : ut simul nos et a peccatis omnibus exuas, et a pœnis quas pro his meremur benignus eripias.

Oratio.

Fidelium Deus omnium Conditor et Redemptor, animabus omnium fidelium defunctorum remissionem cunctorum tribue peccatorum : ut indulgentiam, quam semper optaverunt, piis supplicationibus consequantur.

Oratio.

Pietate tua quæsumus, Domine, nostrorum solve vincula omnium delictorum, et intercedente beata et gloriosa semperque virgine Dei genitrice Maria cum omnibus Sanctis tuis nos famulos tuos, et omnem populum Catholicum in omni sanctitate custodi, omnesque consanguinitate ac familiaritate, vel confessione et oratione nobis junctos, seu omnes Christianos, a vitiis purga, virtutibus illustra, pacem et salutem nobis tribue, hostes visibiles et invisibiles remove, pestem repelle : amicis et inimicis nostris charitatem largire, et omnibus fidelibus vivis ac defunctis in terra viventium, vitam et requiem æternam concede ; per eundem Christum Dominum nostrum. Amen.

Feria tertia in Quadragesima Ordo martyrum, etc.

Sancte Thoma,	Ora pro nobis.
Sancte Sixte,	Or.
Sancte Corneli,	Or.
Sancte Cypriane,	Or.
Sancte Johannes,	Or.
Sancte Paule,	Or.
Sancte Marcelline,	Or.
Sancte Petre,	Or.
Sancte Vite,	Or.
Sancte Modeste,	Or.
Sancte Adriane,	Or.
Sancte Nichasi cum sociis tuis,	Or.

LETANIA.

Sancte Eustachi cum sociis tuis,
                Ora pro nobis.
Omnes sancti Martyres,
                Orate pro nobis.
Sancte Gregori,   *Ora pro nobis.*
Sancte Augustine,   *Or.*
Sancte Ambrosi,   *Or.*
Sancte Remigi,   *Or.*
Sancte Donatiane,   *Or.*
Sancte Eligi,   *Or.*
Sancte Andomare,   *Or.*
Sancte Sulpici,   *Or.*
Sancte Paterne,   *Or.*
Sancte Patrici,   *Or.*
Sancte Dunstane,   *Or.*
Sancte Grimbalde,   *Or.*
Omnes sancti Confessores,
                Orate pro nobis.
Omnes sancti Monachi et Here-
   mitæ,   *Orate pro nobis*
Sancta Felicitas, *Ora pro nobis*
Sancta Perpetua,   *Or.*
Sancta Columba,   *Or.*
Sancta Cristina,   *Or.*
Sancta Eulalia,   *Or.*
Sancta Eufemia,   *Or.*
Sancta Eugenia,   *Or.*
Sancta Gertrudis,   *Or.*
Sancta Ragenfledis,   *Or.*
Sancta Batildis,   *Or.*
Sancta Anastasia,   *Or.*
Sancta Etheldreda,   *Or.*
Omnes sanctæ Virgines,
                Orate pro nobis.
Omnes Sancti,   *Or.*
Propitius esto;
       Parce nobis, Domine.
Ab omni malo,
       Libera nos, Domine.
Ab insidiis diaboli,   *Lib.*
    Etc., ut supra.

Feria quarta in Quadragesima.
Ordo Martyrum.

Sancte Laurenti, *Ora pro nobis.*
Sancte Tiburti,   *Or.*

Sancte Valeriane, *Ora pro nobis.*
Sancte Prothe,   *Or.*
Sancte Hiacinthe,   *Or.*
Sancte Abdon,   *Or.*
Sancte Sennes,   *Or.*
Sancto Thymotee,   *Or.*
Sancte Apollinaris,   *Or.*
Sancte Saturnine,   *Or.*
Sancta Maurici cum sociis tuis,
                        Or.
Sancte Gereon cum sociis tuis,
                        Or.
Omnes sancti Martyres,
                Orate pro nobis.
Sancte Hylari, *Ora pro nobis.*
Sancte Martine,   *Or.*
Sancte Brici,   *Or.*
Sancte Amande,   *Or.*
Sancte Vedaste,   *Or.*
Sancte Germane,   *Or.*
Sancte Ausberte,   *Or.*
Sancte Wilfranne,   *Or.*
Sancte Aruulphe,   *Or.*
Sancte Silvine,   *Or.*
Sancte Taurine,   *Or.*
Sancte Cuthberte,   *Or.*
Omnes sancti Confessores,
                Orate pro nobis.
Omnes sancti Monachi et Here-
   mitæ,   *Orate pro nobis.*
Sancta Agatha, *Ora pro nobis.*
Sancta Susanna,   *Or.*
Sancta Brigida,   *Or.*
Sancta Barbara,   *Or.*
Sancta Marina,   *Or.*
Sancta Martina,   *Or.*
Sancta Felicula,   *Or.*
Sancta Julita,   *Or.*
Sancta Sapientia,   *Or.*
Sancta Fides,   *Or.*
Sancta Spes,   *Or.*
Sancta Charitas,   *Or.*
Omnes sanctæ Virgines,
                Orate pro nobis.
Omnes Sancti,   *Or.*
Propitius esto;
      Parce nobis, Domine.

LETANIA.

Ab omni malo,
    Libera nos, Domine.
Etc. ut supra.

Feria quinta in Quadragesima.
Sancte Vincenti,   *Ora pro nobis.*
Sancte Gervasi,   *Or.*
Sancti Prothasi,   *Or.*
Sancte Tymothee,   *Or.*
Sancte Simphoriane,   *Or.*
Sancte Felicissimi,   *Or.*
Sancte Agapite,   *Or.*
Sancte Albane,   *Or.*
Sancte Gorgoni,   *Or.*
Sancte Achillee,   *Or.*
Sancte Ypolite cum sociis tuis,
    Or.
Sancte Luciane cum sociis tuis,
    Or.
Omnes sancti Martyres,
    Orate pro nobis.
Sancte Nicolae,   *Ora pro nobis.*
Sancte Audoene,   *Or.*
Sancte Romane,   *Or.*
Sancte Laude,   *Or.*
Sancte Machute,   *Or.*
Sancte Sanson,   *Or.*
Sancte Placide,   *Or.*
Sancte Columbane,   *Or.*
Sancte Anthoni,   *Or.*
Sancte Machari,   *Or.*
Sancte Richarde,   *Or.*
Sancte Ethelwolde,   *Or.*
Omnes sancti Confessores,
    Orate pro nobis.
Omnes sancti Monachi et Here-
  mitæ,   *Orate pro nobis.*
Sancta Cæcilia,   *Ora pro nobis.*
Sancta Fides,   *Or.*
Sancta Austroberta,   *Or.*
Sancta Emerentiana,   *Or.*
Sancta Potentiana,   *Or.*
Sancta Oportuna,   *Or.*
Sancta Sophia,   *Or.*
Sancta Juliana,   *Or.*
Sancta Beatrix,   *Or.*
Sancta Crescentia,   *Or.*

Sancta Walburgis, *Ora pro nobis.*
Sancta Ermenildis,   *Or.*
Omnes sanctæ Virgines,
    Orate pro nobis.
Omnes Sancti,   *Or.*
Propitius esto ;
    Parce nobis, Domine.

Feria Sexta in Quadragesima.

Sancte Quintine, *Ora pro nobis.*
Sancte Christofore,   *Or.*
Sancte Lamberte,   *Or.*
Sancte Georgi,   *Or.*
Sancte Marcelle,   *Or.*
Sancte Theodore,   *Or.*
Sancte Valentine,   *Or.*
Sancte Grisogone,   *Or.*
Sancte Felix,   *Or.*
Sancte Adaucte,   *Or.*
Sancte Bonifaci cum sociis tuis,
    Or.
Sancte Kyriane cum sociis tuis,
    Or.
Omnes sancti Martyres,
    Orate pro nobis.
Sancte Benedicte, *Ora pro nobis.*
Sancte Maure,   *Or.*
Sancte Maiole,   *Or.*
Sancte Ægidi,   *Or.*
Sancte Wandregisile,   *Or.*
Sancte Wolmare,   *Or.*
Sancte Philiberte,   *Or.*
Sancte Bertine,   *Or.*
Sancte Winnoce,   *Or.*
Sancte Judoce,   *Or.*
Sancte Petroce,   *Or.*
Sancte Botulphe,   *Or.*
Omnes sancti Confessores,
    Orate pro nobis.
Omnes sancti Monachi et Here-
  mitæ,   *Orate pro nobis.*
Sancta Lucia,   *Ora pro nobis.*
Sancta Katherina,   *Or.*
Sancta Sabina,   *Or.*
Sancta Justina,   *Or.*
Sancta Eufraxia,   *Or.*

LETANIA.

Sancta Fausta,	Ora pro nobis.	Sancte Aniane,	Ora pro nobis.
Sancta Monegundis,	Or.	Sancte Ewrci,	Or.
Sancta Aldegundis,	Or.	Sancte Basili,	Or.
Sancta Radegundis,	Or.	Sancte Maurilli,	Or.
Sancta Pientia,	Or.	Sancte Germane,	Or.
Sancta Benigna,	Or.	Sancte Ausberte,	Or.
Sancta Walburgis,	Or.	Sancte Mamerte,	Or.
Sancta Radegundis,	Or.	Sancte Willibrorde,	Or.

Omnes sanctæ Virgines,
    Orate pro nobis.
Omnes Sancti,   *Or.*
Propitius esto;
  Parce nobis, Domine.

Sabbato in Quadragesima.

Sancte Calixte,	Ora pro nobis.		
Sancte Urbane,	Or.		
Sancte Magne,	Or.		
Sancte Menna,	Or.		
Sancte Ruphe,	Or.		
Sancte Valeri,	Or.		
Sancte Processe,	Or.		
Sancte Martiniane,	Or.		
Sancte Marce,	Or.		
Sancte Marcelliane,	Or.		

Sancte Gordiane cum sociis tuis,
        Or.
Sancte Pancraci cum sociis tuis,
        Or.
Omnes sancti Martyres,
    Orate pro nobis.
Sancte Aldelme, *Ora pro nobis.*

Sancte Leonarde,   *Or.*
Sancte Athanasi,   *Or.*
Sancte Oswalde,   *Or.*
Omnes sancti Confessores,
    Orate pro nobis.
Omnes sancti Monachi et Heremitæ,   *Orate pro nobis.*

Sancta Agnes,	Ora pro nobis.
Sancta Benedicta,	Or.
Sancta Martha,	Or.
Sancta Helena,	Or.
Sancta Euprepia,	Or.
Sancta Candida,	Or.
Sancta Basilissa,	Or.
Sancta Balbina,	Or.
Sancta Ursula,	Or.
Sancta Victoria,	Or.
Sancta Corona,	Or.
Sancta Sexburgis,	Or.

Omnes sanctæ Virgines,
    Orate pro nobis.
Omnes Sancti,   *Or.*
Propitius esto;
  Parce nobis, Domine.
Etc., ut supra.

HERE ENDETH THE PSALTER ACCORDING TO THE USE OF SARUM.

FROM THE

Recent Publications

OF

SWAN SONNENSCHEIN & CO.

LONDON:
SWAN SONNENSCHEIN & CO.,
PATERNOSTER SQUARE

By the Rev. T. B. Dover,
Vicar of S. Agnes', Kennington.

Some Quiet Lenten Thoughts.

A LENT MANUAL. With a Preface by the LORD BISHOP OF LINCOLN. *Small 8vo, cloth boards*, 2s. 6d ; *limp cloth*, 1s. 6d. TWENTY-FIRST THOUSAND.

The Ministry of Mercy.

Thirty-three Devotional Studies of the Gospel Miracles. FOURTH THOUSAND. *Small 8vo, cloth boards,* 2s. 6d. ; *limp cloth,* 1s. 6d. ; *large paper edition, on hand-made paper, demy 8vo,* 5s., *cloth ;* 6s., *vellum.*

"Every page abounds with beautiful and striking thoughts, as well as with serious and solemn lessons."—*John Bull.*
"An excellent book for Lenten reading."—*Guardian.*

The Hidden Word.

Thirty Devotional Meditations on the Parables of our Lord. Uniform with "The Ministry of Mercy". THIRD THOUSAND. *Small 8vo, cloth boards,* 2s. 6d.; *limp cloth,* 1s. 6d. ; *large paper edition, on hand-made paper, demy 8vo, cloth,* 5s. ; 6s., *vellum.*

"A valuable help to overworked priests."—*Church Times.*
"It would be difficult to speak too highly of these short, pithy addresses."—*Guardian.*

Alive unto God.

SERMONS preached at S. Agnes, Kennington, during Lent, 1887, by CANON H. M. LUCKOCK, CANON SCOTT-HOLLAND, REV. H. C. SHUTTLEWORTH, REV. DR. R. E. SANDERSON, REV. AUBREY MOORE, DR. PAGET, REV. WM. BENHAM, REV. H. D. NIHILL. Edited by the REV. T. BIRKETT DOVER, M.A. *Demy 8vo, cloth,* 4s. 6d.

"For educated persons this is quite a Lenten Manual in itself, and will repay attentive consideration."—*Church Times.*

Paternoster Square, London, E.C.

By M. E. Granger.

Lenten Readings.

Arranged for Daily Reading and Meditation, with a Preface by the Rev. R. A. J. SUCKLING, Vicar of St. Alban's, Holborn. Second Edition. *Fcap. 8vo, cloth extra*, 2s. 6d.

"The teaching is sound and practical."—*Guardian.*

"The Author has shown so much good taste in making her selections, and has so fitly arranged them, that the book cannot fail to be of help."—*Church Times.*

By the Rev. Clement René Sharpe.

The Child's Lent Manual.

Suggestions as to the Observance of Lent, with a Collect for Daily Use and Readings for every day in Holy Week. 32mo, *cloth neat*, 1s.

"A really interesting and simple devotional book for the young."—*Family Churchman.*

By the Rev. W. J. Strickland,
Assistant Priest of St. John's, East Dulwich.

The Psalm of Christ Crucified.

Short Lenten Readings on the Twenty-second Psalm.
Fcap. 8vo, cloth, 2s. 6d.

"Devout and practical, not entering into minute details, but seizing the salient features."—*Literary Churchman.*

By the Rev. Wycliffe Vaughan.

The Transfiguration of our Blessed Lord.

Fifty Devotional Studies for the Season of Lent. With a Preface by the LORD BISHOP OF SALISBURY. *Crown 8vo, cloth*, 2s. 6d.

"They are well adapted for devotional reading during Lent, while they will also doubtless prove useful to preachers as suggestive of subjects for discourse."—*Church Times.*

Paternoster Square, London, E.C.

By the Rev. George Edward Jelf,
Canon of Rochester.

Work and Worship.

Sermons Preached in English Cathedrals. Dedicated by permission to the ARCHBISHOP OF CANTERBURY. *Demy 8vo, cloth, extra,* 4s. 6d.

"Earnest, cultivated, devout, and useful."—*Church Bells.*

By the late F. A. Paley, M.A., LL.D.

The Gospel of St. John.

A Verbatim Translation from the Vatican MS., with the notable variations of the Sinaitic and Beza MSS., and brief explanatory Comments. 8vo, *cloth,* 7s. 6d.

"There can be no question as to the gratitude which will be felt by scholars and New Testament students towards Dr. Paley for his new translation."—*Literary World.*

By the Rev. J. T. Bramston,
Assistant Master at Winchester College.

Sermons to Boys preached in Winchester College Chapel.

Crown 8vo, cloth, 3s. 6d.

By the Rev. H. B. Chapman,
Vicar of St. Luke's, Camberwell.

The Religion of the Cross.

A Series of Suggestive Essays on Practical Religion. *Crown 8vo, cloth extra,* 4s. 6d.

"Plain and pithy teaching."—*Church Times.*
"Undogmatic, written in a bright, cheery style."—*Literary Churchman.*

Paternoster Square, London, E.C.

By the Rev. William Bellars,
Vicar of Margate.

Before the Throne.

A Manual of Private Devotion. With a Preface by CANON A. J. MASON. TWELFTH THOUSAND. Fourth edition revised and enlarged. Printed on fine paper. *32mo, cloth gilt, red edges,* 2s. 6d.; *french limp,* 4s.; *calf extra,* 7s. 6d.; *morocco extra,* 7s. 6d.

Editions adapted to the Scottish and American Offices are now published.

"The theological tone is thoroughly sound, and the book has special features of its own, with which we have not met elsewhere. . . . He is clear and accurate on the Presence of the Sacrifice. . . . The principal quality for which we commend the book is its sincerity."—*Church Times.*

The Lesser Hours of the Sarum Breviary.

Translated and arranged according to the Kalendar of the Church of England. *Imp. 32mo,* 2s. 6d.; *fcap. 8vo,* 3s. 6d.

Ceremonial of the Altar.

A Guide to Low Mass according to the ancient customs of the Church of England. Compiled by an ANGLICAN PRIEST. Second Edition. 16mo, *cloth,* 2s. 6d.

The Contemporary Pulpit Library.

Uniformly bound in blue cloth, gilt tops, 2s. 6d. *each.*

1. SERMONS BY CANON LIDDON. Series I.
2. SERMONS BY BISHOP MAGEE.
3. SERMONS BY ARCHDEACON FARRAR.
4. SERMONS BY CANON LIDDON. Series II.

N.B.—The Contemporary Pulpit is published monthly, price 6d., post free, 7d., and contains the Sermons of all the representative preachers of the day. An *extra* Annual vol. of the C.P. LIBRARY is also published.

Paternoster Square, London, E.C.

By the Rev. James E. Denison, M.A.,
Curate of St. John the Divine, Kennington, late Vice-Principal of Cuddesdon Theological College.

Catechising on the Catechism.

With a Preface by H. P. LIDDON, D.D., Canon of St. Paul's.
Second Edition. *Fcap. 8vo, cloth, 2s. 6d.*

"The principle on which this book is constructed is undoubtedly the only real basis of catechetical teaching. . . . We most strongly recommend it."—*Guardian.*

"Mr. Denison's *Catechising on the Catechism* abounds in hints that will be found of value in the Sunday School or for children's services."—*Sunday Review.*

By the Rev. Edward T. Stevens,
Vicar of Sibford Gower.

The Teaching of the Prayer Book for the Children of the Church.

Part I.—Morning and Evening Prayer.   Part II.—The Litany.

Fcap. 8vo, cloth extra, 2s. 6d. each part.   Also a cheap edition in limp cloth, at 1s. 6d. each.

"It compresses a vast amount of information and many interesting dates and details into a small compass."—*Guardian.*

By the Rev. Dr. Lightfoot, M.A.,
Rector of Cross-stone, Todmorden.

Text Book of the Thirty-nine Articles.

Crown 8vo, cloth, 5s.

By the Rev. Edward Ram,
Vicar of St. John's, Timber Hill, Norwich.

Leading Events in the History of the Church of England.

Forming a Concise History of the Church.
Fcap. 8vo, cloth, 1s. 6d.

"Well adapted for parish reading rooms and libraries."—*Guardian.*

Paternoster Square, London, E.C.

OF RECENT PUBLICATIONS. 7

An Illustrated Edition of Thomas à Kempis.
The Imitation of Christ.
Translated from the Latin by CANON W. BENHAM, B.D. With 20 Fine Engravings after celebrated Paintings in the Louvre. *Small 4to, gilt,* 21*s.*

By Jacques Biroat,
Doctor in Theology.
The Eucharistic Life of Christ.
Being the Life of Jesus Christ in the Holy Sacrament of the Altar. Translated from the fifth edition by EDWARD G. VARNISH. 8*vo, cloth extra,* 6*s.*

" The translator has put us under a deep obligation by bringing this work to the notice of English Catholics, and by the diligence and care with which he has rendered it into English."—*E. C. Union Gazette.*

By the Rev. Samuel John Eales, D.C.L.,
Author of " Via Crucis," etc.
The Mystic Vine.
A Meditation on the Passion of our Lord and Saviour Jesus Christ, treated mystically and devotionally. *Fcap.* 8*vo, cloth,* 3*s.* 6*d.*
" A book charming to look at, helpful to read."—*Church Bells.*

By the Rev. William Malam,
Vicar of Buxton ; late Scholar of Caius College, Cambridge.
Black Letter Saints.
Sketches of their Lives, and Lessons derived therefrom. With a Frontispiece after Ary Scheffer. Second Edition. *Royal* 16*mo, cloth extra, red edges,* 2*s.* 6*d.*

" This convenient little volume ought to supply a need. The story of each saint has been well told."—*Yorkshire Post.*

By C. A. Jones,
Author of " Stories of the Catechism ".
The Saints of the Prayer Book.
Second Edition, with 6 outline plates. *Royal* 16*mo, cloth extra, red edges,* 2*s.* 6*d.*

" This dainty little book, with its clever outline illustrations, will be useful to many grown people as well as to children, for whom its simple language makes its suitable."—*Graphic.*

Paternoster Square, London, E.C.

Religious Systems of the World.

NATIONAL, CHRISTIAN, and PHILOSOPHIC. A Collection of Addresses delivered at South Place Institute in 1888-89, revised, and in some cases re-written. *Demy 8vo, cloth, 7s. 6d.*

By Emile Burnouf.
The Science of Religions.

Translated by JULIE LIEBE, with a Preface by E. J. RAPSON, M.A., M.R.A.S., Fellow of St. John's College, Cambridge. *Demy 8vo, cloth, 7s. 6d.*

"The essayist is sure to gain a hearing, as he is the bearer of the great name of Burnouf. He maintains, with unquestionable learning and ingenuity, that the primitive Aryan religions were the source not only of the religions of the Veda and Avesta, but also of Christianity. Many interesting analogies are adduced."—*British Weekly.*

By the Rev. J. P. Lundy.
Monumental Christianity.

OR, THE ART AND SYMBOLISM OF THE PRIMITIVE CHURCH. Fully illustrated. *Post 4to, cloth extra, 31s. 6d.* An important work on Early Christian Art and Ecclesiology.

By the Rev. Arthur Brinckman,
Late of All Saints', Margaret Street.
The Controversial Methods of Romanism.

Third Edition. *Crown 8vo, cloth, 3s. 6d.*

"We strongly recommend to all our readers, alike clerical and lay, this most complete exposure of modern Roman efforts to proselytize."—*Weekly Churchman.*

By H. N., of St. Mary's Home, Stone, with a Preface by the Right Rev. the Lord Bishop of Rochester.
Twenty-three Years in a House of Mercy.

Second Edition, *fcap. 8vo, cloth, red edges, 2s. 6d.*

"I should be sorry for the person who could read the pages which follow without emotion."—*From the Preface by the Bishop of Rochester.*

Paternoster Square, London, E.C.

www.ingramcontent.com/pod-product-compliance
Lightning Source LLC
Chambersburg PA
CBHW031819230426